KU-336-166

WHY AREN'T THEY SHOUTING?

A Banker's Tale of Change, Computers and Perpetual Crisis

KEVIN RODGERS

BUSINESS
BOOKS

To my much loved and often delightful family – Niki, Fred, Eddie and Arthur.

1 3 5 7 9 10 8 6 4 2

Random House Business Books
20 Vauxhall Bridge Road
London SW1V 2SA

Random House Business Books is part of the Penguin Random House group of companies whose addresses can be found at global.penguinrandomhouse.com.

Penguin
Random House
UK

Copyright © Kevin Rodgers 2016

Kevin Rodgers has asserted his right to be identified as the author of this Work in accordance with the Copyright, Designs and Patents Act 1988.

First published by Random House Business Books in 2016
This paperback edition published by Random House Business Books in 2017

www.penguin.co.uk

A CIP catalogue record for this book is available from the British Library.

ISBN 9781847941534

Printed and bound by Clays Ltd, St Ives plc

Penguin Random House is committed to a sustainable future for our business, our readers and our planet. This book is made from Forest Stewardship Council® certified paper.

MIX
Paper from
responsible sources
FSC
www.fsc.org
FSC® C018179

Contents

Foreword to the Paperback Edition

A Clear and Present Danger

In September 2016, I was talking about this book to a group of around 30 or 40 businessmen at the Belgian ambassador's residence in London. A likeable, rather courtly Belgian who had purchased a copy and enjoyed it had invited me there. It seemed slightly incongruous to be talking about irresistible advances in technology in a magnificent old house hung with Gobelin tapestries.

The talk went well but during the Q&A afterwards, a young man from a hedge fund took me to task for my assertion that the FX market had become more fragile. The example that I gave, he said, demonstrated nothing of the sort. He was referring to the fact that the market, once so reliable at providing liquidity during major market events, had completely fallen to pieces following the decision by the Swiss National Bank to remove the cap on the value of the Swiss Franc in January 2015. It had been a bit choppy, he admitted (I smiled at that – it had been utter chaos), but it was the fault of the SNB and didn't prove anything. Another woman (from a bank) asserted that regulatory controls prevented banks from taking risks and *that* was the problem. After a little to and fro we agreed to disagree and I retired to the drinks reception that had been laid on.

Two weeks later, on 7 October, the value of the exchange rate between the British pound and the US dollar – universally referred to in the FX market as 'Cable' – collapsed by as much as 10 per cent in a matter of minutes in early Asian trading, although it recovered swiftly afterwards. The move was dubbed the 'Cable Flash Crash'. It caused consternation. Cable represents the exchange rate between the largest and fifth largest economies on earth. It governs about $100 billion of trade each year. It shouldn't move as violently as this for any reason other than the arrival of enormously significant and unexpected information. But no important information had been released. Speculation as to the cause was rife. Maybe it had been a rogue algorithm spitting out sell orders in automated defiance of its human masters' real wishes? Maybe a hedge fund had sold a huge amount of sterling in an attempt to drive the market lower for its own benefit? Maybe it had been a case of 'fat fingers' from a hapless junior? The Bank for International Settlements, aided by the Bank of England, conducted an inquest to find out.

Their conclusion after a few months of work was that no single cause could be blamed. Rather, the market had simply broken of its own accord. A combination of the time of day, automated systems and general sterling nervousness had rolled up into a 'several lifetimes of the universe' move. In fact, they also concluded that 'sudden moves appear to be happening more frequently as the market becomes faster and more automated.' Fragility was being built in to the FX markets as a result of technological change. Sadly, the report was released too late for my appearance at the Belgian Embassy.

The main idea presented in this book is that the combination of the rapid rise in the power of computers, combined with intense competition, has resulted in unintended systemic consequences for the financial sector. The new brittleness of the FX markets is only one such effect. A much more serious one is the growing fragility of the entire banking system – a gigantic process of weakening that I claim lay behind the Great Financial Crisis. As this event moves from the arena of current affairs to history (this summer will mark the 10th anniversary of its start) it is possible to see it in a wider perspective. First of all, it is clear that the crisis was a dramatic continuation of a sequence of similar events in the past – in particular the smaller but fundamentally comparable 'trial run' that occurred in 1997 and 1998. Second, that the consequences of the crisis have been politically profound – the widespread disaffection with globalisation, which in the last 12 months has resulted in seismic shifts such as Brexit and the election of Donald Trump in the US, was triggered in large part by the fall-out from 2007–8.

Most importantly, I think it is true to say that the danger of another crisis continues to be with us and is growing. The forces that caused the last one are still pressing hard on the finance industry. Computers continue to get more powerful and competition is intense. More banking jobs are being automated. Loosely regulated new competitors are entering banking markets. Nervousness about banks' stability still spikes intermittently: the panic about my old employer Deutsche Bank's stock in the autumn of 2016 – when it briefly traded below €10 per share and speculation was rife that the bank would go under – was a grim echo of 2008.

On top of all this, the regulatory framework that was painstakingly put in place in the wake of the 2008 crisis may be in jeopardy. President Trump has stated that he wishes to 'dismantle' Dodd–Frank – the bill that attempted to regulate American banking more strictly. His election caused a rally in bank stocks on the back of this stated wish. There is every chance, if the US goes down this path, that the rest of the world will follow in a repeat of the regulatory 'race to the bottom' that occurred in the 1990s and 2000s. Certainly the UK has every incentive to do so to protect its finance industry from the possible effects of losing the 'passport' to the EU. So much of the UK's tax take is generated by finance that the country may not be able to afford not to loosen regulations.

In short, far from becoming a period piece, I am afraid that this book's analysis and warning may be more relevant than ever. If it can continue to focus minds on the importance of technology in the stability of banking, it will have done its job.

Kevin Rodgers, January 2017

Preface

Some Disappointing Penguins

It was a quiet day on Deutsche Bank's London trading floor some-
time in the summer of 2012. That it was quiet was no surprise. The
trading business moves according to the seasons, the day of the week
and even the time of the day. January is always busy – Christmas,
quiet. The first Friday of every month (when the US releases non-
farm payroll data) is usually a big day as intense anticipation gives
way to a frantic hour or so of activity after the release. Curiously,
but consistently, the least interesting day of the week, statistically
speaking, is Wednesday. But summers (barring a crisis) are always a
snooze as customers, competitors and colleagues drift off on holiday and the energy drains from the market.

As usual, I was sitting at my desk on the trading floor rather than
in my office and I was doing some kind of administrative chore.
Maybe I was reading some research or answering one of the hundreds of emails that poured into my in tray each day ('URGENT –
Rescheduled GUI priorities meeting', perhaps). Or possibly I was
doing some online compliance training ('Anti-money laundering
basics: estimated time to complete, 30 minutes') while occasionally
flicking my gaze to screens showing the latest market rates. Whatever it was, I was not busy when the phone rang on my private
line. It was a lady from reception and she was flustered. She was
responsible for organising a trading floor tour for a group of the
bank's managers from the retail branches in Germany. These tours
were commonly laid on for out-of-town visitors. If the visitor was
some kind of VIP (a billionaire client, our CEO, regulators), the
whole process was carefully choreographed and sometimes even

scripted in advance. More middling visitors would simply be shown around by a guide, with no prior warning given to the folk actually working on the floor – it was a frequent occurrence to look up from my screen and suddenly find with a start that a knot of eager Cambridge undergraduates or a group of Japanese industrialists was staring at me intently.

That day, the receptionist's problem was that the designated tour guide had called in sick and she needed a replacement – a senior replacement, since the party were all managing directors and, by custom, it was considered the proper etiquette to provide a similarly senior guide. Would I do it? Reluctantly I agreed and met the party at one end of the floor. They were a group of about a dozen men and women (median age about 40 by my reckoning), all serious, sober-suited and polite, who – as was usual with Germans – spoke English impeccably. The trading floor we were on was one of three in Deutsche's London office. Each was stacked on top of the next like tiers in a huge wedding cake. One was given over to the specialised trading of equities, another one was for interest rate and credit products and a third – mine – housed Foreign Exchange, Money Markets and Commodities. In truth, all the floors looked practically identical: row upon row of seats in back-to-back aisles arranged over large, approximately rowing-boat-shaped rooms the size of football pitches. Regardless, I went through the practised stages of my tour smoothly. I pointed out where various teams sat: here was Money Markets; here Commodities; and last, proudly, here was Foreign Exchange, my department. I was starting to explain the various roles of the people sitting there when a lady in the group suddenly interrupted me: 'Excuse me, I must ask you a question.' All eyes in our little party turned to her. 'Why . . .' she said, indicating with a broad sweep of her hand the rows of oblivious traders and salespeople, 'aren't they shouting?' For a split second I was completely confused (What? *Why aren't they shouting?*) but then I saw the look on her face and understood in an instant. It was a look that, as a parent, I was all too familiar with – the unhappy, sulky look of a child unfairly denied a long-awaited treat.

A few weeks earlier, my wife and I had taken our youngest, penguin-obsessed son, Arthur, aged seven, to London Zoo. The aim was to watch penguin-feeding time but we were too late. Instead of watching penguins merrily cavorting and jostling, diving and hopping in pursuit of fish, we merely saw the somnolent after-effects: replete and frankly lacklustre penguins engaged in the slow, lethargic process of digestion. My son's almost tearful expression of disappointment that day was now mirrored in the face of my German colleague. She had heard about trading floors. She had thought she knew what to expect. There would be excitement. There would be people on two phones simultaneously. Maybe there would be some swearing or some wild, primitive gesticulation! Certainly there would be a great deal of shouting. Instead, this! A sea of people tapping on keyboards, walking slowly to and fro, chatting at normal volume: a great susurrating nothingness. I understood that her real question to me was this: why is your zoo so damn boring? Why indeed? I stammered out some words about it being summer and a bit slow and so on, and with that the tour went on and reached its conclusion.

Later, when I was back at my desk, I started to think again about her question. Although it was true that it was summer and therefore quiet, in reality that wasn't actually why people weren't shouting. These days they practically never shouted, I thought. Years previously, when I started out in my career, every single move in the markets, each economic data release, each unexpected news item was accompanied by a deafening wave of noise. But latterly, even in the chaos of the crisis in 2007 and 2008, the volume of sound only rarely reached the heights I would have heard on a fairly ordinary day in the early 1990s. Why? The answer, I realised, was computers. Looking around me, I saw people talking to each other via computers in emails and in chat rooms. Computers were doing some of the tasks that used to be assigned to traders by making prices automatically. Deals were being booked, and their risk often managed, on and by computers. In short, computers had, in all but the direst emergency, reduced the need to shout anything at all. And they'd done more. Compared to the start of my career, they'd altered the very markets themselves: the types of products that were being traded; the types of clients trading them; the types of competitors; even the backgrounds of people employed on a trading floor. In that moment of recognition, other questions began to occur to me. Had these changes occurred elsewhere? What effects had they had? More darkly, did the widespread use of computers have anything to do with the crisis that had engulfed banking a few years earlier? Answering these questions is, in part, the aim of this book. But I get ahead of myself. Why should I be able to provide any answers? Some introductions and explanations are needed.

In the Machine

My name is Kevin Rodgers and I was a banker. I didn't grow up wanting to be a banker. Like many small boys in the 1960s, I wanted to be an astronaut. Sadly, NASA's desperate worldwide appeal for pencil-thin, almost comically short-sighted seven-year-olds never reached my primary school in a suburb of Bristol. To make up for this, I spent my time poring over and copying out hugely complicated diagrams of the innards of spacecraft and aeroplanes and building elaborate models from Lego and Meccano. I'll admit it; I was more than a bit geeky. During my teenage years I tried to tone this image down by playing the drums in various bands – something I hoped would help me to get girls more effectively than displaying my knowledge of the hydraulics of the Lunar Excursion Module. Looking back, I'd give this plan a solid B-minus. When the time came for university I read engineering. It seemed natural:

my father had been an engineer and so had his father before him. I found I had an aptitude for it all. After graduation, I started my first job building large and complex computer systems for oil and chemical companies. This was extremely interesting work, if not exactly lucrative per unit of effort, given the often insanely long hours involved. After four years of doing it, business school seemed like a decent throw of the dice since I had heard, as had all my classmates, that MBAs always earned more money after graduation than they had before – a state of play which I, for one, was all in favour of. At business school I excelled in the finance courses I took. The – to my eyes – comforting and rather beautiful mathematics of the subject appealed to my engineer's sense of order. The slightly louche glamour I imagined would cling to the process of placing bets with enormous sums of money also appealed (most probably to the drummer in me) and in 1990, after the MBA, I ended up taking a job in London as a trader at the US bank Merrill Lynch.

My specialism at Merrill was trading currency options, a form of financial instrument used to insure against, or speculate on, movements in the foreign exchange (FX) markets: markets which were then, and still are now, the biggest in the world. Oddly, as soon as I started work and then in every job after that, each market I traded seemed to heave, spasm and buck as soon as I arrived to trade it. Foreign exchange in 1990 and 1991? Invasion of Kuwait and the Gulf War. In 1992 and 1993? The destruction of the ERM, then one of the market's great bond busts. You get the picture.

In 1993, I left Merrill to join another US bank: Bankers Trust. Bankers Trust at the time was regarded as the leading derivatives house in the world. I worked in my speciality of FX until 1997, then I moved over to the newly created Emerging Markets department. With my angel-of-death-like ability to be close to the centre of any trouble, I was soon caught up in one of the market's greatest ever crises as first Asia, then Russia, then a huge hedge fund called Long-Term Capital Management dragged the banking industry to the brink of disaster in 1998. The market was saved by intervention by the Federal Reserve and, in the chaos, Bankers Trust was purchased by German giant Deutsche Bank. It was here, at Deutsche, from 1999 onwards, that I was to spend the rest of my career.

Having moved banks, my ability to find trouble diminished – at least at first. I had been promoted to managing director in the dying days of Bankers Trust, mainly as a reward from my grateful managers for making (or, probably more pertinently, not losing) a ton of money in the Russia blow-up. This fancy title, although it pleased my mother no end, didn't really mean a great deal at Bankers Trust. It would be inaccurate to say Bankers Trust was disorganised, but it was true that rank didn't matter a great deal and everyone from low to high was expected to pitch in and make money. At Deutsche Bank I found to my surprise that, due to Germanic efficiency and literalness, a managing director was expected to do quite a lot of managing and a fair bit of directing too. My role therefore changed from that of a (fairly expert derivatives) trader to that of a manager of traders.

I found that I was actually rather good at managing traders and handling all the other aspects of the managerial job. The most important of these was overseeing the automation of the business. The world was changing. The power of computers was rising steadily and the Internet was becoming mainstream. The fundamental strategic decision to be made by banks was how to use computers in business. My experience building computer systems and my general unreconstructed nerdiness now came in handy. Although the systems I had once built would have looked laughably old-fashioned to Deutsche's 21st-century computer boffins, we at least spoke approximately the same language. Because I had a natural bent for this most vital of business tasks, over the years I was promoted to do various, gradually bigger roles. These were all connected with Foreign Exchange (where I had started my career at Merrill) and Commodities, in which Deutsche Bank made a big push from 2002 onwards. Finally, having survived the events of the 2008 Great Financial Crisis and the years following it unscathed, the last and largest job I did before I retired in 2014 was running the bank's FX business globally. By many measures ours was the biggest and most successful FX business in the world.

In the last few months of my career before retirement I began to think more deeply about the questions that had popped into my mind after the German trading floor tour – about how computers had changed products, markets and even culture in the banking industry. This book examines how banking changed during the course of my career through the lens of my own experiences.

People and Computers

In most books about banking, computers rarely feature at all, except as bit players. If you think about it, that is surprising, since – these days at least – a bank is in essence nothing more than a lot of people and a collection of legal contracts represented on some very complex computer systems. Put simplistically, banks are just people and computers; all the rest is nice to have but not essential. If that statement surprises you, consider this: virtually all the money you get paid, save or spend is not physical in any sense whatsoever but is merely an abstract representation in ones and zeros on some bank's computer system somewhere. A symptom of this is that I myself have not been into a physical branch of the institution I bank with for many years, nor in that time have I seen a person who works there with my own eyes. Asking around, it seems I am not atypical. In days gone by a bank was defined by its great vaults, its glossy headquarters or its extensive branch network. Increasingly, a bank's true crown jewels are held in the form of bits and bytes in unremarkable data centres on light industrial estates in anonymous suburbs. Similarly, the multi-headed menagerie of mortgages, mortgage-backed bonds, collateralised debt obligations and credit default swaps that teems and writhes through the story of the 2008 Great Financial Crisis was nothing more than a huge number of legal contracts represented abstractly in the innards of thousands of computers. To understand banking, therefore, you must understand how computers have changed and redefined the industry – how they have eaten it.

This book starts with an explanation of how and why automation affected one important corner of finance, the foreign exchange market. I concentrate on FX because I know it well and I was an eyewitness while dramatic changes were happening; indeed, I was instrumental in some of them. That said, the lessons of FX apply to all financial products to a greater or lesser extent. Some of the changes automation has brought about have been beneficial, but others have not. What is definitely the case is that computers have fundamentally altered many markets from top to bottom.

In the second part of the book, I go on to set out my view (initially suggested to me by my German colleague's question) that the huge rise in the power of computers and telecommunications in the 1990s was the essential precursor for the crisis of 2008. Why is that? Faster computers encouraged the development of more complex derivatives, allowed the fragmentation and 'daisy-chaining' of deals and thus led to the huge growth in the size of many markets. Faster computers also tempted banks to rely on quantitative risk measurement that was fundamentally flawed and that tempted some of them to take on too much risk and operate with too much leverage. Last, more powerful computers have allowed banks to grow (since, in theory, technology means that they can still be managed centrally) and become 'too big to understand' and often 'too big to fail'. There have been lots of books about banking since the crisis and in them the themes of complexity, leverage and size have become familiar. But although these explanations are good on the 'why' of the crisis, they are less good on the 'when'. How is it that the crisis happened when it did? The focus on computation gives one plausible answer to that question – in short, the crisis of 2008 would not have been possible without the computers of 2008.

The last two chapters explore a number of questions arising from these two stories. What was going on inside banks that led to these linked developments? How was banking culture changing? Where were the regulators when it was all happening? No book about banking should ignore ethical questions or the multitude of scandals that have surfaced since the crisis and this one doesn't. How did they come about and what part did computers play in them? How should we stop them happening again? More importantly still, will there be another crisis and what may cause it? Finally, the book describes some of the measures that are being taken to fix banking and sets out a couple of modest proposals of my own. The edge of pessimism of this chapter (springing from my belief that another crisis is, in time, inevitable) is lifted slightly by the concluding thought that new technological progress and new competitors may lead, within a new regulatory environment, to a better banking industry in the future.

Truth and Reconciliation

I was intimately involved in most of the developments that I describe in this book and at least a first-hand observer of the rest of them. The stories are therefore told from my perspective. That said, in order to sharpen the accuracy of my memories or to provide a different perspective I have interviewed a few dozen of my former colleagues and competitors to get their views. Some, who are either comfortable with being named or who are so associated with the story I am telling that they are documented in the public domain, have been identified by their first names. Others go by pseudonyms. Yet more are quoted completely anonymously – there is a great deal of reticence about publicity in banking circles these days. I'd like to take this opportunity to thank all of them: you know who you are.

One incident from one interview in particular stands out. It was while I was having dinner with my old colleague and friend Rhom, a thoughtful and perceptive man with whom I have worked, off and on, for 20 years. As the meal came to an end, we began to talk about what had gone wrong with banking. He bemoaned the infantilism of most post-crisis debate on the subject: the unthinking defensiveness of bankers; the generalising hostility of the press, public and politicians. 'What we need in banking is what they had in South Africa,' he said as he sipped his coffee, 'we need a Truth and Reconciliation process. Much more terrible things were discussed in that than ever happened in finance and South Africa managed to move on. We just need to figure out calmly what went right, what went wrong, and how to fix it. It's too important not to.'

I agreed with him then and I agree with him now. It is in that spirit that I present this book.

Acknowledgements

I would like to extend my thanks to all the ex-colleagues and ex-competitors who allowed me to interview them for this book. Thanks also to the friends who reviewed early drafts – Philip, Paul, Mark, Clare, Raven, Mary – I really appreciated your help. Needless to say, any remaining errors are mine, all mine. Thanks also to the staff of Penguin Random House, especially my editor Nigel. Last, thanks to Clive and Tim from *Euromoney* for providing me with the historic details of the *Euromoney* FX Survey that appear in Appendix 1.

PART ONE

Reduced to the Absurd – Automating FX

CHAPTER 1

The Strange Extinction of Mickey the Broker

Oh, What a Night!

My memory of turning up to work in the first few years of my career was that I was generally bleary-eyed as I walked into the office. In large part this was because my day, like that of every other FX professional in London, started early. Foreign exchange is traded around the clock; there is no opening bell. The earlier you get in, the earlier business destined to be transacted with traders in Asia can be transacted with you. Back in the 1990s I would typically be at my desk around 6.45 in the morning or earlier still if a lot was going on. I was probably a fair bit later than that one day in 1993, however, because as I stepped onto the Bankers Trust trading floor I heard my normally calm and unflappable Irish colleague Padraig bellowing my name. What the hell was happening? I broke into a jog then a sprint as fear gripped me. We didn't have any particularly terrible risk on the books and, according to my portable 'clicker' (a primitive plastic unit the size of a matchbox which showed live indicative FX rates), nothing much had been going on in the markets overnight or as I walked in from the Tube. But as I got to my desk, Padraig's pale blue eyes were bulging in excitement: 'Quick! Frankie Valli! Four Seasons! Is it September or December?' he yelled at me. 'What the fuck are you talking about?' I replied, gently. 'Is it September or December back in '63?' he went on, then, seeing my irritated bafflement, he explained.

For reasons unknown, two spot brokers at a firm called Marshalls had been discussing a Frankie Valli and the Four Seasons song called 'Oh, What a Night!' But then they got into a dispute about whether the song refers to a night in 'Late September, back in '63' or, alternatively, 'Late December'. The thesis and antithesis of this important dialectic had, sadly, not reached synthesis. Voices had been raised. Testosterone levels had spiked. There was no agreement. The brokers' clients (of which Bankers Trust was an important one) had been polled over the phone and there was an even split of opinion. Perhaps inevitably, money had been wagered and so by the time I had strolled, then sprinted, into the office, thousands of pounds from all over the market were stacked up on both sides of the argument. So what did I think, asked my friend, what was it, September or December? By coincidence, I knew the answer with 100 per cent certainty. My wife (then and now) was born on Christmas Day, 1963. The Four Seasons' song had become a sort of private joke between us. Knowledge is power, as they say, or, more accurately in this case, money. 'Is the betting still open?' I asked Padraig urgently. He thought it was. I raced to the desk of our chief spot dealer and clicked the button to allow me to speak to a broker at Marshalls who was running this particular book. After some delay (most people who cared had bet already) he found someone to take £300 on September to offset my bet on December. Satisfied, I walked back to my desk and got to work. It was late in the afternoon before the matter was finally settled. Someone at Marshalls obtained the number of Frankie Valli's record company and managed to get a definitive ruling from a confused but compliant junior employee. The answer, as I knew full well, was December. The winners and losers were notified and I got my money handed to me a few days later in a pub. And, yes, since you ask, it was a very special night for me.

Now, if you are under 30 years of age, or even if you are older but have forgotten what the world used to be like, the first thing that might strike you as peculiar about this story is this: why didn't they just look the answer up? Indeed, if such a dispute had arisen at any time from about 1996 or so onwards, a quick look on the Internet would have yielded the answer. As a test, I just used my iPhone to search for 'Oh What a Night lyrics' and got the correct wording within a few seconds. But, of course, in 1993 very few people had heard of the Internet and it was certainly not available inside banks. The information that was needed to bring the great September/December trade to settlement was not readily available. To modern eyes that looks odd. But for me the really quaint detail of this story is the appearance of spot brokers and the firm of Marshalls.

Spot brokers were employees of so-called interdealer brokerage houses; one of the biggest of these companies was Marshalls. Their role was to put together deals between banks in the FX spot market. For this the banks would pay a commission and the brokers themselves would be paid a fraction of that as a bonus. Spot (where one currency is exchanged for another for delivery in two business days) is arguably the single simplest product in the whole world of banking but, despite this, it was, and still is, the most important part of the FX market. When you hear on the news that 'the pound weakened today against the dollar' it is the spot market that is being referred to. Spot brokers were some of the biggest stars in FX. Their job of matching buyer and seller for hour after hour, deal after deal, though monotonous, required immense concentration and speed of thought. One well-known broker's party piece each evening was to 'check out' (that is, confirm all the deals he had done during the day) with Bankers Trust's traders purely from memory. Given that he would typically have done hundreds of trades, this amounted to the equivalent of memorising several pages of a telephone directory, daily. The best and most successful brokers were paid spectacularly well. Legends abounded: the broker who had given his desk assistant a £50 note to get him some lunch and 'something for yourself', only to wait for an hour and see his junior return with a beef sandwich and a new shirt. The broker who, on being asked by a US-based realtor how he would pay for a property he'd just bought in Florida, responded, 'Two hits – June and December.' The brokers with Ferraris or Lamborghinis or Aston Martins; the brokers' restaurant bills; their hangovers. In many ways, at the start of my career, spot brokers *were* the FX market.

And now, today, they are gone. Although a tiny number of spot brokers still exist to broker some peripheral, illiquid emerging markets currencies, the vast majority are no longer employed. Marshalls, the spot brokerage house *par excellence*, has been subsumed within another larger firm, and its name has been erased from the market's consciousness, save in the memories of some ageing old-timers. Spot brokers have gone for exactly the same reason that my story's other odd and archaic element (lack of ready Four Seasons lyric data) has gone – the rise in the power of computers and the spread of information. How did it happen?

When You Trade You Begin With A B C

To understand how spot brokers became extinct it is important to understand how the FX markets work. It is possible that you already know this very well, in which case feel free to skip through a few pages. It is more likely that you have as little idea as I did when I first stepped onto the Merrill Lynch trading floor in the spring of 1990. True, having specialised in finance at business school, I was bursting with knowledge of Ito's lemma, stochastic calculus, rational markets and the capital asset pricing model. That meant nothing. It was like I was claiming to be prepared for the Tour de France because I'd studied Newton's laws of motion and a treatise on advanced metallurgy. I needed a practical guide. Luckily, I had one to hand in my first boss, a young Frenchman named Loic. If you imagine asking for 'a young Frenchman' from central casting,

Loic is who they would send you. By turns garrulous and mood-ily silent, good-looking, his elegantly turned-out frame usually wreathed in a cloud of fumes from the Marlboro Reds he chain-smoked all day long, he endeavoured to educate me on the ways of banking and FX.

He explained to me that, although banks make money from a bewildering number of different business lines, every one of those business lines could be categorised as using one of two underlying methods. In the first, a bank provides a service for a client in return for a fee. This is known as the 'agency' model. A classic example might be advising on a merger; an example from outside banking would be an estate agent finding you a house to buy. What is impor-tant is that, as an agent, the bank (or the estate agent) doesn't take any risk. The bank never owns the company at any stage but merely helps someone else buy it. The bank is being paid for its people's ex-pertise. Loic had little time for the Merrill Lynch bankers and their agency business: 'They are photocopy monkeys, Kevin. They went to the right schools and have nice cufflinks. Besides that? Nothing.'

The second type of business does require the bank to take risk. (We, in FX, were one of these; Loic was naturally keener on this model.) In these businesses, a bank will deal on its own account and attempt to make a profit by obeying the age-old adage of 'buy low, sell high'. This is known as the 'principal' model. Most parts of a bank operate on this basis. The core activity of taking deposits and making loans is a principal business. If you borrow money from your bank, the bank is at risk. In part, that is because the money the bank itself has borrowed in order to lend it to you might have a different maturity to your loan, or it might have a floating interest rate versus your fixed one (or vice versa). This is 'market risk'. But primarily, the risk comes from the fact you might not pay back the loan. This is 'credit risk'.

Away from the aeons-old business of lending money at interest, many large banks run various trading businesses, most of which use the principal model. Merrill Lynch was no exception. Merrill's bankers traded bonds; they traded interest rate swaps; they traded loans; they traded short-dated deposits. Loic would take me around the cavernous trading floor during quieter moments and point out where all these businesses were located, their staff hunched over tightly packed rows of desks. These tours were useful, but the most vital part of the education I got from Loic in those first few weeks was about how our department, FX, functioned.

'You have to imagine', he once said, waving his cigarette in emphasis, 'that we are on a great big production line. Clients and deals come in one door, we work on them, and they leave through another.' I nodded eagerly: this was like the value chain from business school! I was back on familiar territory.

First of all, he explained, there were a number of activities that happened 'pre-deal'. Researchers provided reports outlining their views on the market, for example. There were teams of people working in the background who 'adopted' new clients (that is, sorted out all the paperwork and made sure that they were not drug smugglers and the like and – vitally, to reduce credit risk – made sure that they had enough money to cover any losses). But the most important purveyors of 'pre-deal' services were the salespeople whose job it was to speak on the phone to the bank's customers. These days, FX salespeople are virtually all expensively educated, well dressed and charming. Back when I started with Merrill, they were well dressed and charming too, but the degree of education was, shall we say, a little less uniform. The waves of MBAs and PhDs that had begun to break over other areas of banking in the 1980s had not yet washed up on the shores of FX to any large extent. Early in my career one of the most senior salespeople I dealt with was Bev, a one-woman tsunami of chat and charm who had worked her way up from the back office she had joined aged 16. Perpetually tanned and habitually encrusted in a medieval monarch's ransom of gold, diamonds and other gems, Bev spent every moment of every working day on the telephone to her hedge fund clients. The word 'persuasive' conveys but a wan shadow of the effect of her patter. Bev, like all salespeople, needed to do two things while on the phone: first, to tell her clients what was going on in the market and, second, to advise them when and how to access it. The first of these is crucial. Rather like the brokers being in ignorance of the lyrics of Frankie Valli songs, Loic explained that all but the most sophisticated clients didn't really have a clue what was going on in FX. They couldn't see the prices at which currencies were trading. Even the really switched-on clients (major corporations, hedge funds, pension funds etc.) who had eye-wateringly expensive subscriptions to market data services like Reuters, Bloomberg or Telerate could only see indicative levels (posted manually by banks) for a subset of the most widely traded currency pairs. The salespeople were their eyes and ears into the reality of price formation and liquidity. And it was the pricing and transacting of deals that was, and is, the core of the business.

Central to this 'dealing' part of the production line were the FX traders. We all sat together in two rows of seven seats segregated into three subgroups according to our specialities. First, and most important, were the spot traders who sat across from me. Each had a currency or currency pair that he (it was inevitably a 'he') was responsible for. One did the Swiss franc, another the Japanese yen, for example. The royalty of the spot desk were the traders of dollar/mark and of Cable. Dollar/mark was the exchange rate between the US dollar and the German mark, which, because of the global clout of those two huge economies, was the most heavily traded pair. Running it a close second was Cable (the exchange rate between the British pound and the US dollar), which, as Loic told me on my first day in the job, got its slang name in reference to the transatlantic cable that had once transmitted information between New York and London. Now, although some spot traders were university educated, many had career paths that were similar to Bev's.

Not that this mattered one jot. Success as a spot trader was more a matter of stamina, quick wits, a cool head and native cunning than any knowledge of Milton, Goethe or the atomic weight of molybdenum.

The second set of traders was found on the forwards desk; they sat to my right. A 'forward' is an exchange of one currency for another at a date in the future. Three things determine the correct price of a forward for a particular currency pair and date: the spot rate, the interest rate of currency one and the interest rate of currency two. Thus, because the parameters of their market were more various, the typical forwards trader was, by and large, a somewhat more cerebral beast than his equivalent in spot. One in particular, an Italian in his thirties called Maurizio, was exceptionally well read and had an obsessive and encyclopedic knowledge of military history, which he would discuss at length on the flimsiest pretext. 'Kevin, this-a market reminds me of the attack on La Haye Sainte' was one typically odd utterance.

Last, and regarded as the most cerebral of the lot, were us options traders: Loic, a Swiss chap named Bernd and me. Although only a small part of the FX market (options make up around 5 per cent of the total volume of FX), there was always a mystique about the products we traded. They were considerably more complex than spot (what isn't?) and came cocooned in their own impenetrable silken web of jargon: call, put, straddle, strangle, strike, pin, vol, smile, skew, theta, gamma, vega, delta, rho, and so on. Maybe as a result, or maybe because all three of us were university educated and a touch geeky, our colleagues regarded us options traders as odd fish (indeed, with my master's degree in engineering *and* an MBA, I was considered to be an overeducated freak). I'm pretty sure that the older members of the spot desk thought there was something just a little bit effete about us. One spot trader named Ian almost choked on his tea when he found out I was a fan of West Ham. 'You like football?' he goggled. 'I'd have thought you'd be more into . . .' (he paused as he visibly struggled to think of a sport unmanly enough for me) 'l dunno, lacrosse or something.'

Fun in the Jumper Market

So how did trading actually happen? The trigger was commonly a request from a client for a price. The request was transmitted over the phone to a salesperson, whereupon said salesperson would stand up and yell across the trading floor – it was quicker, and louder, that way. Sometimes the request was just for a 'level' – that is, a non-binding indication of where a particular exchange rate was currently trading. As you will recall, many clients didn't really know where the market price was and so this was a useful service. Most times, however, the request was for a binding 'price' at which the client could subsequently transact. It might have crossed your mind that there is an inherent problem with clients not knowing at what level a market is trading: how could they keep the bank honest? It certainly crossed mine and I pumped Loic for answers. In part, he said, they did it by pitting banks against each other. Dozens of banks provided FX services in cut-throat competition and most clients would talk to five, six or even more of them. A phoned request to a couple of FX desks simultaneously would do the trick. But the chief way clients kept banks honest was to ask for a 'two-way price'. To illustrate how this worked, I'll repeat the explanation Loic gave me all those years ago. I like it because it uses a real-world transaction and shows – as was Loic's intention no doubt – how odd two-way pricing is.

Imagine, he said, you walk into a shop that sells jumpers, or 'sweaters' if you are American. You find one you like and you ask for a two-way price. The assistant quotes you, '38 at 40'. You can pay the 'offer' (aka 'the right-hand side', 'the top', 'the lid') of £40 like any normal shopper, hand over the cash and walk out with the jumper.

Alternatively, you can 'hit the bid' ('the left-hand side'), whereupon you'd whip out a plastic-wrapped medium lambswool in navy blue that you'd bought elsewhere, hand it to the assistant and demand £38. Two-way pricing means you can either buy at the offer or sell on the bid. Now let's say there are lots of jumper shops nearby all selling identical products – you are in the fabled 'jumper district'. If the same jumper in all the nearby shops is trading at 34/36 (that is, you can buy a jumper for £36, sell for £34) then you are presented with a chance of a profit: you could buy your navy lambswool in a rival shop for £36, run across the street and hit the first shop's bid at £38. In return for the slight risk that the 38/40 emporium could have a change of heart about its pricing policy between you accepting the jumper in the cheaper shop and managing to sell it, you could make a quick £2 and, as an added bonus, not end up with a jumper to lug around. Do that often enough, for industrial quantities of jumpers, and you would quickly get wealthy. In this fictional world of two-way pricing of jumpers, it would be important for every shop to keep track of what every other shop was quoting – where the jumper market was trading, in other words. As a customer, you would be confident, as long as the difference between a shop's bid and offer – the so-called 'spread' – was not too wide, that you were buying or selling at an approximately fair rate. If you weren't, then someone would be putting themselves at risk like the 38/40 shop we just saw.

It was two-way pricing that gave customers confidence in the FX market where spreads, even back in the early 1990s, were already very, very tight. A typical two-way quote for a 'clip' of $10 million of dollar/mark might be 1.6820 at 1.6825 Deutschmarks per dollar. This means that if you were to buy $10 million it would cost you 16,825,000 Deutschmarks; if you were to sell $10 million you would receive 16,820,000. The spread of 5,000 Deutschmarks amounts to approximately 0.03 per cent (or three one-hundredths of 1 per cent, aka three 'basis points') of the

notional – that is, the size of the deal. To make life easier, most of
the numbers in the rate were rarely spoken out loud. The price we
just saw would be quoted as 20/25; these are the 'pips' and so this
price is 5 pips wide. The 1.68 piece of the rate would be left unsaid
and simply understood. The number 8 in this piece of the price
was commonly referred to as 'the big figure'; the number 6 was
occasionally referred to, if it was referred to at all, as the 'big, big
figure'; and, as far as I know, the number 1 had no name whatsoever.
No name, but a numinous kind of occult significance: changes in
this number for major exchange rates (for instance when Cable
broke above 2.0000 in 1992) were greeted by the FX market with
the same mix of superstitious awe, fear and excitement with which
I imagine primitive man would have greeted a solar eclipse, or the
eruption of a long-dormant volcano.

Once he'd been asked for a two-way price by a salesperson on
behalf of a client, how would a trader decide what he would quote?
Loic gave me some pointers but ultimately, in his mind, there was
no other way of learning this most vital of skills than by pure trial
and error. 'You try. You see how it goes. It's simple, no?' To help
me learn, I was briefly asked to leave the rarefied world of options
trading and do a stint on the spot desk. It was in the summer; some
traders were on holiday and one was ill. Loic's boss, an immensely
likeable Italian called Michele, believed that it would be a good experience – toughen me up, that sort of thing. Instead, it damn near
killed me. Despite the fact that it was relatively quiet and I was
trading Japanese yen (which was not a huge market focus), I found
the constant hours of concentration intensely difficult. I didn't dis-
grace myself but nor did I excel and after a couple of weeks I was
grateful to return to options where I belonged. That said, the lessons it taught me on price-making lasted my entire career.

The process of providing prices to customers (or 'making rates')
needed to be done at breakneck speed. Early in my stint on the
spot desk I hesitated fractionally too long in replying to a bellowed

request from Gary (a large, bull-necked salesman who'd joined the desk after some time in the army). This made Gary unhappy: 'You'd better get fucking quicker at this if you want to make a living out of it, mate!' was his loud and helpful advice. To 'make a rate', the first and most vital piece of information I used was the current market price for the exchange rate of the currency pair I was being asked on (usually dollar versus yen). I would have some clue about this from deals I had already done recently and from deals I had seen my colleagues do in other, related, currency pairs. For instance, the prices of dollar/mark and of dollar/yen were somewhat correlated since the biggest driver of the price was demand for dollars. But the best source of information was the broker market. Traders would often place bids or offers with the brokers simply to find out what other banks were doing (or to manage risk, as we shall see). The brokers would then keep up a constant stream of chatter about these rates and about any deals banks transacted with each other. This information would be broadcast through loudspeakers (called 'broker boxes') on the trading desk via open phone lines linking bank with broker, thus providing a steady bedrock of decibels above which the din of the trading floor would need to rise. Noisy though it was, the brokers' chatter would provide me with an idea of the current rate; my next decision would be how wide the spread should be.

Spreads were, to some extent, a matter of custom. There was an accepted price for relatively small deals in the most heavily traded pairs. Beyond that, it was purely up to me on a deal-by-deal basis subject to the extreme competitive pressures of a very heavily banked market. The size of the deal mattered – the larger it was the more risk I would be taking and so the wider the bid-offer spread. It mattered whether the market was relatively calm or whipping around in a frenzy. The more volatile, the more spread was needed to protect the bank. Last, the type of client played a part. Certain clients were considered 'important'; these clients commanded tighter than normal spreads (so-called 'aggressive prices') as a result. Salespeople, who were acting as their clients' mouthpiece as well as being employed by the bank, were caught in the middle of any dispute about spreads. 'I need dollar/mark in 200,' shouted a salesman once to an expert but irascible trader of the old school named Gus. (By 200 he meant 200 million; nobody actually says 'million' on a trading floor.) 'I'm 25 at 35,' came back Gus after a few seconds thought. 'Oh, come on,' shouted back the salesman, 'this is for a top client; I need an aggressive price.' 'An aggressive price?' Gus replied, standing up, his voice gradually rising both in volume and in pitch to reach an ear-splitting, fire-alarm scream. 'OK. I'm 25 at 35, you fat, bald, useless, TWAT!' I can't recall whether he dealt or not.

Actually, it was vitally important for me to know instantly whether I'd dealt after making a price. Because (as you will recall), FX is a principal business – once a client deals with a bank, the bank is at risk. Also, in a market where spreads are razor-sharp, any delay or ambiguity can eat into, and even eradicate, the spread very quickly. One straightforward way for a salesperson who was glued to the phone to let me know if a deal had happened was simply to shout at me at soon as the client made a decision. 'Mine!' indicated that the client had paid the offer, 'Yours!' the opposite. These two words insinuated themselves into the very fabric of everyday discourse on the trading floor. 'Mine', apart from its narrow technical meaning, had expanded its reach to become a general-purpose word of approval in virtually all circumstances: 'What do you reckon to these new shoes?' 'Nice, mate, a solid "mine".' The exact opposite was true of 'Yours', which had become shorthand for contemptuous dismissal: 'Did you meet Linda's new boyfriend?' 'Yeah. He's a doofus – a total "yours".' The London management of my bank once ran a competition to find a new name for the execrable little coffee and sandwich shop that nestled in the corner of the trading floor (which was previously called 'Nibbles' or something equally toe-curling). It amused us greatly that, reputedly, in their innocence, they almost went for some wag's suggested name of 'Yours!' on the grounds that it would represent the noble and intertwined concepts of sharing and accessibility. Sadly, management got wise to the ruse and chose another name so anodyne that I have totally forgotten it.

Unambiguous as screaming was, its one drawback was that if everybody did it, especially simultaneously, mistakes and misunderstandings could occur. To prevent this, most deals were also accompanied by hand signals. To point your forefinger upwards in a sharp jabbing motion or, alternatively, to bring your flattened palm in towards your face like a weights-free biceps curl meant 'Mine'. A finger moved threateningly towards the floor or a palm thrust away from you (a gesture which, if done too enthusiastically, had an unfortunate resemblance to the now rather unfashionable Nazi salute) meant 'Yours'. Thus, back then, a busy time on the trading floor was a real tourist attraction with enough shouting and arm-waving to have delighted the disappointed German lady I mentioned in the Preface, had she been around to witness it.

Do I Feel Lucky?

Once a deal had put me at risk, I had to make some quick decisions. Should I keep the risk on the books or should I get rid of it? Like Clint Eastwood's unfortunate adversary in the film *Dirty Harry*, I had to decide, 'Do I feel lucky?' If I was extremely lucky, another client would come along then and there and do the opposite to the first deal thus taking me out of my risk and allowing me to lock in the spread. In my entire career (not just the brief time on the spot desk), I only saw this happen a dozen times at most. So, in most cases, I was left at risk. What would sway my decision about what to do? In truth, it was a huge number of factors. Did the client who had just dealt know what he was doing? Was he the kind of client who might do sufficient size to move the market his way and thus hurt the bank? A particularly unloved behaviour from certain clients was to call up a number of banks simultaneously and sell each of them a large amount of currency – which made up a gigantic amount in aggregate – and then to stand back and watch them all struggle while the market collapsed. This is known in the trade as a 'drive-by', usually perpetrated by 'important' clients. Another crucial factor: what position did I already have? If I was already long (i.e. had already bought) a lot of dollars, could I tolerate the risk of being given even more? How was the tone of the market? Did it look firm (aka 'well bid' – another universally applied and generic term of judgement, by the way) or, on the contrary, 'offered' (ditto)? For these decisions I would rely partly on my – at that stage, undeveloped – instincts and partly on the information, and sometimes advice, coming from the spot brokers. As the trading day progressed, my mind was a constant whirl of shifting probabilities as deals, and new information, came in from all sides. It was not, and is not, an easy job.

How would I manage my risk, practically speaking? Let's say I decided that I would like to cut down the size of my position since I had been given (sold) a lot of dollars in a flurry by clients; I was a shop that had been sold a large number of jumpers. In market parlance I would be long dollars and (if I had been trading dollar/yen) would be correspondingly short Japanese yen. If the dollar strengthened against the yen, my position would start making money (and vice versa if the dollar weakened). To reduce my exposure to moves in the exchange rate I would, naturally, need to sell dollars. I could employ two broad strategies to do this: passive or active.

A passive strategy relied on others paying me out of my position. One way for this to happen was to show offers to sell dollars to a spot broker. Then, if any other trader at any other bank needed to buy, the broker would match that bank up with me. Another way was to try to get clients to play their part. As more clients asked for prices, I could 'skew' my two-way rates lower in order to show a more attractive selling price. Say I thought that the market price was 20/25; I might make 18/23. This had two advantages. First, if there was a cry of 'Mine!' (customer buys) I would have sold dollars, reduced my risk and, in the jargon, have 'had my spread crossed'. That is, I would have sold dollars more expensively (23) than if I had hit someone else's bid (20) – a good thing. The second advantage was informational. If a client did not deal, that in itself told me something rather worrying: the client was probably looking to sell dollars too. This client's dollars would add to the general selling pressure in the market and could potentially result in the dollar weakening. Thus, as a consequence, it could lead to losses for me – a very bad thing. The significance of a client not dealing (or 'passing') on a skewed price was such that it was always communicated to the trading floor by the familiar and simple means of shouting; a lusty cry of 'Client X just passed on a low one!' would grab everyone's attention. But if the client who had been shown a skewed price (or 'had been read', in the slang) actually hit a low bid – then the intensity of the shouting was redoubled. I had attempted to protect myself by lowering my price and showing an uncompetitive bid, but the client had dealt anyway! The client didn't care about mere pips! The client wanted out! 'I read him lower and he HIT ME!' was a shout loaded with significance. At this point, possibly seeing the writing on the wall and having just got even longer dollars, I'd turn to strategy two and get active.

Active trading in this context would mean going out and selling by hitting other people's bids. Not clients' bids – clients did not hold out prices for banks to deal on, they were 'liquidity takers' in the market parlance, not 'market makers'. No, I would need to pass on the risk to other banks. A perfectly good way of doing this would be to use a spot broker to find bids from other banks who would like to buy. An alternative was simply to call another bank directly and ask for a rate. In the so-called 'direct market', banks would act as market makers to each other exactly as if the bank calling up for a price was a customer. There was a strict etiquette about this. Back then, it was considered extremely bad form to ask for liquidity and not provide it in return when required. Traders took immense professional pride in being able to do so. 'What happens if I don't make a rate?' I once asked Loic. 'Then you are just an amateur, my friend,' was the unambiguous response. All the conventions of two-way pricing, mine-and-yours, skewing and reading that applied to client price requests also applied to these requests between banks. Whether to use a broker or to 'go direct' to another bank was a matter of circumstance as well as individual preference and taste. Each method had advantages and disadvantages. Calling up other banks was usually faster and kept your dealing a little more private than the – quickly visible to a lot of other banks – use of a spot broker. However, it did oblige you to provide liquidity back to the bank being asked and that could be a problem at a later date. It also meant you would cross a bank's full bid-offer spread, unlike the case with the broker, where you might find bids or offers at mid-market.

In extremis, if I needed to get out of a lot of risk very quickly I could trigger a piece of FX action that, in its frantic, choreographed intensity, would have made the day of any tour group. Much to my regret, but probably to the relief of my managers, I never had enough risk during my short career as a barely-average spot trader to invoke this procedure. But other, more senior and expert traders often did. In the metaphorical FX zoo, this was the crowd-pleasing equivalent of feeding the lions by letting them into the wild pig enclosure. Its name was 'calling out' or, simply, 'calls'. Whatever you were doing – whether you were on the phone, loitering near the desk of the attractive new PA, making your way to 'Nibbles' (or whatever the hell it was called) to fetch a mediocre cup of tea – when you heard the yell of 'Calls!' you dropped everything and grabbed your call list.

In my mind's eye I can still see the chaos as, say, Ian, our normally quiet Swiss franc trader, would stand up and suddenly start to shout. 'Calls! I'm selling! Hit anything 15 or better!' was the cue for everyone to start calling their pre-assigned banking counterparties to ask for a price. If the bid they showed was 15 or above, you'd hit it and then holler out the fill – 'I sold 25 at 16, Dresdner Bank'. Ian would tally up what had been sold amidst a cacophony of yelling. Normally, for run-of-the-mill call-outs, only the 'A' team of senior spot traders would be involved, calling the big market-making banks. Loic, Bernd and I on the options desk were in the 'C' team with a responsibility for getting prices in smaller size from a list of peripheral banks. For us to be roped in on any call-out meant that things were getting serious and the bank really needed to shift some risk – thus I was always in an agony of nerves throughout the process hoping that I wouldn't make some kind of highly visible rookie error. After the shouting was done, or when he was satisfied that enough risk was out of the door, Ian (or whoever had asked for calls) would signal a halt and begin the process of totting up what had just happened. The sharp-eyed among you might be thinking that this whole procedure sounds a little like the despised 'drive-by' perpetrated by clients. And in that, I must confess, you would be right. I make no excuses for the double standards.

Thus it was that the trading day progressed from early morning until early evening: clients asking for prices, the shouts of traders and salespeople, the background drone of the broker loudspeakers ('80/83 dollar/mark, 80/83, 83 paid, comes back 81/84 . . .') all rising and falling in volume as news hit the wires or data was released. The noise of a churning, heaving market where risk was being taken from clients and offloaded from bank to bank like a pinball rattling inside a gigantic arcade machine, bells and buzzers sounding, the score rising and falling. Ultimately, somewhere, the dollars (say) would pop out of the machine into the hands of a client who needed to use them somehow. You could be forgiven for thinking at this point, why go through this complicated, noisy procedure? Clients loaded the ball (the risk) into the pinball machine and other clients eventually took it out; why couldn't they just deal with each other? The answer is convenience and timing.

Imagine you are going on holiday and you need to exchange your pounds for euros. Now imagine that when you get to the Cambio (currency exchange booth) at the airport you can't just transact there and then and take away your euros. Imagine that you have to wait for another passenger to come by who wants to do the exact opposite of what you want to do. It's possible that you could get lucky. Or you might get unlucky with a crowd of people all trying to do the same thing as you, forcing you to wait and to miss your plane. The Cambio, standing as market maker, ready to transact when you want, provides a guarantee of liquidity. It is, in effect, a miniature version of the FX market with its banks and brokers standing ready to process client requests. And, incidentally, just like at the Cambio, the bulk of clients of the FX market back then actually needed to use the currency. In popular imagination, the FX market was simply a den of speculation. Naturally, speculation went on but its importance was less than you might imagine. Research done by my colleagues at Deutsche Bank as late as 2007[1] showed that only about 25 per cent on average of the flows Deutsche saw were unambiguously speculative (although in certain periods this percentage might rise). Half were definitely not and the remaining 25 per cent were difficult to classify.

The Coming of Computers

Looking back, for all its seemingly clunky mechanics, the FX market worked very well. It provided continuous liquidity to tens of thousands of clients ranging from private individuals and small businesses to giant pension funds and globally famous industrial concerns.

During the first years of my career it coped well with the macro-economic shocks of Saddam Hussein's invasion of Kuwait and the subsequent Gulf War and with turmoil in the former Soviet Union and its satellites. More controversially, it functioned as the market-place for the speculative and (equally important, though less widely reported) commercial flows that blew apart the European Exchange Rate Mechanism in 1992. Views differ strongly on this event, which reverberates in European politics to this day. I would argue that subsequent history shows that the countries affected were better off as a result, my own (the UK) for one. It also seems pretty obvious that Italy, say, a country that is struggling economically to some extent within the euro at current parities, would have fared even worse had it joined with the Italian lira 25 per cent stronger than its entry point in 1999. Whatever your opinion, the FX market played its part efficiently and effectively in this and other crises of the first part of the 1990s. What is strange in retrospect, given how the market has developed since then, is that it did so with very little help from computers.

That is not to say that computers played no part. Then, as now, if you looked at a typical desk on a trading floor you would see a large number of screens in front of every person; each of these was attached to a computer somewhere. But many of the screens back in the 1990s were connected to data providers like Reuters or Bloomberg that would stream data about a plethora of financial markets in return for a fee. Each provider would give a trader that firm's own proprietary screen, inevitably a softly humming cathode-ray job. These screens took up a lot of desk space and, what's more, threw off so much heat that, taken in aggregate, they often made the trading floor a very, very hot place, especially in summer. But you could not interact with the screens; they were just showing information. In essence, they were like little televisions, each tuned (to any normal person's eyes) to a particularly boring set of text-based programmes. Some screens, however, allowed you to do things that were a little more interesting.

Reuters, which back then had an armlock on providing FX-related services (Bloomberg was more about bonds and equities), had a product called the Reuters Dealer. This allowed a trader to type a message to any other trader in the world who was attached to the system, whether in his own bank or a rival. In effect, it was a glorified two-way typewriter but it found its place in FX by allowing traders to call out for prices. Although earlier I described the process of calling other banks as if it was done entirely on the telephone, a number of the calls would be made using Reuters Dealer since it was possible to have up to four conversations open at the same time – a distinct advantage during a call-out. The procedure was to type in the four-letter code of the bank you wished to contact and a short text specifying what you wanted. Usually, each separate desk in a bank had a different code but not each trader. So for example, if someone wished to contact the Merrill Lynch options desk, they would have typed in the code MLOP – this would sound a beeping alarm on the Reuters Dealer screen of each options trader. To this day, despite not having used Reuters Dealer for about 16 years, I can still recall many of the codes, so ingrained were they in my daily routine: CIOP was Citibank, GSOP Goldman, etc. A typical call for a spot price would be the quintessence of brevity. 'USDDEM 50; 20/25; URS', meant a request for a spot price for $50 million against the Deutschmark; a price of 20/25 being made; and the 20 bid being hit. It was crude, but effective.

Computers also played a part in the very last stage in the FX production line – 'post-deal' processing. FX deals require a two-way electronic transfer of currency from one bank's accounts to another's. Each of the hundreds of deals that would be transacted every day would need to be settled. This process employed a large number of back-office staff since, back then, each deal would need to be typed in manually to a universally used system called SWIFT that would then automatically make the appropriate payments. Question: how did the back office get to know what deals had been

done? Answer: traders or salespeople would need to type the details into yet another terminal on their desks. Adding to the din
during the day would be the pleading of traders for salespeople
to enter deals that had been done with clients ('For fuck's sake,
can you PLEASE get those Soros deals in?') or their angry shouts
as they discovered mistakes had been made. As you might expect
from fallible humans typing under time pressure, mistakes were
common and, since entering the deal into the so-called 'risk management system' not only fed the settlements process but also allowed a trader to keep track of his position, could also be extremely
costly. An 'out trade' (where, say, a purchase of dollars was entered
incorrectly as a sale) could fool a trader into thinking he was short
when he was actually long. This was especially a problem during
busy periods where so many deals were done that it was difficult
to keep track mentally of what was happening. Despite this, the
markets – in their flawed human way – worked. Computers were
an adjunct to human beings: they showed humans information;
they kept a tally of deals; they took some of the drudgery out of
settlements. But they were not yet replacing humans. They were
not making decisions. That was still to come.

Let's All Meet Up in RD-2000

I can't remember when it was that I saw an EBS screen for the first
time; it must have been around 1994 or so. By this time I had left
Merrill Lynch and was working at Bankers Trust. A group of us
gathered around the desk of a spot trader like schoolkids as he demonstrated what it did. EBS (which stands for Electronic Broking Services) was a company owned by a consortium of a couple of dozen
of the biggest banks in FX; Bankers Trust was one of them. The EBS
system was an attempt, in electronic form, to replicate the functions
of the spot broker. On a screen installed among the crowded nest

of other screens on a trader's desk, driven by a chunky little beige plastic keyboard that also joined two or three others, a trader could post prices and could deal FX just like he could with his favourite broker. Along specially installed communications lines – this was before trading routinely occurred over the internet – traders' orders to be placed into the market would be transmitted to the EBS central computer system where they were matched. Notification about filled orders (buys or sells) would be transmitted back to the trader. It was a simple, but quite slick-looking product.

Why had the consortium of banks decided to create this system? Only in very small part was the answer a purely economic one. True, the levels of brokerage (the fee per unit of FX transacted) would be lower over EBS than via a traditional 'voice' broker and so, other things being equal, banks would save on their brokerage bills – not an insignificant plus. But the jointly held company itself was not designed to make money; it would break even as a 'utility'. The real reason the banks acted was that they were supremely nervous about a rival product that had been launched by Reuters: Reuters Dealing 2000-2 (usually shortened to the Star Wars acronym, RD-2000). Functionally speaking, this was designed to do the very same thing as EBS in an almost identical way. As such, its aim was to displace brokers. Reuters' motivations, however, were straightforwardly commercial. The brokerage that was being paid to interdealer brokers to fund the purchase of Porsches and Aston Martins would instead flow to the shareholders and staff of Reuters. To make this happen, the company could capitalise on two of its major strengths: first, a great deal of technical know-how about running the technology of global communications between banks, since this was the core of Reuters' existing business; and, second, Reuters' already strong presence in FX. This was not just a matter of perception and branding: Reuters' existing products were already sitting on traders' desks. In the jargon, the company had 'desk real estate' and this made it much easier to install upgraded kit on a bank's packed and overheating trading floor. The banks, in response, had clubbed together to create EBS because they feared that if Reuters displaced the brokers and controlled the market-place for FX, they would ultimately be able to use that power to act against the banks' interests; EBS was an attempt to stop that happening. EBS was therefore, in strategic terms, a defensive play.

But why were these systems being developed in the 1990s? Why not before? The simple answer is because they *could* be developed. The cost per unit of performance of computers had fallen to the point that it had become feasible to create a broker killer. The availability of technology had dictated strategy. It was to become a familiar theme.

Eaten by Computers

At first, though, neither EBS nor the Reuters system made much of an impact on the market. Despite the insistence from the consortium's constituent banks that their traders must use EBS, it took a while for screens to be installed and, even when they had been, because traders were unfamiliar with the systems' operation they were not the first place to go to deal, especially in times of market volatility. The EBS system acquired the dismissive nickname of 'the Toy'. Maybe it was fine to do little bits and pieces on, but it was not for real men doing real size. Behind this attitude was a deeper problem: traders liked dealing with brokers. They had got used to it over the years and, what's more, many traders actually liked the brokers personally. After the trading day was done, brokers would regularly entertain the traders and were often excellent company. A man called David, who back in 1990 on my second day in the market was the first broker I ever spoke to, is still a good friend and is godfather to my youngest son Arthur – he of the rubbish penguins. Lots of other traders have similar tales. How could this newfangled combination of plastic keyboard and flickering screen replace a broker? Would it go to the pub with you? Would it go to the football? Would it tell jokes? No, it would not. At first, then, brokers were safe.

But as the months and years went on, the systems gradually started to win. First off, they were genuinely rather convenient. Most banks built a means of downloading deals straight from the machine; this meant less work for the traders, who didn't have to type the details of what they had done into their own systems. Even better, it meant fewer mistakes and 'out-trades'. Also, because the numbers displayed on the screen were real, dealing prices, not just levels, traders started to look at them to gauge what was happening in the market. When they did, they paid just a little bit less attention to the chatter from the broker boxes. Some traders started to use the screens as part of the complex game of bluff and double bluff between them and the other banks. For instance, if you were just about to sell a large amount of dollars via a call-out, why not buy a few on the Toy to make other banks think the market was well bid? Maybe the banks you called would then read you up, show better bids and let you sell dollars more expensively. Once other traders started using the screen in this way, it made sense for you to show prices on the Toy because then you would see Citibank on it (for instance) and be forewarned. A positive feedback loop had been formed: as more traders at more banks started making prices and doing deals on the automated systems it made them more important – this drew in more liquidity. There was no definite tipping point, but the signs of the extinction of the spot broker started mounting from the mid-1990s until the end of the decade: EBS and Reuters routinely announced record trading volumes through their platforms; traders began to ask for the screens rather than accepting them on sufferance; more and more banks signed up to the systems. It became common to be introduced to a new options broker (the options market, being more complex, was not automated at all at this stage) who had 'moved over from the spot side' – sadly, few made the transition successfully.

The remaining spot brokers redoubled their efforts like John Henry in the famous folk song, who burst his heart while laying railway track in a heroic but doomed competition with a steam hammer: they entertained more, they stayed later. But it was hopeless. In time, EBS and RD-2000 took over more or less completely and broker boxes fell silent. Interestingly, the battle between the rival computer systems didn't end with the eclipse of one by the other like the classic business-school case study of VHS versus Betamax in home video recorders. Instead, they divided the FX market along currency lines. It was a little like the division of post-war Europe. EBS was the king in dollar/mark (and, later, euro/dollar) and dollar/yen. Reuters reigned over the 'colonial currencies' (Australian, Canadian and New Zealand dollars) as well as emerging markets. Cable, rather like an FX version of East and West Germany, was split between them. In 1999, the symbolic end of the spot broker came with the merger of M. W. Marshall & Co. (established 1866) with Prebon Yamane, another broker with its roots in the bond market.[2] After that, though honoured at first in the title of the combined entity, the name Marshall quietly disappeared.

But what about the spot brokers themselves? A few drifted to banks where they became traders or, more commonly, salesmen. Some simply retired or found work outside finance. Anecdotally, a number of them became London black-cab drivers. In around 2003 I met one who had done just that. I struck up a conversation with him as he took me home from the office; his name was Mickey. 'I used to be a spot broker,' he told me after he found out where I worked, 'it was great.' We reminisced for a while about the way the FX market had been, then, as we approached my street, he said, a little sadly, 'But it had to end, we couldn't beat the computers – they ate us all alive.' We arrived outside my house where I got out and paid him. As he began to drive off, he slowed down and shouted back at me, 'They ate us alive – and they'll do it to everyone!' With that, he turned the corner and drove out of sight.

CHAPTER 2

Whales Don't Eat Elephants

Triangle Man and the Clackatron

It was spring 1999 and I was bored. The takeover of my employer Bankers Trust by Deutsche Bank had been agreed late the previous year after the Russia crisis and the collapse of a major hedge fund called Long-Term Capital Management (LTCM) but had not yet been consummated. Like every other trader in Bankers, I had been given strict instructions by management on how I could help the process, namely do as little as possible and don't screw up. My boss Ron, a crop-haired and intense Israeli ex-paratrooper, packed around 20 of us emerging markets traders and salespeople into a cramped, anonymous, overheated meeting room to explain. 'Don't add any risk to the books, just unwind things. If a customer wants a new trade, send him to Deutsche. Cooperate fully with any of their guys looking over our positions to value them.' He paused, then scanned the room. 'Oh, and try to get yourself a job. They'll be doing interviews soon.' My heart sank. I certainly needed a job; the previous year I had bought and moved into a bigger house and now my wife was heavily pregnant with my second son. The first, Fred, was three. But the prospect of a job with Deutsche Bank looked remote. The Deutsche Bank emerging markets people were, to put it mildly, not very keen on Bankers Trust as a result of a number of market-related disputes and run-ins between the two banks in the recent past. Predictably, when, one after the other, we all trudged the short walk to the Deutsche Bank offices to make our pitch to be employed there, the resulting interviews were mostly car wrecks. No sale; redundancy beckoned.

As I wearily started to prepare my CV to send out to other banks, I was saved the bother by an offer to join Deutsche's FX department, which, just as at Bankers Trust, was a separate team from Emerging Markets and was run by a wiry and almost intimidatingly focused Australian called Hal. His bold and rather clever strategy was just to scoop up everyone from Bankers Trust who knew about FX and add them to his existing staff. He'd take the best from the Bankers and Deutsche Bank people later after he'd seen them all in action. Aside from the fact that I would be spared the prospect of touting myself around the market or, worse, of facing immediate unemployment, I was genuinely excited by the prospect of joining Deutsche's FX team. They had a fast-growing reputation and in the past had hired a few Bankers Trust people I was still friendly with. With my immediate future sorted out and with months to wait until the official completion of the takeover and the start of my new job, I cheerfully began to dedicate myself to the other of Ron's instructions: doing absolutely nothing on full pay.

At first, this was fine. I made a hit list of novels I wanted to read or reread and ploughed through them with serious intent. Appropriately, given what I'd been trading for the last couple of years, most were by Russians. In time, though, even the company of Tolstoy, Pushkin and Dostoyevsky began to pall and serious ennui set in. Then, one day, as I was walking somewhat aimlessly around the now becalmed and enervated trading floor, I noticed an unfamiliar FX trader whose bursts of frenetic activity were in sharp contrast to the general torpor. I watched him for some time. A young, fit-looking guy in his mid-twenties, he would remain utterly silent for tens of minutes on end watching his screens intently like a suit-clad cobra. Then, suddenly, he would frantically begin to pound the keys of his stubby little EBS or Reuters keypads, his fingers a blur of motion. Afterwards, he'd fall silent and motionless again. Occasionally, after a noticeably intense period of keyboard manipulation, he'd shout, 'Free cash!' to no one in particular and to everyone in general; then, silence. Eventually, I asked one of his colleagues what he was doing. 'Oh, he's prop, mate,' I was told. 'He's doing triangle arb in Swiss. He's great at it. Basically he's autistic, a regular fucking Rain Man. We call him Triangle Man.'

Triangle 'arb' (or arbitrage) is a more involved variant of the trick we saw with jumpers in Loic's explanation of two-way pricing, whereby a customer could make risk-free profit by buying a jumper for £36 and (almost) simultaneously selling it at £38 to another shop. Triangle arbitrage, which is a specialised subcategory of proprietary or 'prop' trading (aka 'gambling with the bank's money', if we are being pejorative), relies on the fact that the most heavily traded currencies are quoted in a number of ways. For example, the Swiss franc is commonly quoted against the US dollar and also against the euro. Naturally, the US dollar itself is also separately quoted against the euro. Usually different traders make each rate. If the three rates (the three sides of the 'Swiss currency triangle') ever get out of line, then a sharp-witted trader can make a quick profit. If you are curious about how this works, see the example in the footnote.* For Triangle Man (whose mother had actually named him Paul) to be able to exploit arbitrages required his constant and unrelenting focus on the market and lightning-fast reflexes. But more curious was his ability to pick out arbitrages in the first place. I asked him how he did it. He looked a little abashed. 'I just sort of "see" when the rates are out of line,' he explained. He'd use a calculator to check sometimes, but often he just knew.

---

* Let's say US dollars and euros are worth exactly the same; if so, the exchange rate is said to be 'at parity' (or, to write that like a professional, USD/EUR = 1.0000). If the Swiss franc per euro exchange rate is at 1.0500 (CHF/EUR = 1.0500) and the Swiss franc per US dollar rate is at 1.0400 (CHF/USD = 1.0400) then there is an arbitrage assuming that you can buy and sell at the same rate; i.e. a zero bid-offer spread. How would Triangle Man take advantage of it? First off, he'd buy $10 million using 10,400,000 Swiss francs. Then he'd sell those dollars for €10 million. Last, he'd sell the euros for 10,500,000 Swiss francs, netting him a quick profit of 100,000 Swiss francs. In reality, of course, the opportunities for profit were much less obvious and very much smaller than in this example and would need to take into account the – albeit tiny – bid-offer spread.

This slightly spooky skill allowed him to net the bank many millions of dollars in profits. Despite this, he admitted that sometimes he simply wasn't fast enough to capture an opportunity; it disappeared before he could trade.

If I had been a cartoon character, a light bulb would have popped into view above my head at this point. 'Can't we just do what he's doing with computers?' I asked a friend of mine in the IT department soon afterwards. 'A computer would always be fast enough and would never get bored or tired. Why don't we just build something to mimic him?' There were numerous reasons we couldn't do it, he explained patiently with the air of a sceptical builder looking at extravagant architectural plans. First off, and easiest to cure, the exchange rate data on EBS and Reuters screens was meant for humans to read, not computers. To get the prices into a form that a computer could perform calculations on, the data would need to be extracted in real time by a clunky process called 'screen scraping'. But the insurmountable problem came after the computer had identified arbitrages: how could it execute the trades? The only way to trade on either dealing system was to use the keyboard – and computers don't have fingers. He also reminded me that the rules of EBS and Reuters specifically forbade any such automated trading in an attempt to make their market safer for fallible humans. 'Besides,' he said with a heavy sigh, 'we're all under instructions not to do anything new until the takeover is finalised so we'd never get the funding.' Scrub that idea, then. It was only many years later, while in casual conversation with an official from the Bank of England, that I found out that in the early 2000s one bank, Lehman Brothers, had created an ingenious (if somewhat ethically dubious) solution to these problems: they had given the computer some fingers.

The 'Clackatron', as the collection of mechanical digits was dubbed, was a box-like device that sat above the EBS keyboard. As the computer that it was attached to identified suitable trades, the Clackatron would use an array of metal prodders to press down on the appropriate EBS keys, so creating a rattle of loud 'clacking' noises. One minor issue was that the device was against the rules; this meant that it was hidden away in case any visitor to the trading floor from EBS ever saw it. Even more problematically, it had a habit of regularly going a little bit haywire and breaking keypads and so, I was told, the Clackatron's keepers needed to come up with ever more outlandish excuses to EBS for why they were getting through them at such a lick. It made money but, in time, the machine was made redundant by better technology and, like human spot brokers before it, was cast aside (albeit into a cupboard rather than onto a taxi rank). If the story of the computerisation of banking was told as natural history, with its progress indicated by a succession of gradually more complex forms, the Clackatron would be the missing link, a strange mechanical archaeopteryx combining elements of the familiar and analogue with the new and digital. And like the archaeopteryx it was destined for extinction.

Of course, I was ignorant of the Clackatron back in 1999 and so my IT friend's discouraging words dampened my enthusiasm for my first idea. But a fire had been started. I began to obsess about the question of what could be done with computers in the FX business that I would shortly be joining at Deutsche Bank. I had made some efforts in this direction in the past. With my colleague Darren, a shrewd, funny, skinheaded son of Blackpool, Lancashire, I had built some very elaborate spreadsheets to automate the pricing and booking of deals in the Russian bond and FX markets. The sheet took 'scraped' pricing feeds from various screens and calculated and published hundreds of prices in real time. The idea was to avoid making stupid human errors in the excitement and noise of trading. It worked well, but it was small-scale stuff; I dreamed of bigger things. Why couldn't all FX options prices be made automatically? Why did humans need to book deals? Why couldn't all prices be shown to customers online rather than going through a salesman? Why weren't FX options brokered electronically like spot was on EBS? There was no way I could address these ideas in my final few months at Bankers Trust, but I started to sketch out plans of how I thought we could do it at Deutsche.

Those Who Cannes, Do

The takeover became official over a weekend in June 1999 and thus I started my new job. Adding to the strange mix of excitement and apprehension I experienced (which was akin to how I'd felt starting a new school) was the disorientation of also having a new child. On the Friday before so-called 'change of control weekend', I was a Bankers Trust employee with one child; on the Monday after it, my business card said 'Managing Director, Deutsche Bank', and I was a father of two. My middle son, Eddie, was born on the Saturday. Amid the chaos of finding my seat in Deutsche's unfamiliar and brand-new offices and getting all my screens working that Monday, I was introduced to my future workmates. My boss was a man called Jim whom I had known at Bankers Trust – a few years previously he had left to join Deutsche Bank and he was now being reunited with some of his old colleagues. Friendly and personable and with a rugby player's build (he'd been outstanding at the sport as a schoolboy), he masked his sharp mind and determination with an air of clubby affability. He immediately set me to work, not as a trader, but on a number of minor but complex and rather politically delicate managerial tasks concerning the integration of Bankers Trust's FX business with Deutsche's. Looking back, I suspect it was a test. If so, given that I stayed at the bank for another 15 years, I must have passed it. However, despite all our efforts to fit in, my fellow Bankers Trust refugees and I were regarded by the Deutsche natives with some suspicion. 'We should have fired the lot of these Bankers bastards,' I once overheard one say to another before suddenly falling into embarrassed silence as he clocked me. Hal, the head of FX, decided to address this problem head on; we would have a meeting of the entire FX department away from the office – what was called an 'offsite'.

The offsite Hal planned was on a grander scale than anything I'd experienced at Bankers Trust, where penny-pinching was institutionalised. This trait was exemplified by the often-told story of the bank's pugnacious CEO Charlie Sanford (who always insisted on travelling in an economy seat on flights between London and New York) pointedly teasing a managing director who had travelled in first class on the same plane as him. 'See here, Kelly,' he said in his Southern twang as he ran into the discomfited man in the arrivals hall, 'I got here the exact same damned time as you did and I saved $2,000 for the shareholders.' Accordingly, offsites I had experienced had been very low-key affairs. Not this time. Hal got the bank to approve his plan to have ours in Cannes. The logistics alone were daunting – the FX department's traders were based in half a dozen cities around the globe and salespeople were based in a dozen more. How could we get everyone together and still keep the business functioning 24 hours a day? A complex plan of skeleton staffing and staggered flight times was engineered to get a couple of hundred staff into one – rather elegant – hotel for the two-day meeting. Hal's intention for the offsite was twofold: first, to use the unfamiliar and convivial setting (and freely available alcohol) to try to break down the antipathy between the Deutsche Bank and Bankers Trust contingents; second, to discuss and 'socialise' (banking jargon for 'share') what strategy the department should pursue. In both aims he succeeded.

He was due to make his opening speech to all of us in a large auditorium in the hotel on the morning of the first day. I can't say that he was facing an audience at the peak of its attentiveness: we had arrived the previous evening and many of us were jet-lagged and most were suffering the after-effects of vigorously pursuing Hal's bonding agenda the night before. We were jolted from our lethargy by his entrance. The lights were lowered and, in the darkness, pounding nightclub-volume trance music filled our ears. A film started up, projected on a huge screen behind the podium, showing fast-cut footage of all the department's trading floors and offices overlaid with bullet point statistics showing its enormous scale. It was as slick and professional as a music video. The contrast to a typical Bankers Trust meeting (information on hand-produced acetate sheets thrown up on a screen by an ancient, humming overhead projector) couldn't have been more violent. 'Holy shit,' I muttered to the man on my left, 'is he going to come on wearing a jet pack?' Hal didn't, but his speech made a deep impression nonetheless.

Deutsche Bank's FX business was at a crossroads, he told us. Like the rest of Deutsche Bank's investment banking arm it had been built up quickly since 1995 when the bank's main board had decided to get serious about investment banking. Previously, Deutsche's efforts had been, let us say, a little lacklustre. Back then, he said, Deutsche Bank had not excelled at FX. I stifled a hoot of spontaneous laughter at that; Deutsche had been a standing joke in the market – 'not excelling' didn't begin to do its former incompetence justice. He told us how, in the hugely influential poll conducted annually by the magazine *Euromoney*,* Deutsche had ranked 22nd in terms of market share in FX – an extraordinarily poor ranking for a bank of its size. After a hiring spree and a brutal process of rationalising the number of trading locations (Germany alone had contained a dozen or so), the bank's strong relationship with its corporate clients and its push to deal with hedge funds had netted it business that had catapulted it to second place. In this position it now looked up at Citibank, which had retained the number one slot every single year since the survey had started in the 1970s. The progress had been good, Hal told us, but not good enough. The aim

---

* All the *Euromoney* survey results mentioned in this book are set out in a table in Appendix 1.

was to become number one: not just in market share, although that was important, but in profitability, customer service and, in short, 'general all-round excellence'. But, he continued, his gaze sweeping accusingly over the room, to overtake Citi we couldn't just repeat what had been done in the past few years; Citibank were too big, too entrenched. We would have to do something different: 'That's why we are here today, to figure out what to do.'

Hal was not exaggerating the scale of the task. Citibank was everywhere in the FX market; the bank's salespeople were based in virtually every city I had ever heard of and their client list was gigantic. To try to replicate their model would be so cripplingly expensive as to be unfeasible. Deutsche Bank's costs in FX were already high before the complication caused by adding the Bankers Trust people and computer systems. But the prize, Hal concluded, was worth the effort: 'If we get this right, it could mean billions of euros for the bank in the years to come. So we need to get it right.'

After another few formal presentations and a hurried lunch, we split into groups of 15 or so to discuss various questions that Hal had set us. The group I was in was sent to a plushly furnished meeting room to consider 'how to expand the reach of sales'. Various ideas were thrown around. One very loud French salesman lobbied for the idea of a call centre in a cheap location where smaller clients could be directed. Another, from our Singapore office, suggested hiring a lot of salespeople in Singapore and have them cover the rest of the Asian region by means of frequent flights: 'It's got to be cheaper than opening up offices, right?' Maybe, I thought, but the cost of replacing the jet-dazed salespeople's burned-out husks every two years might not run cheap.

We quickly homed in on the idea of reaching clients electronically. It was 1999 and in the heat of the dot-com boom, after all. If we could make prices in small amounts of currency available via screens, then our customers could just click and deal without bothering our sales staff. All the salespeople in the room liked this

idea since they hated doing the same amount of keyboard bashing
for a tiny deal as a big one. The traders liked it too – small deals
were actually more profitable per unit of risk than big ones – but
they worried about their workload if hundreds of tiny price requests started pouring in. Thinking of my Russian bond spreadsheet and the ideas I had been working on in the months before I
started at Deutsche, I pitched in and started to talk in lyrical terms
about the benefits of automating price-making. 'We could make all
small prices automatically and book the deals automatically too,' I
raved to the room at large. 'It could generate a ton of profit but we
wouldn't need to hire more people.' Others joined in enthusiastically. Freed of the crushing obligation of handling the multitude
of tedious tiny deals – the small fry – salespeople would be able
to use their time to concentrate on bringing in large, profitable
and noteworthy trades (so-called 'elephant deals') and then bask
in the resulting glory. Traders would be able to spend their time
handling more risk. Every one of us started dreaming of an Elysian
future where we could focus on the fun parts of our jobs and let
the machines take care of the boring but profitable bits, like a crew
of well-behaved digital domestic servants. It was perfect! I dubbed
the idea the 'Plankton Strategy', noting to room-wide nods of approval that the largest animal on earth, the blue whale, didn't survive on a diet of elephants but rather on tons and tons of krill. On
the strength of this extravagant wildlife-based metaphor, the group
chose me to present our recommendations to the full auditorium.

Looking back years later on any major change it often seems obvious that it had to happen in the way that it did. Certainly, I feel
that now about the way Deutsche Bank's FX department became
automated. But, although my presentation that day went down well
and was echoed by the views of several other teams who had drawn
very similar conclusions on other questions, in truth there were
other plausible and competing visions set out. Maybe we should
formally team up with small regional banks in Asia to provide FX

prices to their customers? They would provide the sales force and would deal directly with their clients before passing on the risk to Deutsche Bank, which would, in effect, become a wholesaler. Maybe we should increase profitability by doing more proprietary trading? So much flow was passing through the books that, if it were properly analysed, we should be able to glean sufficient clues to enable Deutsche to trade at a profit on its own account. But it was the electronic strategy that won out – partly of course because this was what Hal had planned from the first. It is an infallible rule of management that if you let the people who work for you think they've come up with an idea they will strain to make it happen much more willingly than if the idea is seen to be yours.

Building a Better Money Machine

Back in the office after the offsite, work began in earnest. How vast a task we'd set ourselves was made plain by Mark, the head of the IT team responsible for the FX department. Mark, as befitted his birthplace in the north of England, was renowned for his bluntness. A senior colleague of mine once asked him whether his team could complete a piece of analysis by an insanely tight deadline. 'No,' came the reply. Shocked silence – IT people were normally a walkover. 'Well, I suppose we could come up with something by then,' he said at last (at which my colleague's face brightened for a moment), 'but it would be shit.' Happily for us, his bluntness was matched by his competence and a refreshing disinclination to use jargon.

'What we're proposing to do', he told me and the other assembled managing directors during one of a series of meetings, 'is like swapping out all four engines in a 747 while flying across the Atlantic.' It wasn't just that we'd need to create software to make prices and to book deals. If we were serious in our goals, all the computer systems that processed deals further down the production line would need to change in order to cope with a far greater volume of small tickets (i.e. the 'plankton'). Further complicating the job was the need to make the changes while continuing to run FX to make money for the bank; we couldn't just stop dealing during the years it would take. He produced a diagram showing how the various systems we already had in place all fitted together. It was a mind-boggling mess. Computer systems built internally at Deutsche jostled with others provided by software vendors. There were separate versions of the same system in different parts of the world. There were Bankers Trust systems; there were spreadsheets; there were ominous gaps with boxes marked 'manual process'. My mouth sagged open a little. And then he whipped out another diagram entitled 'Potential Future State'. I smiled; this one was as orderly as a Mondrian. The current maze of incompatible risk management systems (which allow traders to see what risk they have on the books) was replaced by one box. The same was true of the settlement systems that made sure all the cash flows into and out of the bank were handled correctly. No longer would separate products and separate countries have different technologies; one system would rule them all. And it went further than that. We realised that to get the most out of the change, we'd need to deal wherever possible in one legal name around the world (Deutsche Bank London AG was the choice) in order to allow us to standardise our contracts. The result of all of this was, in effect, a plan to smash together a diverse set of businesses fragmented along product and regional lines to create one big, seamless global team.

If I had seen all of this written down as a case study at business school it would have been an easy one to analyse. FX is a high volume, low margin business – cost was critical. What we were planning to do was to drive down the marginal cost of providing the service, to offer it more cheaply and thus to gain a bigger share of the 'FX wallet' (that is, the total amount that customers all over the world spend on transacting FX). With the extra profit we would make as a result, we'd be able to spend more on technology to push down the cost even further. It would be a virtuous circle wherein we would drive the concentration of market share. After the Cannes offsite, the expression 'The Big Are Getting Bigger' started to be bandied around as a justificatory catchphrase in any discussion of what we were up to. However, what is striking to me in retrospect is that I can recall no attempt at the time to figure out the precise numbers around how this plan would work. We were embarking on a very ambitious programme of change so it would have been natural to seek answers to a few obvious questions. How much would costs reduce? How much extra market share would we get? How would other banks respond?

In the course of writing this book, I interviewed a number of people who had been my colleagues around this time. I asked them if there had there been any cost/benefit work done (which I had been unaware of) to justify the decision. There had been back of the envelope stuff but very little even of that, I was told. Did we ever think of getting McKinsey or some other set of consultants to opine? At that, one of my interviewees spluttered with laughter down the phone: 'McKinsey? How the hell would they have helped? They like numbers and we didn't have any.' That, at heart, was the reason for the seeming lack of rigour – the data that would have been needed to construct the classic investment case simply wasn't available. Banking is a very secretive business and although we had a vague idea of market shares in the FX market (from not very scientific surveys like the one run by *Euromoney* magazine) our knowledge of other banks' revenues was sketchy and our knowledge of their costs was well-nigh zero. Extremely limited too was any idea of how customers would respond to changes in bid-offer spreads (which, as we saw in the last chapter, is the critical pricing decision in FX), not least because we didn't keep the data on how they'd responded in the past. Once a trader had yelled out 20/25 and then had either dealt or not, the fact that he'd quoted 5 pips wide was lost forever because the whole shouting-pricing-dealing process was manual.

Last, it was even difficult to figure out how the changes we were planning would affect our own costs. Banks, even back then, were extremely complex beasts; Deutsche was no exception. For a department like FX, although a chunk of its costs were spent directly on wages and travel for the folk actually doing Foreign Exchange-y stuff, the biggest portion of its costs came from spending in support departments. These costs came back to FX as a series of bills presented for services rendered: the IT department would present a bill; so would research; so would the legal department; and so on. Even the costs attached to the office of the board of Deutsche Bank were allocated. 'You see Breuer's right thumb?' the department's chief accountant asked me once when an interview with our then CEO Rolf Breuer was shown on one of the many televisions that festooned the trading floor. 'Yeah,' I said. 'We pay for that thumb,' he claimed, deadpan. How the billing from these many departments was arrived at was often opaque and so it was a tricky job to figure out exactly how these allocated costs would respond to anything we did. It would be extraordinarily difficult to figure it out for the massive changes we wanted.

In short, the programme of automation was started as a leap of faith. Like Triangle Man just 'knowing' about arbitrages without resorting to his calculator, a dozen or so of us, led by Hal, just felt that it should work. 'One thing that drove me was fear,' said one of my ex-colleagues when I spoke to him. 'It seemed so obvious after everything that had happened with EBS and with the buzz at the time about the Internet that FX was ripe for automation. If we didn't do it, we'd surely be killed by another bank that did.' I can't say I felt fear but nor was my excitement about the programme motivated primarily by thoughts of riches. FX, because of the simplicity of its most important product (spot) and its slightly rough-round-the-edges air, was, at the time, regarded as a deeply unfashionable place within Deutsche despite the strong financial contribution it made. Pay, as a result, although absurdly high compared to the outside world, was unexceptional by banking standards. Besides, the pay-off for the plans we were making might not happen for many years, if at all. It is difficult to drag yourself into the office in the early hours of the morning day after day purely on the promise of an uncertain pay cheque years in the future. No, what really excited me was the prospect of building this new money machine and seeing if it would work. It was same feeling I got as a small child rummaging through my box of Lego to build elaborate spaceships on a Saturday afternoon as my dad listened out for the football scores. In this I was not alone: the FX market, and Deutsche in particular, had attracted many more geeks in the ten years since I had started my career.

As we set to work, did I ever think at any stage what the wider consequences might be? Did I wonder how the market would develop if other banks copied us? How many FX staff, like spot brokers before them, could be made redundant? Where it might all end? Not really. As the (possibly apocryphal) quote by quantum physicist Niels Bohr has it, 'Predictions are very hard to make, especially about the future.' I suppose I just had a touching faith that if we gave our customers what they wanted, all would be well; the invisible hand would make things turn out fine. I was partly right.

Meetings Monkey and Cat Herder

A few months later, in early 2000, FX was reorganised. Jim was promoted to a role running FX in Europe and I was asked, along with my colleague Matt, to take over his old job running the options business globally. This made me happy, but nervous. Happy because Deutsche's options business was a large and successful one and because I was returning to the product where I had started my career and which I knew best. Nervous because previously, at Bankers Trust, I had only managed three or four traders in one location and I would now need to manage dozens scattered around the globe. Although the options business was less important than spot or forwards, it still contributed around a quarter of departmental revenues. The bank couldn't afford for us to screw it up, a fact made plain to me by Hal ('Mate, don't screw it up'). Although we were co-heads, Matt and I split the workload. A likeable, good-natured and cheerful (if occasionally short-tempered) Anglo-German, he was an outstanding mathematician and an expert in the more abstruse end of the derivatives market – so-called 'structured products'. He concentrated on that and I focused more on the day-to-day concerns around simpler products (which made up the bulk of the trades) and the automation project.

Managing a trading business was, and still is, like being in charge of a factory with a very active arbitration department. Along with the daily routine (checking risk reports; watching the markets; making sure there was cover for a trader who was on holiday or who was ill), Matt and I were constantly called on to intervene in disputes. Salesman A's customer thought trader B's spreads were too wide. Salesman C believed credit officer D was being too difficult about a credit line. Traders E and F were at loggerheads about cutting or adding to a position. All needed to be dealt with. And for me, along with this, running in parallel, was the effort to upgrade and automate the business. The broad outlines of the plan were what we'd agreed after Cannes: the risk management and settlement systems would be rationalised and we'd create a means of automatically publishing option prices. This was easy to say, but challenging to achieve. Even looking at options in isolation, Mark's system chart was a jumble. A number of different systems needed to talk to each other in order to report risk to traders, for example. This resulted in frequent errors and meant that junior traders were often obliged to stay at the office until 10 or 11pm each night to reconcile positions. Having had to suffer through this myself early in my career I was determined to put a stop to it. The plan was to take one home-grown risk management system (which Mark had dubbed RMS in a fanciful Northern flourish of imagination) and to extend its scope away from its original purpose of handling a small number of complicated derivatives to a new role covering all of our needs. A similar proposal was put in place for settlements. Last in the new blueprint were some brand-new pieces of software that would automatically show live options prices in small size to salesmen anywhere within the bank; they could then quote the prices to their customers. It wasn't quite my vision of allowing customers to click and deal directly with the bank but it was a good start towards that goal and would save a lot of effort and shouting.

I soon discovered that there was a very simple, if not very glamorous trick to getting new technology created. Meetings: lots and lots and lots of meetings. Meetings to thrash out the exact design requirements; meetings to discuss hiring new programmers for the IT department; meetings to assess progress. I once even went to a meeting to discuss the exact way to organise another, separate series of meetings (about how to control the release of new pricing models, if you care). To be honest, it was a slog. But gradually, as the months passed, I started to see some progress – in the spring I was shown a prototype version of the system to broadcast prices to salespeople. In time, this system went live and I discovered that building computer systems was the relatively easy bit; as had been the case with EBS in its first years, getting the traders to use them properly was a great deal harder.

To make sure that the option prices on this new system were correct (and that Deutsche Bank didn't turn into the shop quoting the price of jumpers at 38/40 when you could buy them for £36 everywhere else), the traders had to do some work. Option prices are determined by a number of factors (exactly how is not important right now) but one of them is so central that the entire market uses it as a proxy for price. It is the predicted 'volatility', or 'degree of choppiness', of the currency pair in question. To allow the correct prices to be shown to the salespeople, traders had to keep the system updated as to where the market was pricing this parameter. It wasn't a massively onerous task. Back then, except in very violently moving markets, three or four updates in a ten-hour trading session would suffice and the system had been designed with features to make the task as easy as it could be. But the traders wouldn't do it. Like spot traders in the early days of EBS, they were used to how things had always worked and what I was asking was something new and strange and bothersome. As a result, salespeople would try to use the system and it would very often flash back, 'Prices stale – refer to trading desk'. This was worse than no progress at all. I appealed to the traders' better natures. I cajoled and threatened. In some weeks there was a slight improvement, then back to 'Prices stale'. The nuclear option was just to turn off the 'stale price' system check and let salespeople deal for their customers on whatever was shown on the screen, wrong or not, but this would necessarily result in losses for the bank – definitely a step too far. I was a new manager and, despite progress since Cannes, I still had the taint of being one of the 'Bankers bastards'.

Then, like Doctor Seuss's 'Grinch Who Stole Christmas', I had a wonderful, awful idea: I'd let our prop traders loose on the screen. I took this slightly controversial plan to Jim who, when he had finished laughing, endorsed it heartily. The small team of proprietary traders looked at me hungrily in wonder and disbelief when I announced that they could deal on the new screen even if prices were wrong. All their birthdays had come early! The options traders were appalled in equal measure. The beauty of the scheme was that I knew that the prop guys would scour the screens all day long looking for discrepancies but, if they found them and dealt, the money that they'd make (and the options guys would lose as a consequence) would stay within the FX department and, more importantly, within the bank – the shareholders wouldn't lose out. What made it even neater was that there was little love lost between the two teams: the options guys thought the prop team was a bunch of cowboys and the proprietary traders looked down on what they saw as the dull, coupon-clipping, customer-facing farmers on the option desk. Losing money to the proprietary team was the options traders' worst nightmare and, as I had hoped, they set out to make sure it didn't happen. Within a day, the number of volatility updates went up from a desultory and inadequate one a day, to ten a day or even more for the more important currencies. The system was now fit for our customers' needs. It had been a rotten low trick of mine, I admit, but it had worked. A small milestone had been reached on a long journey.

Automated Risk Manager

Another milestone was reached in May of 2000. Deutsche Bank won the *Euromoney* FX survey. Although this news quite rightly made no difference to the vast, happy majority of people in the world who were not in the FX business, within the FX community it was an astonishing event. There had never before been any doubt which bank was the biggest and baddest FX shop – it was Citibank. This was an immutable law of nature like the value of pi or the orbits of the planets. But now, they had been overtaken. In truth, our win was a bit of a fluke. The survey required customers to report to *Euromoney* how much volume (in terms of notional dollars traded) they had transacted with various banks in the previous year. No one relishes filling out survey forms so customers had to be pleaded with and pestered to do so by their sales contact during a three-week survey period. The result was thus a function of two things: the actual volumes that had been transacted and the extent to which a bank's sales force could be browbeaten by their management into becoming a complete pain in the ass for three weeks. The addition of the (relatively small) Bankers Trust FX volumes had increased Deutsche's market share in 1999, but the real advantage we had was the meticulously organised way our salespeople had been marshalled into a vote-begging machine.

The win set off rejoicing the like of which I had never witnessed. There were messages of congratulation from every senior manager up to and including the CEO. There were raucous celebratory drinks. Each managing director was presented with a heavy glass paperweight inscribed with the message: 'Deutsche Bank – Number One in FX'. Beautifully designed posters went up all over the building saying the same thing. 'Bloody hell,' said an ex-Bankers friend of mine, who, like me, was unused to such hoopla, 'it's like we all went to sleep in the UK and woke up in North Korea.' Cynicism aside, winning the survey created genuine benefits for us. The number one slot (regardless of its flukiness) was a great calling card for our salespeople. Each of them now recited the same mantra: if you are a firm or fund with FX to transact, you need to speak to us – we're number one. But, despite this outward confidence, we were starting to worry.

As my colleague had feared, other banks were starting to pursue an electronic strategy too. Dresdner Bank's FX business, led by an ex-colleague of mine from Bankers Trust called Achilles, had developed a product called Piranha that allowed customers to deal spot online. The British bank Royal Bank of Scotland was doing the same. Most worryingly, so was Switzerland's UBS. We had to move fast. An existing Deutsche-developed system called Autobahn was selected as the way to show spot prices to customers. Autobahn had actually been created a few years earlier to show indicative bond prices but it made sense to strap FX into it to save time. A newly created team of salespeople bustled around our clients showing them demonstration versions of the system and trying to get them to take it. Like the battle to get dealing systems like EBS onto traders' desks in the 1990s, the key aim was to capture 'desk real estate'. Happily, unlike in that battle, Autobahn didn't need to be used on yet another stand-alone screen on a crowded desk but could be installed on clients' own computers. That made things easier and so gradually commitments to take Autobahn for FX started to trickle, then pour in. Unbeknown to our clients, however, behind the scenes there was a massive internal scrap taking place. It revolved around two related questions: how would prices get onto the screen and who would manage the risk after a deal?

Just as I had found while trying to make options traders change their habits, messy human characteristics of inertia, habit and pride were formidable obstacles to change. Salespeople were belatedly waking up to the complications associated with the idea of customers dealing through a screen. For one, how would they know what clients were doing? It was a cornerstone of salespeople's craft to tailor their commentary and advice against a background of intimate familiarity with what their clients were doing and thinking. With screen-based trading their fear was that this knowledge, or at least a good part of it, would disappear. More self-servingly, they worried whether they would still get credit for business going through the screens. Deutsche Bank, like every other bank it competed with, had a process of awarding 'production credits' to salespeople based on the volume and type of deals they brought in. The idea was to use this data to assess both the salesperson and the customer. If the deals came through the screen, would the salesperson still get the credit for 'his' customer? This was a serious matter – a salesperson's pay depended on it. The solution to both problems, some on the sales team argued, was simple: let salespeople themselves make the small prices that customers would request via Autobahn. But this idea utterly horrified the FX traders. 'Traders are called traders because they trade. Salesmen are called salesmen because they sell,' heatedly opined an excited trading manager at one meeting, banging his fist down for emphasis, 'you can't mix

that up.' Despite this rather tautological reasoning, there was arguably already a precedent for the approach in the bank. In the equity
department (which dealt with stocks and shares) some salespeople were allowed to execute customers' orders. They were called
'sales-traders'. But, shot back the FX traders, equities are different
from FX. The equity business operates an agency model; equity
salespeople simply execute customer orders to get the best fill and
charge a fee; they don't take risk. FX is a principal business; FX
traders do take risk; you can't compare the two! The sales department's idea got nowhere.

More serious was the fight over whether spot traders or computers would make the prices on the screen. Armed with screen-
scraped market data from EBS and Reuters, a computer could easily
have been programmed to show a price. But what would happen
afterwards? If a client dealt, the bank was at risk and someone or
something would need to manage that position. It couldn't be a
computer, hampered as it was by its lack of fingers, so a trader would
need to do it. But then how could it be fair, argued the spot traders, to expect someone to manage a position resulting from prices
that he himself had not made? His profits could be affected by the
mistakes made by the programmers of the pricing system – it was
unnatural! Once again, the powerful spot trading lobby won out.

The dealing process resulting from these arguments was unsur-
prisingly a messy hybrid. Customers could ask for a price up to a
certain limited size via a screen on Autobahn. This would flash up
a 'request for quote' (RFQ) in a pop-up on the relevant trader's
screen. He would then type in the price he wanted to make and
send it back to await the customer's decision. What we'd come up
with was in every way the same as the traditional way of dealing,
with the exception that no salesperson was called on the telephone
and there was no shouting across the trading floor. To mollify the
salespeople, the production credits for deals transacted in this way
were still granted to the 'owner' of the client even if that person

did no work for them. In short, our approach was a patchwork of compromises. Some of us in the FX team's more resolutely pro-automation faction gave Autobahn the rather unkind nickname of 'the Mechanical Turk' after the famous – supposedly clockwork – robot chess player that had delighted and amazed the courts of late 18th-century Europe but which had been an elaborate hoax animated not by cogs and gears, as people supposed, but rather by a tiny, hidden, chess-playing midget.

Maybe we were being a little harsh. In retrospect, it is clear that at least this way of doing things gave our customers something tangible and got them used to dealing on Autobahn. That said, ugly creaking and grinding noises from the system soon became apparent. Things went tolerably well when the market was quiet or only moderately busy. When it became even slightly more interesting, shouting was redoubled. Mingled with the normal, heartily voiced requests for prices in sizes too big to be routed through the system came the anguished cries of salespeople reminding traders to make prices on the smaller-sized RFQs (pop-up price requests) that inevitably piled up on their screens: 'How many times do I have to ask? PLEASE make that five lot in euro Swiss! Come on! My client's been waiting over a minute.' The plan wasn't working quite as we'd foreseen. Our optimism was further dented by the result of the *Euromoney* survey released in early 2001. Citibank, stung by the ignominy of being displaced as the number one FX house the previous year (in fact the bank had been narrowly shunted to third by Chase Manhattan), hit back with a well-organised campaign of its own. Deprived of the advantage of superior organisation, we were pushed back into second place in overall market share. This was bad news, but the Mechanical Turk continued to operate in its clunky manner for the whole of 2001. Why was this? Partly because it was difficult to undo the hard-fought compromises of the previous year; partly because the huge, time-consuming and continuing task of reengineering our risk and settlement systems distracted our managerial attention; partly because of the strain of coping with the tragic consequences of the 9/11 attacks. Whatever the reason, little changed during the year.

But the *Euromoney* survey released in 2002 shocked us into determined action. Deutsche had come third! We were going backwards! The second slot was taken by our bitter European rivals UBS. What made this an even more embarrassing blow was that UBS had gained market share in exactly the same way we had planned to, with an electronic platform that all our clients told us was significantly better than ours in terms of pricing and reliability. Jim (who by now had taken over the job of head of FX from Hal) was adamant: we needed to change and change fast. Enter the 'small deals book'.

The idea behind the small deals book was to create a team selected from the spot desk (which numbered dozens of traders globally) to specialise in making the pesky little prices that so gummed up the works when things turned busy. It wasn't a popular assignment. No one wanted to boast to his friends or to the girl he was trying to impress in a nightclub that he was 'on the small deals book'. It sounded so . . . insignificant. But the man chosen to lead the team saw its potential. Simon (not his real name) had been a forwards trader and had already experimented with building spreadsheets to automate pricing in his previous job. With his pale, moon face and his intelligent eyes peering from behind a pair of round, wireframed spectacles, he resembled a benign maths teacher, or a large owl. Habitually precise and softly spoken, he was as far from the cliché of a spot trader as one could imagine. At first, he and his team concentrated on creating relatively rudimentary software to automate the pricing of spot; they did this by the familiar torturous procedure of 'trial by meeting'. Within months this worked well enough to silence the cries of complaint from clients and their salespeople about delays in pricing little deals. But then he started down a more radical path.

As we saw in the last chapter, one of the things that a human spot trader thinks about when making a price is how much risk he already has from previous deals: if he is long (i.e. has bought) US dollars, he will be inclined to show better offers to sell them than he might otherwise. Simon's pricing software attempted something similar, automatically. The goal was to 'internalise' as much flow as possible: that is, keep customers paying our bid-offer spread while minimising the number of times that we paid another bank's spread to get out of the risk ('Calls!'). So far, so conventional. But, Simon thought, what risk should I be looking at when I make a price? For a human spot trader the answer was simple: he should look at the risk on his own book, usually in one currency pair. But at the level of a bank, that made little sense. One trader might be long US dollars and short euros but his neighbour, or even a trader on a different continent, might be short an equivalent amount of US dollars but long British pounds. Thus, the bank would only have risk of movements in the euro versus the pound; the US dollars would cancel out. Because Britain and the eurozone have very tightly interlinked economies, this risk is usually much less than the risk of movements against the US dollar. The portfolio (i.e. the combination) of the two positions is, to use the jargon, 'self-hedged' to some extent. So, Simon reasoned, if I make my pricing and risk decisions at the level of all the deals in all the currencies that are coming in to the small deals book, I will necessarily be doing a much more efficient job than individual traders looking at risks in isolation. To satisfy himself of this, he spent weeks meticulously analysing the data from tens of thousands of deals that had previously come through Autobahn. He was right! Simon immediately began to lobby for resources to build a powerful pricing machine that would take into account all the risk coming in from electronic deals. He dubbed it ARM for Automated Risk Manager. Convincing the senior management of Deutsche to stump up the funding was a tough sell; we had been pouring money into the automation project for three years with little tangible progress. 'We were pushing hard on the gas pedal but the dials just refused to move,' as one colleague described it. To their credit, with Germanic patience, the board wrote the cheque.

Work on ARM started too late to affect the market share rankings in the 2003 survey (which measured dealing done during 2002) and Deutsche Bank finished third again with UBS beating Citibank to the top position. The electronic strategy was working, but infuriatingly we weren't the beneficiaries. Then, in 2003, ARM came online and was an instant success. All the years of seemingly quixotic efforts to create one legal entity and one risk system (the option desk's system had recently been further extended to spot) now began to pay off. Because of it, ARM could look at all the electronic flow coming in from all over the world and react accordingly – it was a massive advantage that other banks did not have. ARM had been carefully programmed to continue to make prices and to accumulate risk until certain limits were reached, whereupon its human handlers (Simon and his team) would reduce risk on its behalf – the computer's lack of fingers was still a limitation. But, while it operated within its parameters, ARM was a wonder. It dealt in a blur! When the market became busy, the screen showing completed deals scrolled so fast it was impossible to focus on it. And it was so cool under pressure! Lacking human emotions, it never got flustered when holding a big position but would simply continue to deal and skew its prices as it had been programmed. It could never be arbitraged by Triangle Man or the Clackatron because it continuously checked all its prices to make sure that could not happen. I once stood next to one of the human spot traders (now dubbed 'voice traders' to distinguish them from the robot) as we observed it in action. 'God,' he whispered in awe mixed with a little fear, 'it's *so* fucking good.'

Almost from the word go, ARM began to make money. It didn't do it like a regular trader with some weeks up and some weeks down; it was consistently profitable. This allowed ARM to be tweaked to show tighter bid-offer spreads. Emboldened by success, Simon's team (no longer referred to limply as the 'small deals team' but rather by the much more glamorous title 'e-trading') started to show 'streaming prices'. What this meant was that, instead of waiting for a customer to ask for a price and then responding, the computer would hold out a price constantly, just waiting for a customer to buy or sell. This, and the tighter bid-offer spreads, attracted an even greater volume of deals as more and more clients noticed the improvements. Eventually, word of the machine attracted the attention of board members. One was shown ARM on a tour of the trading floor. He listened in polite but slightly baffled silence to an explanation of its intricacies with the same practised, neutral facial expression that the Queen uses while being entertained by a particularly odd South Sea Island fertility dance. At the end of the recital of gigantic volumes and tiny spreads he observed that 'this is all very impressive, but it sounds like trying to eat soup with a fork'. 'True,' he was told, 'but remember – it's a very, very, very fast fork.'

The progress in the FX business was dramatic but not quite enough to dislodge UBS from top slot in the 2004 *Euromoney* poll. Disappointingly, Deutsche came second by less than 0.2 per cent of market share – a whisker. But after another year of the e-trading team finessing how ARM worked, and the resulting surge in volumes, the 2005 poll (reporting 2004 volumes) was a walkover. Deutsche won it with an overall share of 16.72 per cent, the highest single market share of any bank in the survey's 25-year history. The gap to UBS in second was over 4 per cent, a volume which, in itself, would be a respectable share of market for many long-established FX houses. This time the celebration of the *Euromoney* win was warranted. It had taken five years since Cannes, but the whale was finally gorging itself on plankton.

Elsewhere, though, harpoons were being sharpened.

CHAPTER 3

Code Wars in the Kingdom of Microseconds

The Thirty-Billion-Dollar Blink

It was around midday in early 2011, six years after the ARM-inspired *Euromoney* win, and over a dozen of us were seated around a large table in one of Deutsche's biggest meeting rooms. Several other people in Asia and the US had dialled into the meeting on a conference-call line. All around us on the walls were lurid examples of Deutsche Bank's famous post-war art collection. (Were they by Jörg Immendorff? Unusually, that day I was blind to them.) It was over an hour into the meeting, but no one was getting bored or starting to flag – the topic was too important. We were discussing the plans for a brand-new computer system called RAPID, an acronym for Revolutionary Application Program Interface Development. RAPID was to be the spot-trading superweapon that was meant to shore up Deutsche's hard-won and increasingly threatened position as a leading FX house. The discussion looped through, over and around a number of interlocking questions. What precise functions would RAPID perform? Who within the IT department would be responsible for building it? When would it be ready? Where, how and to which of our customers should it be rolled out? Would it take over completely from the now elderly workhorse ARM or just supplement it? How much would it cost? Despite the technical nature of the arguments and the presence of the preternaturally calm Simon (who because of his team's success was now a managing director), tempers were starting to fray as a result of competing egos, intellects and departmental jostling – I, as chairman of the meeting, was the person responsible for keeping things moving along.

I had this role because, weeks earlier, I had taken over the job of heading all Deutsche's FX trading globally. This meant that Simon and his e-trading team now reported to me and, as a result, the tricky task of developing RAPID was ultimately my problem. My boss, the global head of FX, a man named Zar, had been clear about this in his typically forthright fashion: 'All the rest of your teams can run themselves for a while, just focus on RAPID. Get this train out of the station and on the right tracks – you're on the hook.' Zar, who had taken over running the department from Jim four years earlier, was a brilliant, likeable, sometimes infuriating whirlwind of energy who would pepper me and others in his management team with emailed questions, ideas and suggestions at all hours of the day and night; I was determined not to let him down. Thus it was that gradually, over another couple of hours, with as much diplomacy as I could muster, I corralled all the competing views into a plan that looked sensible.

There was one last topic. 'I'm going to need to pitch this to the IT budgeting committee next week,' I told the room. 'We're looking for a chunk of new resources. Help me out, guys – in your view what's the simplest way for me to explain to them why we're doing this?' The markets have changed, I was told. Our customers were increasingly technology-savvy and huge volumes of FX were being done by hedge funds operating with lightning-fast computer systems. ARM was old and, despite being fine for normal flows, was simply not designed to deal with these HFT ('high frequency trading') firms. I already knew full well that, long term, we couldn't just take the easy route and refuse to quote them – their trading volumes were now so important that to ignore them risked losing our number one slot in the *Euromoney* survey, which, since we'd now won it for six years in a row, was both a source of pride and a powerful marketing tool for the department. We needed a pricing and trading system more flexible and, above all, much faster than ARM. 'How fast?' I asked. 'Give me a sound bite. I need to wow the committee, I won't have long to pitch.' 'Blink,' commanded Simon. I blinked. 'That will have taken about 0.3 seconds,' he said in his customary, precise tone. 'If a fund's trading system has a tick-to-trade time of 10 microseconds, which would be very, very fast but wouldn't be utterly exceptional' (at this, the IT guys in the room nodded vigorous assent) 'then, if they deal a standard little clip of $1 million each tick-to-trade cycle, they can trade $30 billion in the time it just took you to blink. Thirty billion – it's the market capitalisation of Deutsche. *That's* how fast we could be competing with.' The room fell silent. 'Heaven help us,' I thought as I wound up the meeting and took the lift back down to the trading floor.

Hooking up Skynet

As was quickly becoming obvious to me, in the six years since ARM's debut the FX spot market had been transformed into a high-tech battleground dominated by computer scientists rather than traders. My job as a trading manager, instead of being focused primarily on the markets and on risk as it always had been, was now largely concerned with high-speed communications networks in Asia or with advanced pricing algorithms. A bewildering variety of trading venues and new trading firms were crowded into what had once been a simple market made up just of banks, brokers and customers. How had we come to this? What had happened in those years?

In fact, most of the changes that had paved the way for this transformation were already in place by the time ARM was sucking in plankton. One important development had been the advent of dealing APIs. An API (Application Program Interface) is a way for one computer system to talk to another. The planned RAPID system was an advanced example of one – hence API as the middle three letters of its name. Early in our automation programme, in 2001 or so, both EBS and Reuters made a pricing API available – this streamed information about FX rates that a bank's computers could understand without having to go through the laborious process of screen-scraping data which had been designed to be read by humans. More importantly and contentiously, in late 2003, after years of vacillation resulting from its unwieldy multi-bank ownership structure, EBS made an API available to banks to allow their computers to deal directly through the platform. Having access to a dealing API meant that a bank's computer no longer needed fingers to do a trade – it could bleep its orders in ones and zeroes directly to EBS without bothering with the inconvenient, slow-moving lumps of meat gathered around its terminals. Simon and his team raced to connect ARM to EBS to allow them to program the computer to manage risk on its own; a few other banks followed suit. And it wasn't just the electronic brokers that began to connect to banks – other so-called Electronic Communication Networks (ECNs) did so too. Since 2000, a number of different and competing companies had set up to allow FX customers to see prices from multiple banks simultaneously. In the old days, a customer would need to phone around to a number of banks to see competing rates; through these new 'multi-dealer platforms' they could see a blended rate on one screen – a bid from Deutsche Bank and an offer from UBS, say. The biggest of these firms (sporting modish names like Lava FX, Hotspot or Currenex) were independently owned, but one, FX All, was owned by a consortium of banks, a little like EBS. Regardless of ownership, the presence of these trading venues and their rush to create APIs for banks led to a market that was increasingly fragmented but also increasingly automated. Although the percentage of flows transacted via API was small initially (around 5 per cent of

EBS's flows by late 2005 for example[1]), the lid of Pandora's box had been prised open a fraction. The means had been found to remove human beings from the trading loop entirely.

Another major change was the rise of so-called 'retail aggregators'. These are firms that allow the regular man or woman in the street (hence, 'retail') to dabble speculatively in the FX markets. They started popping up from around 2000 onwards in the wake of the craze for day trading stocks and shares and, although the way they work varies to some extent between firms, the basics are always the same. You, the client, make a down payment (called 'margin') to the retail firm and you can then deal FX up to a notional amount that is a multiple of that payment (in the jargon, you are 'leveraged'). If you lose money and cannot post more margin, your positions are closed out. Anyone unfortunate enough to have to watch the business channels on TV for any significant length of time will no doubt have seen endless adverts for these retail FX firms in between the market updates. They compete on bid-offer spreads (just like banks in the professional market) and on the multiple of margin they offer. Astonishingly, multiples as high as 200 times margin used to be available. This meant that for $1000 down, you could trade $200,000 of FX – tiny by the professional market's standard, colossal by that of most individuals.[2]

The most unlikely people started accounts. I was once introduced to a man called Tony who was a friend of a friend and who was (and I hope still is) a professional pianist. When he found out what I did for a living he was extremely excited. 'You're an FX trader!' he beamed. 'I want to do that!' It turned out that his plan was to supplement his income by trading FX from home on a retail platform, possibly in the gaps between Chopin Nocturnes or Liszt Variations. I quizzed him for a while on his methodology: how much money was he looking to make; how much time could he dedicate; what was his expertise. 'Do you have any advice for me?' he asked at last. 'Stick to the piano,' I said.

But thousands, then tens of thousands, then hundreds of thousands of people had a similar idea to Tony's and persevered. Their collective decision was important for the FX markets in two ways. First, over the course of time, retail flows grew to the point that, as early as 2007, they made up around 10 per cent of all customer spot flows – including all those from professionals at corporates, hedge funds, pension funds and the like.[3] Retail 'investors' have become so important in Japan, for example, that a shift in their collective positioning moves the market. As a group, Japanese retail clients are known in the markets as 'Mrs Watanabe', as in 'Mrs Watanabe is cutting long yen here' or 'Mrs Watanabe is staying on the sidelines'. Whenever I heard this term during risk meetings I always imagined a gigantic, office-block-sized, bespectacled Japanese housewife in a huge kimono clutching a phone the size of a car and barking orders down it. Sadly, the reality is more prosaic. The second reason for retail flow's importance is how banks responded. Seeing a new set of customers, banks (including Deutsche Bank) courted them diligently. What did they want? Apart from the usual, eternal requests for yet tighter prices, what they wanted, given the huge volumes of tiny tickets that they were seeing, was to be able to trade automatically to offset their own risk without calling salespeople or even typing into screens. Eager to oblige, we and other banks built pricing and dealing APIs to allow them to do so. In time, so did the multi-dealer platforms. Another link had been forged: customers' computers could now talk to the ones sitting in banks.

After APIs and retail aggregators, the third alteration that enabled the transformation of the FX market into a microsecond-obsessed computerised battleground was the rise of 'prime brokerage', colloquially known as PB. Imagine you are running a hedge fund and that your traders deal with a lot of separate banks. You will need to negotiate legal contracts with every one of them before they allow you to deal. What's more, as your trades make or lose money, you will need to settle with, and post margin to, a number of different banks with different computer systems. With enough back-office manpower all of this is possible, but it is a pain and, besides, people and the offices to put them in are expensive. This is where a bank (Deutsche Bank, say), acting as a prime broker, steps in. Your fund's traders can still deal with other banks but, after they have dealt, your fund 'gives up' the trade to Deutsche. What this means, legally speaking, is that your fund will have a deal with Deutsche Bank; Deutsche will, in turn, book an offsetting, 'back-to-back' deal with the bank that made you the price. The prime broker stands in between your fund and the bank taking the market risk. Instead of a plethora of banks to settle with, you only need to settle with one. You also only get one statement of the deals your fund has done. What's even better is that offsetting deals (say if your traders have bought US dollars from one bank and sold them to another) cancel out at your prime broker and so you won't be asked to stump up margin on any of them. 'Prime brokerage is great,' a fund manager once told me. 'It's like I only have to rip open the envelope of one credit card statement each month.'

Obviously, this convenience isn't free: the price is in the form of fees based on the notional amount traded. Although this looks like an agency business at first sight (i.e. take no risk and charge fees), in fact the prime broker is engaged in a principal business and is taking plenty of risk – credit risk. If your fund loses a lot of money on a position and cannot afford to post margin to pay for the loss, Deutsche, as prime broker, would still have to make good the loss on the back-to-back trade. For a bank to succeed as a prime broker requires a very solid grasp of funds' creditworthiness as well as excellent computer systems – few things excite a fund manager's ire more than having trades go missing from his reports. In fact, the rise of prime brokerage, initially in the equity markets of the 1990s, was only possible with the advent of computers powerful enough to keep track of all the deals. The prime brokerage idea in FX was eventually stretched to include not just funds but also smaller, less creditworthy, often regional banks – a development that led to a subtle but vital twist on how the market worked. The spring of 2004 saw the launch of a service called EBS Prime. This allowed banks that were not set up on EBS (primarily for credit reasons) to access the prices shown on it. They did this not by dealing in their own name as other banks did, but rather by using that of their prime broker, inevitably one of the FX trading giants. At this stage, mindful of the traditional demarcation between banks and clients, EBS carefully excluded funds from the proposal. The service was envisioned as a way to 'level the playing field' (and, of course, to generate more brokerage for EBS). Small banks would plug away gamely in their artless way, it was thought, all the while dealing in the name of (and thus being backed by the credit of) their prime broker, like kids let loose in the shopping mall with their dad's Amex card. Harmless enough, except that ultimately it didn't stop there, as we shall see.

By the start of 2005, then, the decades-old walls delineating who did what in the FX market were already tottering. Human spot brokers had been all but eliminated and banks dealt directly with each other through EBS and Reuters, with computer-to-computer APIs increasingly bypassing human involvement altogether. Customers' computers could also deal directly with those of banks, and the way had been opened, via the magic of prime brokerage, for customers to deal in the interbank market, albeit cloaked in another name. The barriers preventing the market from becoming a playground for high frequency traders were now almost down. A few more nudges would complete the job.

'You Are all a Bunch of Assholes'

'Have you seen what those clowns at Barclays are doing?' Jim was asking his assembled team of managing directors. The question was rhetorical because we all knew the answer – they had 'gone decimal'. We were in our normally routine weekly meeting of the FX management committee. This one, however, was not routine since the talk, which grew quite heated, was all about 'decimalisation'. It was mid-2005 and we in Deutsche Bank were still warm from the glow of our ARM-led *Euromoney* victory but Barclays' announcement a couple of days earlier had stunned us and all of our competitors: we felt an FX version of the shock the US had once felt over Sputnik. Since time immemorial, and certainly for my entire career and the career of every person in the meeting, FX rates had been quoted to four decimal places. Thus, the US dollar to euro rate would be 1.3278, say. What Barclays were now doing via their computer system BARX (the equivalent of Autobahn at Deutsche) was to quote an extra decimal place so that the rate could be 1.32783. This may strike you as being a trivial change – why did it matter? First off, it meant that the team at Barclays now had the ability to undercut our spreads without hurting themselves too much. In the past, if one bank had been quoting prices 3 pips (i.e. 0.0003) wide, the only way to quote narrower was to go to 2 pips – a 33 per cent reduction. This would be hugely significant in the context of very large volumes. But now Barclays had the ability to go to 2.9 pips (i.e. tighter by only 3 per cent). In our imaginations we could hear the feedback from customers already: 'You lot are quoting 3 pips wide; Barclays are quoting 2.9 pips – we're going with them.' But worse still was the knowledge that it might take many months, if not years, to respond.

As we had planned back in Cannes, what is called the 'architecture' of our computer infrastructure was now much simpler: for instance, we had one risk system rather than a patchwork of a dozen. But each system within this now much cleaner structure was still very complex. What's more, the assumption of the 'four-decimal-place-ness' of the FX markets was running through each of them like the pink lettering in a stick of rock. One small example that we all could identify quickly: all the screens that Autobahn provided to customers to allow them to click and deal showed rates to four decimal places with the last two, the pips, in larger font than the others. But much more subtle manifestations of the four-digit assumption undoubtedly lay hidden in the millions of lines of code that made up our systems. We'd have to find them all. 'Wonderful,' said Mark the IT guru laconically. 'It's like Barclays have just given us our very own Y2K bug.' We concluded the meeting by giving Mark's team an urgent task to figure out what would need to be done to decimalise our systems; then we all braced ourselves to see what impact Barclays' move would have.

The cause of our discomfort was a forceful Australian named Ivan, the head of FX at Barclays. I was acquainted with him since he was also an old boy of Bankers Trust: tall, clean-cut, usually tanned, to me he always looked like a particularly photogenic US senator. With the intervening years bringing some greying around his temples, that impression was even more striking when I interviewed him during the course of writing this book. I wanted to know why Barclays had taken the decimal decision. 'We didn't really have much choice,' was his view. 'Barclays wasn't even a top-ten-ranked FX house in 2002 when I took over – it was embarrassing.' Barclays' revenues had been as limp as its market share and Ivan had come quickly to the same conclusion as ours at Cannes: the only way to gain scale and revenues was automation. But Barclays was late to the game: customers already had dealing systems provided by Deutsche Bank, UBS and others. Why would they need another? 'We did the rounds for two or three years and struggled for desk space,' he said, 'but then two very smart options guys I'd hired came to me with this decimal idea and we went for it.' At a stroke, Barclays would have a 'killer app' – decimal pricing (branded 'Precision Pricing') was unique to BARX; any fund that needed to guarantee best execution on behalf of its fund-holders would now need to have it. 'Competitors were livid,' he said, laughing (I smiled ruefully). 'One guy took me aside at a conference and

told me we were all a bunch of assholes.' But Ivan and Barclays
didn't care. 'We needed to be disruptive – and, let's face it, you
can be a cannibal if you have nothing to lose.' Barclays' innovation
gained it instant traction; decimalisation was here to stay. Gradually over the next couple of years, most of the ECNs (multi-dealer
platforms) and many banks converted their systems to allow it.
Few people then foresaw how decimal pricing would play into the
hands of high frequency funds.

The last nudge to the walls protecting the old model of FX also
came in mid-2005. The management of EBS, seeing the success
of EBS Prime, extended the reach of the product to include 'the
professional trading community' – that is, hedge funds. This was a
totally different matter from letting regional banks into the heart
of the interbank market; hedge funds knew what they were doing!
The bigger banks, though, perhaps because they were shell-shocked
by the pace of change, perhaps through complacency, perhaps because of internal disagreements (since in the majority of banks the
prime brokerage business – the winners from this move – operated
out of the equity department which cared little for the precious de-
marcations in FX), all let this change happen. Nothing now stood
in the way of any fund dealing automatically in the central hubs
of the market. Fund to bank to bank to fund, a complex network
of APIs began to link vast numbers of dealing computers together.
Prime brokerage, retail aggregators, multi-dealer platforms, APIs
and decimal pricing had transformed FX. The old market was
dead! Long live the new!

Latency? Schmatency!

In truth, the effect of the change wasn't immediately apparent. The
trends in market share continued unstoppably, it seemed. In the
2006 *Euromoney* survey (measuring flows in 2005), the advantage

we at Deutsche got from the excellence of ARM meant that our survey-topping market share grew to an eye-watering 19.3 per cent – to put this in perspective, the combined share of the top three banks in the 1999 survey was about 21 per cent. Barclays, with their decimalisation strategy starting to kick in, had risen to fourth with 6.6 per cent. What was changing was staffing in the industry. At Deutsche, the absolute number of people we employed in FX hadn't altered very dramatically, but the balance of what those staff did certainly had. There were far fewer 'voice' spot traders, for one thing. This wasn't because there had been a big cull at any point. It was just that Simon's small e-trading team was handling more and more of the flow, so if a voice trader quit, he simply wasn't replaced. On the other hand, the e-trading team was expanding and to a greater extent so was my derivatives (options) team, especially the section of it called 'complex risk'. Interviews for these posts were often conducted in an impenetrable, blended patois of English and maths and the whiteboards in the interview rooms were inevitably covered in a dense thicket of equations afterwards; the geekiness of the FX trading team was increasing rapidly. All told, though, the effect of the changes in the market didn't strike us at Deutsche particularly hard. At smaller banks, on the other hand, there was carnage.

FX is a very secretive market despite its huge size and it is difficult to get accurate numbers of how many people are, or were, employed in the business; it is more difficult still to break that down into the jobs that they did. What was clear at the time, however, was that smaller FX banks were steadily shedding spot (and to a lesser extent forwards and options) trading staff. Articles about a bank downsizing would appear in the FX trade press; the phone would ring and a headhunter would be trying to find a job for someone ('Hi, you don't know me but it would great to grab a few minutes of your time or even a coffee to discuss a very interesting CV that has come my way . . .'); emails would come directly. The reason is clear from the market share numbers. In the 1999 *Euromoney* poll, almost 48 per cent of market share was held by banks outside the top ten; by the 2006 poll, that number had halved to about 24 per cent. These banks did not have a business large enough to justify spending the money needed to automate. In fact, the collective market share decline of smaller banks masked a shift in behaviour that was even worse news for the career prospects of the traders who worked in them. Increasingly, FX giants like Deutsche would give these banks access to systems like Autobahn or the equivalent. Their salespeople would simply quote the Deutsche Bank (or Citibank, UBS or Barclays) rate to their customers with a small spread to offset the credit risk. No need for expensive traders. In effect, the smaller banks had shifted from 'manufacturing' FX rates to being distributors to clients with whom they had a strong relationship based on regional expertise or history. 'You guys just sucked us dry,' complained an old friend and adversary at the time – he was in his late thirties, from a smaller bank, and we were at his 'leaving-the-industry' drinks. 'But,' he added resignedly, with a slightly drunken grin, 'I guess that's just that old whore Capitalism for you.' He became a maths teacher.

Despite the privileged position Deutsche Bank had in terms of staffing, soon Simon and his e-trading team started noticing other worrying signs of change – it looked as though we were consistently losing money to certain clients. In the (manual, pre-electronic) past, no bank had any clear idea of how much money it was making from dealing FX with a particular client. In my days at Merrill and Bankers Trust there was a general feeling that some clients were 'friendly' and thus profitable to deal with, and that others sometimes weren't as profitable, especially if they were fond of perpetrating the despised 'drive-by', but no formal reckoning was ever done other than just adding up volumes. But now, with a large proportion of flows being handled electronically, the data existed to get more precise. At first this was a very crude calculation done in a spirit of almost idle curiosity. All customer flows were marked to market against the FX rates observed (or 'snapped') at the day's formal close of business. Given the round-the-clock nature of the FX market this was arbitrarily set as 4pm London time, simply to make things easier. The limitations of this approach were glaring and obvious to all. If a customer bought US dollars, say, early in the trading session and the dollar subsequently gained in value, then, because the customer's trade made money, the calculation would show a loss to Deutsche. But, in reality, Deutsche's position would almost certainly have been offset within seconds of dealing. Never mind, reasoned the e-traders, over a long period the random impact of luck should cancel out and it might be possible to observe something useful, though at this stage they weren't really sure what. They were right. Predictably, the largest section of customers, whose flows were 'bidirectional' (i.e. they sometimes bought and sometimes sold a currency), were profitable for the bank; a proportion of the tiny bid-offer spread was being captured; this is what Simon and his team expected. A few customers were very profitable or very unprofitable but it was easy to see why – their flows, for whatever reason, tended to be in one direction (maybe they were European exporters that constantly needed to sell US dollars) and, by chance, the market had gone with them or against them over the sample period. But one American fund defied all expectations – it chopped in and out of the market all the time but its flows consistently lost the bank money. This was a real shock. Could it just be a fluke, happening by random chance? Technically yes, but, Simon calculated, the odds against it were astronomically high. What was going on?

Simon set out to find out. He got one of his team to shout out when this fund dealt and then he would instantly check the EBS screen to see what was happening in the market. The same pattern emerged again and again. The market on EBS for US dollars per euro would be trading 20/22, say, and Autobahn would be showing the same price; then the fund would pay Deutsche's 22 offer (i.e. buy) via Autobahn and, instantaneously it seemed, EBS would jump to 23/25 – an immediate gain for the fund and a loss for Deutsche. The e-traders quickly realised that the fund was engaging in 'latency arbitrage'. Its computers would constantly monitor the market and wait for a large order or an information release to move prices on EBS or elsewhere. Then its computers would 'look' around the prices shown by its banking counterparties and deal on any rate that was too slow to respond. ARM was programmed to alter its prices in this event in a fraction of a second, but the fund was faster. In the gunfight at the FX corral, ARM was being beaten to the draw.

This was a disturbing discovery. No one had ever seriously questioned the mantra (upon which Deutsche's, Barclays' and other banks' FX strategies had been based) that if you added more clients and traded more volume, you'd make more money. Hence the obsession with the *Euromoney* rankings that were volume-based. This 'latency arb' fund was proof to the contrary. The first, urgent response was to get much more serious about measuring the profitability of customer flows. Maybe other customers were up to the same thing but couldn't be spotted? Gigantic quantities of tick-by-tick pricing data from EBS and elsewhere were captured. Now, instead of the very blunt method of marking customers' flows to market at the 4pm 'snap', flows could be tracked against market moves minute by minute through the day. This analysis suggested that a number of funds were in the same latency game but playing it less successfully than the one that had spurred the e-traders into action. The second response was to try to improve the speed of ARM. 'You have to remember ARM had been built to be faster than humans,' reminisced an ex-colleague (now senior, then new to the desk) when I spoke to him. 'Nobody worried much about beating other computers.' One problem was that the electronic channels that transmitted messages from ARM to EBS (for instance) and back – colloquially known as 'the pipes' – were also used for all sorts of other things in Deutsche. 'It was mad. We were trading billions and we were in competition for bandwidth with people looking up the lunch specials at Wagamama.' More seriously, a hoggish, high-priority user of bandwidth was the internal video messaging system. That this system was a problem for ARM was obvious as New York came in each morning and the resultant extra traffic slowed things down noticeably. But switching off this system was simply not feasible – people loved the ability to be able to see their colleagues while they spoke. Arguably, the way it helped our teams work together had a bigger impact on profits than any problems with latency. 'We lobbied for months to get a higher priority for our messages,' my colleague recalled; 'we eventually succeeded and it helped, but the battlefront kept moving on.'

A technological cat-and-mouse game quickly began to escalate. Most of the new e-trading funds that were entering FX were expanding from the equities market where electronic trading (aka 'algorithmic trading') was already well established. This was because equities are a largely exchange-traded product, which means that there has always been a natural single place to deal (the exchange), and so the pressures to trade electronically were felt earlier than in FX. The newly interconnected and API-heavy FX market was a happy hunting ground for them – especially happy because money was becoming harder to make in the highly competitive equities market. The predator's techniques that worked in equities were now being ported over to this new, big, relatively unsophisticated ecosystem. For instance, one common way to shave fractions off response times in equities was for a fund to put its computers as close to the exchange's servers as possible – so-called 'colocation' or 'colo'. Few banks in FX had thought to do it with the servers of EBS and other trading venues.

But what really made latency specialists lick their lips was the global nature of the market. If they dealt US dollars versus yen in

Japan, the deal could be offset against an opposite deal in London, say – since a dollar is a dollar and a yen is a yen, equities tended to be much more regionally based. The huge distances between trading hubs in FX (between Tokyo and London in this case) meant that, compared with equities, messages took longer to arrive, so the scope for arbitrage by making your fund's 'pipes' faster was much greater. FX departments in banks were now engaged in a struggle with real experts who, freed from any obligation to make markets or look after customers, could dedicate all their attention to speed and flexibility – the banks needed to learn fast. At Deutsche, urgent upgrades were made to ARM. Messaging priorities were upgraded; code was scoured for obvious bottlenecks; eventually, rather than everything being London-based as had been the case from ARM's inception, servers were placed in New York to be nearer the EBS servers for the US. It began to work. 'It's like being a gazelle in a herd', my ex-colleague explained, 'when a lion is after you; you don't need to be the fastest, but you're a blood-caked carcass if you are the slowest.' For now we were staying ahead of the slowest gazelle.

As we and other banks fought back on latency, funds brought other, more sophisticated techniques to bear. Rather than pure latency arbitrage (where, rather like the canny shopper in Loic's jumper market we met in Chapter 1, a fund could buy at one price and sell at higher one almost simultaneously), funds looked for 'relative value' trades. What this meant was that by observing the bids and offers and deals in the market, a fund's computers would predict the future evolution of prices over a very short time frame and would get ahead of the expected market move before it happened. To make their algorithms (or 'algos') more effective, funds would engage in massive number-crunching analysis of past trades to set the rules by which the algos operated. In this they were helped by the availability of colossal quantities of tick-by-tick data that the main trading venues started to sell as an adjunct to charging brokerage. In time, relative value trading was made easier by the availability of decimal pricing – if a fund's algorithm signalled that the US dollar was likely to weaken in the next split second it could enter an offer to sell a tenth of pip under the best offer in the market and then hope to be paid (and thus go short) before the predicted move happened. It was a blisteringly fast version of price skewing that had always been practised by human spot traders. 'Decimalisation was a gift for high frequency traders, and it was one that kept on giving – to them,' as my ex-colleague put it rather sourly; 'it meant you needed to be way more careful pricing to an HFT fund via an automatic link than to a human at a corporate treasury clicking prices on a screen.' The Deutsche Bank e-trading team responded by making ARM tailor pricing to different client types (previously it had been one price for everyone) in order to try to offset the funds' advantages. Good human spot traders had always done this instinctively; increasingly, the computer was being taught to be more like them.

In April 2006, EBS was bought for $825 million from its bank shareholders by the brokerage house ICAP.[4] This was significant: between them in 2006 Reuters and EBS accounted for around 60 per cent of all flow between banks[5] and now neither venue had any banking representative sitting on their board. Both were now free – and indeed duty-bound – to maximise the profits for their shareholders without worrying that much if it suited banks. Increasingly, since a broker's revenues depend primarily on volume (via agency fees), the rules of engagement on their platforms were nudged to encourage more trades and the fastest growing driver of volume was the HFT community. How dramatically the market was changing was starkly illustrated in 2007 when the triennial Bank for International Settlements (BIS) survey was released.[6]

This three-yearly snapshot, taken in April of the year of release, is one of the most comprehensive views of the FX markets available – it is always pored over by banks and their regulators for months after publication. The startling headline in 2007 was that FX volumes had grown to $3.2 trillion a day – an increase of 63 per cent since the last survey in 2004. To put that in context, in the 12 years between 1992 and 2004, volumes had grown from $0.88 trillion per day to $1.97 trillion – a growth rate of approximately 7 per cent each year, roughly in line with the growth of the world economy. From 2004 to 2007, though, the annual growth rate was close to 18 per cent. The biggest driver of the change was that the volume of deals transacted by 'other financial institutions' had exploded – up 110 per cent since 2004. This category of market participant (which included hedge funds, HFTs and retail aggregators) now transacted 40 per cent of all flows and was almost as important as 'reporting dealers' (old-school banks like Deutsche), who accounted for 43 per cent of flows, sharply down from the 64 per cent they traded in 1998. The centre of gravity of the FX market had shifted decisively. Despite the significance of this shift, by the time the report was released in late 2007 my attention and the attention of my colleagues was elsewhere – the Great Financial Crisis was under way.

Reduced to the Absurd

The FX market was not the source of the crisis. The earthquake's epicentre was the US mortgage market, which sent tremors to the money markets and to the equity markets with sickening speed. But FX was not immune. Prior to the first warning signs of catastrophe in July 2007, the FX markets had been becalmed to an unprecedented degree. By one measure – a Deutsche Bank index of volatility called CVIX – the FX markets were at the most stable and uninteresting they had been in more than 30 years. That soon changed – volatility started to rise inexorably. At first this was good news for banks like Deutsche. Uncertainty made our non-HFT clients trade more as they rushed to hedge FX exposures that had seemed so unthreatening in the pre-crisis calm. Spreads widened to compensate for the extra risk – this did not suit HFT firms that relied on very tight markets to operate in and so the volume of the trickiest flows diminished. In time, though, as the crisis deepened in 2008, our initial joy at more volatility turned into alarm, then fear. 'It's like being on a runaway roller coaster,' complained my boss Zar at the time; 'at first it's fun, then it gets faster and faster until you hear the track creaking and you realise you are strapped in with no way out.'

After the bankruptcy of Lehman Brothers in September 2008, FX market volatility rocketed to unprecedented, historic highs. Normally stable currency pairs heaved and bucked. An example: between July and October 2008, the exchange rate between Australian dollars and Japanese yen (the currencies of two sensible, developed countries) plummeted from 104 yen per Aussie dollar to around 58 – almost a 50 per cent decline. A panicking Mrs Watanabe was in the driving seat for much of this move. In the chaos, most of our thoughts were focused purely on the survival of the business. Our days, and often nights, were spent managing risk as the market lurched crazily – incremental upgrades to our dealing systems were far from our minds. But Zar had been thinking ahead and had hired several new members for the e-trading team who had direct experience in the savage world of equities. Their advice was unambiguous – when the market eventually calmed down, the technology battle (which had been put on hold somewhat) would be renewed with even greater intensity and Deutsche needed to be prepared. Specifically, we would need to be able to trade in the market more like an HFT than a bank. The gloves would need to come off.

The leader of this tendency was a newly-hired German named Dierk. He had the ascetic look of a 16th-century Protestant martyr and I expected him to be as gnomic as a monk. Instead he was voluble and intense. The market would keep changing, he insisted repeatedly all through 2008. In time, even customers whose flows were easy to cope with now would resort to the same techniques as HFTs. Banks would eventually offer computerised trading tools that would give all their customers an edge. In this he was right: so-called 'algorithmic execution' rapidly became an increasingly important way of dealing. 'Algos' allow a perfectly ordinary, non-high-frequency customer (a corporate treasurer or a pension fund manager, say) to instruct a computer to slice up an order into little bits and execute it automatically – often over multiple venues – rather than just clicking and dealing himself. Besides, the HFTs themselves would not stand still – they'd keep spending to compete. We weren't prepared! We didn't have the right people! We didn't have the right systems! We needed to change! Although Dierk didn't stay long at the bank (ironically, he left in early 2009 to be the founder of a very successful HFT fund), his message got through. We started to hire specialists to crunch data like the HFTs did and come up with better, faster dealing algorithms. These people, many of them Russian, were not like any FX professional any of us had ever seen. One, on his birthday, sent out an email to everyone in the London FX team telling us we could have a slice of his cake if we could tell him the first derivative of X^x. I sighed to myself – quizzes on calculus weren't really a great way to fit in with the others on the trading floor. But the feisty old spirit of FX wasn't quite dead yet. Within minutes Paul, a New Zealander and one of the few remaining voice spot traders in London, arrived at the birthday boy's desk with the correct answer. 'I never knew you were a mathematician,' said the e-trader. 'I'm not,' replied Paul bluntly in his Kiwi drawl, 'I just looked it up on the Internet. Now give me my cake.' He returned to his seat with some chocolate gateau to the sounds of laughter and applause.

Dierk's other suggestion – that ARM be scrapped and we start all over again with a system designed from the outset to be optimised for low latency – was much more controversial. If our plan after Cannes was like taking out the engines of a 747 in flight, this would be like trying to change the engines of a fighter jet with heat-seeking missiles on its tail. During 2009 and 2010, everything that could be done was done to wring the last drops of performance out of ARM but, as predicted, when the markets calmed down and volatility began to decrease, the HFTs came back with a vengeance – faster and more sophisticated. Some of them were simply too hot for us to handle and, reluctantly, we decided that we needed to stop quoting them. Our market share, which had peaked at a probably unrepeatable 21 per cent in the *Euromoney* surveys in 2008 and 2009, now started to slip. After months of debate, the decision was made to invest again and RAPID was born.

By 2014, RAPID was up and running and the algorithmic FX arms race was going strong.[7] True, there had been some movement away from a computerised free-for-all – in 2012, EBS, under pressure from its bank customers and seeing its market share drop, decided to step back from full decimalisation and to quote in half pips – but the overall picture was of an intensifying struggle. The practice of electronic quoting and risk management had spread from spot and was taking over the forwards and options markets; some banks had started quoting to six decimal places; some funds had even begun to use microwave technology for communication between trading sites since it is marginally faster than light through fibre-optic cables. The market was continuing to grow. The 2013 Bank for International Settlements survey showed a daily FX turnover of $5.3 trillion – up 66 per cent from 2007.[8] More significantly, 'other financials' (funds etc.) accounted for 53 per cent of flows, bigger by far than the 39 per cent for large market-making banks. In virtually every way, the market I left behind in the summer of 2014 when I retired was almost unrecognisable from the one I joined in 1990 – the shouting had gone and the computers had almost taken over.

Illusion and Paradox

The FX market has become bigger and faster – but is it better? I confess that, like someone viewing a clever optical illusion (is it two white faces in profile or a black vase?), I can see the picture both ways. The argument for why the market is better is an easy one to make. For one thing, prices are much more readily observable these days – type 'FX prices live' into Google if you would care for a demonstration. In 1992, in the early, keener years of my career, while on holiday in Florence and curious about what was going on in the markets, I needed to ring the office to find out. Twenty years later I was able to see live rates on my phone while on a rutted road in a minibus in rural China. And it isn't just observing the market that is easier; dealing is easier too. Professional FX traders have a smorgasbord of ways of accessing the market. They can use a single-dealer platform like Autobahn; they can use a multi-dealer platform like FX All. They can deal by clicking on a screen; they can deal by setting up an API; they can deal by using a bank's 'algo' service to have a robot trade for them. They can deal from their desks; they can deal from their smartphones. If they are feeling particularly retro they can even call up a human being and execute over the phone like it's 1999. Curiously, these days most remaining voice spot traders talk to clients, usually while executing large and sensitive orders that the client does not trust to a computer – the despised 'sales-trader' model from equities has taken over. And, for the non-professional, a dozen or so retail platforms allow everyone from Japanese housewives to concert pianists to speculate away merrily in FX from anywhere there is an Internet connection. Away from gambling, if you buy something on the Internet and the seller does not share the same currency as you, the small FX deal is handled automatically and smoothly behind the scenes by a network of systems. Lastly, spreads – at least for small quantities of currencies – have tightened so that is cheaper to transact. Not that it was ever very expensive, even at the start of

my career; FX was super-cheap, now it is ultra-cheap. And yet . . .
despite all of this and despite the fact I spent a large chunk of my
professional career helping to push the market to where we are now,
I have my doubts. The picture shimmers and I see the vase.

One concern – a major one for most central bankers I have met – is
the possibility of the computers running amok and causing systemic
damage. Indeed, within Deutsche Bank and its rivals (and, I'm told,
algorithmic funds) this is the main focus of internal controls – how
to ensure that systems don't 'go rogue' and accumulate huge positions
that could cause financial harm. In the very early days of ARM in
2003 or so, I noticed a large red button on a metal box wired to a thick
cable behind the computer screens of the head of spot (Simon's boss
at the time). Seeing my puzzlement, he answered my unvoiced question: 'If I hit that, it kills ARM,' he told me. 'Think of it as the loaded
tranquiliser gun at the zoo in case the bear escapes.' It was never used.
But whether computers have gone rogue or not, the new electronic
fragility of both the FX and equity markets has been shown several
times in recent years and the short-term effects have been spectacular.

Late evening London time, 6 May 2010: 'the Flash Crash'. Within
a few minutes, driven by computerised orders, the Dow Jones Industrial Average records one of its biggest ever losses as it plummets
1,000 points (9 per cent), sending markets into pandemonium.
Funds playing the correlations between markets start automatically hedging in FX and the Japanese yen rockets 4 per cent versus
the US dollar in minutes.[9]

Early morning, Tokyo, 17 March 2011 – another extraordinary
4 per cent surge in the yen happens in 25 minutes as computerised
stop losses for Mrs Watanabe hit an illiquid market with London
and New York asleep.[10]

1 August 2012, Knight Capital, the largest trader on the New York
Stock Exchange, is effectively wiped out as a computer glitch results in 4 million spurious executions in 154 stocks for more than
397 million shares in approximately 45 minutes.[11]

Academics, regulators and lawyers are still arguing about the precise causes and lessons of the Flash Crash but no one doubts that the hair-trigger response of interlinked computers exaggerated the move and sent it radiating out to other markets. Regulators have responded by instituting new exchange circuit breakers in the equities markets. No such controls are possible in FX.

Another shadow across the rosy picture of a better and faster FX market is the issue of spreads. In 2012, as I took over from Zar as head of FX at Deutsche Bank, I did some work to look at the chief drivers of FX bid-offer spreads. To my surprise, spreads could be explained almost perfectly (in a statistical sense) by looking at two, and only two, factors: the volatility of the currency pair and the passage of time. By far the most important influence was volatility – as the market gets choppier, spreads get wider and vice versa; incidentally, this is why FX businesses in banks tend to do better when the market is 'interesting' since more flow is transacted at greater spreads. Behind volatility, as a faint background trace, the influence of time passing and technology improving could be discerned. But for all the decades-long investment in computers, this effect was quite small – low single-digit percentages each year. I recently had lunch with a partner of a specialist financial management consultancy firm and he confirmed that his (unpublished) research came to exactly the same conclusion: '... but it's not a popular message at banks,' he confessed. What's more, both his and my work focused on spreads for small size at the 'top of book' (i.e. the best bid and offer at any time). What about spreads for larger sizes of deal? Here there is little but anecdotal evidence. For example, from a 2011 survey by the Bank for International Settlements into high frequency trading: 'Some contacts argue that HFT provides liquidity at "top of book" for small order sizes, but is detrimental to liquidity for larger order sizes ... spreads in [yen versus euro], for example, have narrowed 20 per cent for deals under €5 million in size but widened for larger deals.'[12] In other words, if you are shopping for one or two jumpers you are now better off – but the spread you are paying these days could be worse if you are looking for a price on a truckload of them.

Behind these concerns about stability and spreads lies a deeper and more serious one – has computerisation compromised the fundamental purpose of the market? In other words, has the structure of the market altered so much that it is now more fragile and worse at providing liquidity, especially in extreme conditions? That the structure has changed is beyond doubt. For example, when it comes to market making and the provision of liquidity, the 1999 *Euromoney* survey showed that the five largest banks accounted for 33 per cent of market share. By 2014, this had grown to over 60 per cent. The nature of the users of the FX market has also changed. Highly leveraged speculative retail flow is now a significant fraction of turnover. Funds, which have no – even informal – duty to make markets, are dominant. When I spoke to Simon (who has now left banking) in the course of writing this book, he expressed the same worry. 'What we now have is dangerously concentrated *real* liquidity,' he told me; 'there might not be enough people willing to make markets in the event of a market shock.' He was right to worry – on 15 January 2015, the Swiss National Bank gave the FX market its biggest test since the height of the Great Financial Crisis in 2008. Sad to say, it failed.

The build-up to the test had taken years. Four years earlier, all through 2011, the Swiss franc had been gaining in value versus the euro. Investors, worried by the growing turmoil in the periphery of Europe, were piling into Switzerland as a safe haven. At the start of the year, the euro bought around 1.3000 Swiss francs, but as the year wore on, the rate plunged to under 1.0000 – the last few per cent of this move in one frantic trading session on a sweltering day in August. The Swiss National Bank, growing nervous about the effect of a very strong currency on Switzerland's exporters and tourist industry, took radical action – in early September they imposed a cap on the value of the franc (that is to say, a floor on the Swiss franc per euro exchange rate which goes lower as the franc

strengthens). 'With immediate effect, [the SNB] will no longer tolerate a EUR/CHF exchange rate below the minimum rate of CHF
1.20. The SNB will enforce this minimum rate with the utmost determination and is prepared to buy foreign currency in unlimited
quantities,' they announced.[13] This move briefly caused turmoil
but, as the weeks and months wore on, the market got used to the
cap and grew to believe in its permanence, having unsuccessfully
tested the SNB's resolve on a number of occasions.

A new, common, but lazy trading strategy began to emerge in the
market – buy euros with Swiss francs at a rate slightly higher than
1.2000, then wait. The idea was simple: if there was good news for
the EU and the euro the position would make money as the euro
strengthened versus the Swiss franc and the rate rose to 1.2500, say,
or higher. And if the news wasn't good? Well, the rate could not
go below 1.2000 – the SNB guaranteed it! It was a one-way bet,
the dream of all traders. Swept up in this dream was the European
cousin of Mrs Watanabe – a group known within Deutsche Bank as
'the dentists' since, for some reason, dentists are said to love retail
FX. They certainly loved this trade and did it – cumulatively – in
enormous size. Their brokers, the retail aggregators, hedged the
risk electronically in the market by buying euros. Despite this, the
exchange rate never budged very far from 1.2000.

Then, after three and a half years of the cap, on 15 January 2015, the
SNB simply walked away from their commitment to it, a commitment
that had been reaffirmed publicly a few days before. Why? Rumours
abounded afterwards about the SNB's motivation: worries about the
imminent imposition of quantitative easing in the eurozone; worries
about the upcoming Greek election; worries about the Swiss money supply. Whatever the reason, the result was immediate, dramatic
and, for some, catastrophic. The euro collapsed in value against the
franc. The FX market, for all its computerised sophistication and
split-second response times, ceased to function. Screens went blank.
One large retail aggregator called FXCM reported receiving wildly

different simultaneous bids for euros from two bank market makers some three minutes after the announcement – one for 1.1220 Swiss francs per euro and one at 0.6734 (just over half the 1.2000 rate!).[14] Things turned ugly. Enraged by the incessant shouting of salespeople for prices (in this regard the market briefly revisited the 1990s), I am told that one bank's Swiss trader ripped his EBS screen from its stand and turned it, devoid of bids or offers, for his tormentors to see. 'I said there are no fucking rates,' he screamed. 'Do you believe me now?' Around 40 minutes (2.4 billion microseconds) passed before the market gradually stabilised around a price just above 1.0000 – a 16 per cent decline in the value of the euro. Some deals were done way below this level. Losses were widespread. Retail aggregators rediscovered the eternal truth – if you allow leveraged customers to deal on margin, then, if it all goes wrong, at some point they can walk away with a limited loss (albeit personally painful and collectively large) but you are on the hook for the full loss on all your hedges. In effect, aggregators had become the unfortunate prime brokers of 100,000 dentists. Some retail platforms, like the firm Alpari (sponsor of West Ham United football club), sustained such serious losses that they went under.[15]

Who was to blame? Naturally, market ire was focused on the SNB – how dare they do this? Some participants even railed against the SNB's perfidy in saying that they were keeping the cap a few days before they ditched it (as if they would say anything else). Regardless of blame, what I believe this incident demonstrates is that, for all its sophistication, the new FX market is not really any better, and may indeed be in some ways worse, at coping with shocks than the old one. Simon's worry about the limitations on real liquidity has been made manifest. How it will cope with another major crisis is – or should be – a matter of urgent debate.

After years of change, then, this is where we are: an FX market that is more transparent and more convenient but is also more concentrated and maybe more fragile than it used to be. Do we see two faces or a vase? The fact that there is any debate at all is telling, given the years of investment in automation. The FX market is a paradox. For all our efforts, for all the expense, has society really benefited that much from an FX market that can turn over $5.3 trillion a day; that is to say, the entire value of the GDP of the world in two weeks? From one where inefficiencies at the level of milliseconds and microseconds – time intervals too short for human comprehension – are ruthlessly eradicated? Where it matters that signals are transmitted by microwaves because light through optical fibres isn't fast enough? I'm not sure. But what I am sure about is that at every stage in the long transformation of the market, the people responsible for it acted rationally.

One of my e-trading ex-colleagues was worried about the message of this book when I interviewed him for it. 'You're going to make my mother hate what I do for a living, aren't you?' he asked, rather plaintively. In truth that is not my aim. I think he can say that he served his employers, the shareholders of Deutsche Bank, extremely well. The remorseless logic of technological change wasn't his doing – he responded to it. So did the managers of HFT funds who looked out for their investors. For what was the alternative? Not to compete? Whether the motivation was the fun of building systems, the desire for money or glory, the fear of losing your job or, as became the case for me in the latter stages of my career, the fear of having to announce layoffs to people who were my colleagues and friends – no task in business is more depressing and unpleasant – whatever the motivation, the urge or need to compete would have had the same result. The Prisoners' Dilemma caused by the power of computers prompted us all to push the market to a new, shaky equilibrium. The only unknown was whether in the process, to paraphrase General Patton, you would get fired from your firm, or whether you would make sure that the other poor son of a bitch would get fired from his.

At least when computers ate the – relatively straightforward – FX market most of the results were positive. In other parts of banking, where complexity was higher, their effects were much less benign. And it is to this we now turn.

PART TWO

Creating the Crisis

CHAPTER 4

Making Mayhem with Monte Carlo

MMVII

Turning points in history are not always obvious, even in retrospect, but I know exactly where I was when I was first made aware that the banking industry I had worked in for most of my adult life was sliding into an abyss. It was 12 July 2007 – I was in Barcelona and I had just been watching the Rolling Stones play. And not watching them in some giant stadium with 60,000 others, forced to peer at dot-like geriatric rockers through binoculars – oh no! – I had watched them perform a one-off show to a tiny crowd of 500 of Deutsche Bank's most important clients and most senior investment bankers on a fully rigged-out stage specially constructed in a museum. The Stones had been hired to play a private gig as the entertainment during that year's two-day 'Deutsche Bank Derivative Conference' – the most meticulously organised and eagerly anticipated client event in our calendar. Apparently, the head of Deutsche's investment bank at the time and Sir Mick Jagger came up with the idea one day when they met at Lord's cricket ground (both are avid cricket fans). They figured Deutsche's clients would love it – and they were right. When I first started out in banking I rather foolishly imagined it would be glamorous. Seventeen years of staring fixedly at screens, arguing interminably in glass-walled meeting rooms and being patted down over and over again while jet-lagged in foreign airports had rather tarnished that idea. But I will admit that watching the Rolling Stones loud and up close was a bit more like it. Sadly, my retrospective enjoyment of the memory

of that evening has been marred by the conversation I then had
with a couple of my colleagues in the elegant and packed bar of the
Hotel Arts after the show.

One of them was called Greg, a forthright, talkative, slightly vul-
pine man who at the time was the head of mortgage trading at
Deutsche in New York. I knew him vaguely from events like the
conference we were attending and I knew his reputation within
the bank as an expert in his field. He was talking urgently about
the American sub-prime mortgage market and why it was doomed
and why he was betting that bond prices would crash – why he
was shorting it, in the jargon. He seemed convincing even though
I wasn't catching all of what he was saying. To be honest, I wasn't
really concerned that I wasn't catching it either – the mortgage
market, especially an obscure segment of it, was a faraway country
of which I knew nothing. It might surprise you to learn, given the
turmoil that followed, that very few non-specialists within banks
were focused on mortgages at the time. As far as I was concerned –
although I was always sensitive to any information that might be
relevant to the foreign exchange markets – mortgages had never
been a worry for me because they traded in an American market
funded in US dollars. No matter what happened, how could they
seriously affect FX?

But then another colleague of mine joined in; David, a short,
cherubic Canadian, was the bank's leading authority on how
money markets work. Money markets exist to provide short-term
funding to banks, funds and companies and, while they are not
considered glamorous, they are huge and vitally important. If they
fail to function, banks and companies struggle for cash and shortly
thereafter begin to thrash around like a scuba diver with a block-
age in his air pipe. This, according to David, was exactly what was
about to happen. A few weeks earlier, two troubled hedge funds
that had invested $20 billion in instruments linked to sub-prime
mortgages (and which were operated by the bank Bear Stearns)

had been bailed out with a multibillion-dollar loan from their parent. 'That's just the start!' said David with a manic, almost gleeful giggle that I learned, during frequent meetings with him in the long months ahead, to associate with imminent terrible news. If Greg's views were right, David said, more and more funds would hit the rocks. But if Greg's bet really paid off and the mortgage market collapsed, the effects could be utterly catastrophic because banks had a colossal amount of mortgage risk on the books. The money markets could seize up and there could even be bank runs. Bank runs! This was a frightening, archaic threat, redolent of panic and of grainy, sepia photos of long uneven lines outside banks with now-forgotten names. His parting recommendation that night was both chilling and prescient: 'Sell any stocks you own and don't buy anything expensive.'

Disastrously for people the world over, both Greg and David were soon proved completely correct. That very day, as we were happily watching the Rolling Stones, credit rating agencies in the US were issuing the first mass downgrades of investment products linked to mortgages. By 20 July, the rescue of the Bear Stearns funds was unravelling as investors rushed to get their money out and the lenders looked to seize the funds' assets to cover loans. Shortly afterwards, both entities were declared bankrupt. On 6 August, the American Home Mortgage Investment Corporation (a retail mortgage lender) also went bankrupt. Ameriquest went on 31 August. By mid-September, on my side of the Atlantic and with money markets now in meltdown, the mortgage lender Northern Rock was the scene of the first bank run in the UK for 150 years. By now, volatility and fear had returned with a vengeance to equity, bond and FX markets after years of gradually increasing calm. It was clear that the previous period of unusual stability was just the water rushing from the beach before a tsunami. From late 2007 onwards, until the end of 2008, the succession of failures and forced takeovers of financial firms reads like the familiar but dolorous list of battles in a terrible, lost war: Countrywide, Bear Stearns, Indy-Mac, Fannie Mae, Freddie Mac, Lehman Brothers, Merrill Lynch, AIG, and on, and on. How had it gone so wrong? How could an industry, which had felt so confident that it could, among other similar gestures, hire the world's most famous rock group for a private party, have come apart so badly and so quickly?

The now well-rehearsed story of the sub-prime crisis is in essence one of systemic fragility – sub-prime was simply the trigger. Ben Bernanke, Chairman of the Federal Reserve, put it like this: 'Prospective sub-prime losses were clearly not large enough on their own to account for the magnitude of the crisis . . . rather, the system's vulnerabilities . . . were the principal explanations of why the crisis was so severe and had such devastating effects on the broader economy.'[1] And what were these vulnerabilities? First, complexity: both the complexity of products and that of the web of linkages between firms. Second, leverage: the risk banks took compared to the amount of shareholders' capital they had to absorb it. Last, size: the sheer size of institutions made the problems worse – the familiar 'too big to fail' syndrome. Each of these vulnerabilities came about as a result of years of gradual change, which, just like the transformation of the FX market, was prompted, enabled or accelerated by the availability of more and more powerful computers. All through my career, these changes had been occurring around me. The link between complexity and computers was clear right from the very start.

My Future in Options

'What is the most important law in finance?' demanded our business school finance professor as he glared out into the ranks of us students. There was silence; the professor had a well-deserved reputation for sarcasm and no one wanted to say something foolish and risk his ire. 'The tax code?' some brave soul ventured, finally. 'Good try . . .' came back the reply (the courageous student beamed for a split second) 'but completely wrong. It is the law of one price.' Thirty or so biros scratched that phrase onto notepads. It was 1989 and I was at London Business School in the first lesson of an elective class called 'Options and Futures'. At that stage, I had no plans to be a banker – regardless, I found the lecture and the ones that followed it fascinating. The law of one price, we were told, is that a security must have the same price wherever it trades otherwise arbitrageurs will step in and close the gap. Recall Loic's jumpers in Chapter 1 – it is obviously untenable that the same jumper can simultaneously be offered for sale at £36 and bid at £38. Both Triangle Man and the Clackatron, and then all the increasingly sophisticated computer systems that took over from them, based their trading on the same fundamental law.

The example of spot FX is a very simple one, however. The law also applies to combinations of different types of securities. 'Imagine you are a market maker and you have to determine the price at which to offer a very simple derivative – a share for delivery in a year's time,' our teacher instructed us, 'how would you do it?' The answer is rather straightforward. Let's say you can buy or sell the share for £100 for delivery today and that you can also borrow or lend money at 10 per cent per year (note, to make things simple, there are no bid-offer spreads – the buying and selling price are identical – also, assume the share pays no dividends). The price of the share in a year (the 'share forward') must be £110. Assuming, as we have, that there are no bid-offer spreads, this would be a price at which you would allow a customer either to buy or sell the share. To see why £110 is the correct price, let's imagine that you, as market maker, decided to show a price of £120 instead. A canny customer could borrow £100 for a year, use the cash to buy a share at its current price and simultaneously sell you the share for future delivery at £120. In a year's time, he would give you the share, you would give him £120 and he would use this money to pay back the loan with interest (£110) and, importantly, have £10 profit. Needless to say, your long-term job prospects as a market maker may have taken a dent during the year. In time, if enough customers did enough of this trade, the current price of the share would rise, the future price of the share would fall and – possibly – even the interest rate would rise in order to make the riskless profit disappear. A similar trick could be applied in reverse if the price was too low (that is, below £110). In essence, because the share forward can be 'manufactured' using other components (the 'share now' combined with borrowing or lending) – its price must be the same as the sum of the components. 'Pricing derivatives: just find the way they can be made from other things,' I scribbled down hurriedly as the lecture ended.

It was a useful lesson and under our professor's steely gaze we learned to apply it to a large number of different markets: currency forwards, interest rate swaps, commodity futures and so on. But all the derivatives in these examples have one thing in common – they have a linear payout, which is to say the profit or loss from holding them is a straight line depending on the price of the underlying asset. In our simple share example, if the correct price of £110 was shown to a customer who agreed to buy the share for delivery in one year's time, then, if the current price of the share went up 5 per cent, so too would the value of the customer's deal since the share forward would now not be worth £110 but £115.50 – this is simply the new, correct forward price with a current share price of £105 and 10 per cent interest rates for a year. The same, in reverse, would be true of a 5 per cent decline. This made a lot of the derivative pricing calculations easy to perform. But there is another type of financial product where things are much more complicated: these are called options and they are the cornerstones of most derivative markets.

'An option is the right, but not the obligation, to buy or sell an asset in the future at a pre-agreed price,' intoned our teacher in words that, unfamiliar then, have now become as automatic and as ingrained in me as a prayer learned in childhood. How do options work? Let's go back to the share example. The customer, rather than agreeing to buy the share in one year's time at £110, could instead buy a 'call option' on the share at the same price. (If he wanted the right to sell, the option is called a 'put'.) In terms of the option catechism, this call option would give the customer 'the right to buy the share at £110, but not the obligation' – that is, if he does not want to buy it in a year he need not do so. And what would influence the customer's decision? In a year, if the market price of the share for current delivery had risen above £110 (say to £130) he would want to exercise his right to buy a share for £110 from you as a market maker (and seller of the option) since he could instantly make a £20 profit. But if the price was below £110 (say, £90), he wouldn't exercise his right – it would be cheaper just to buy the share in the market. This all sounds too good to be true for the customer – he can't lose! But the option he bought is not free; he must pay a premium to you as the market maker. This is a little like paying an insurance premium; indeed, a very important use of options is to protect – that is, insure – the value of financial assets. The tricky question is this: how much premium should you, as market maker, charge the customer? What is the correct price of the option?

'Options have existed since the time of the ancient Greeks,' our professor informed us while pacing back and forth, 'but until quite recently there was one big problem with them. Anybody?' I had a sudden rush of blood to the head. 'Is it that no one knew how to value them?' I blurted. 'Correct,' he said, 'no one knew how to value them' (I grinned foolishly in pure relief). The reason for this, he explained, was that no one could figure out how to manufacture the option payout. In the example of the 'share forward' delivering in one year it's obvious – to offset (manufacture) the risk of selling a share forward a market maker would need to buy one share right now and combine it with a loan (technically speaking, buying one share now is a 'hedge' for the simple derivative). But how many shares should you buy as a market maker to hedge the sale of a call option? You might need to deliver one share if the eventual share price was above the agreed purchase price (the 'strike price' in the jargon) or no shares at all if the price finished below.

Economists and traders had been trying to work out a pricing formula for options (i.e. the correct way to manufacture them) since the 19th century to no avail. True, they knew what factors must influence the price. It was clear that the relationship of the option's strike price to the current market price of the asset must play a part – if the share is currently trading at £100 you'd charge more for the right to buy it for £110 in a year's time than you would for the right to buy it for £1,000. Ditto, the choppiness or 'volatility' of the share price – if the price bounces around chaotically you would charge more for an option than if the price hardly ever budges, since the chances of a big 'win' for the customer at the option's maturity are much higher and – remember – he can walk away if the price goes in the wrong direction. Last, the time until the option's maturity must also be important; the right to buy the share at £110 in a year should be worth more than the right to do so tomorrow – once again the chance of a big 'win' is higher the longer the wait. All this was clear, but there was no pricing formula. That is, no formula until 1973, when two economists at MIT, Fischer Black and Myron Scholes, aided by their colleague Robert C. Merton, solved the centuries-old problem.[2]

Their argument was brilliantly elegant – the way to manufacture the option was to hold a blend of shares and borrowed money and to rebalance the proportions as the share price moved. So instead of the 'static' way we saw of making a linear share forward (i.e. borrow money, buy a share and sit tight), this was 'dynamic' – the balance of shares and borrowing would be altered continuously every time a tiny movement in price occurred. In this way, they argued, you (as market maker) could be sure of having the right hedge at every stage – as the price rose you would buy more shares such that, at maturity, you would be able to deliver shares to the customer if the price was above the strike – and vice versa (sell, and thus hold no shares) if the price fell. From this reasoning, using nifty mathematics after making some simplifying assumptions, they derived an exact formula for the price of options – the famous Black–Scholes formula – which allowed a price to be calculated using a handful of parameters: the asset price, the strike, the option maturity, the volatility and yield of the asset and the interest rate. Their work ushered in a revolution in finance. I sat in the lecture theatre entranced by all this. Afterwards, I gushed to my classmates about how cool it all was! They smiled politely while eyeing me with the nervous suspicion with which you would regard a talkative lunatic on the Tube. But I wasn't the only one who was impressed. In 1997, the Nobel committee awarded Scholes and Merton (Black was dead by this time) the Nobel Prize in Economics for their work in the field. More importantly, throughout the 1970s and 1980s, stock option trading volumes began a dizzying rise, bolstered by the confidence that having a pricing formula gave the market. In time, so did the trading of options on a number of other assets, including FX. By my entry into the banking industry in 1990, partly as a direct result of the 'Options and Futures' course, options were everywhere.

Greeks Bearing Gifts

'Kevin! Another set of risk runs please! Wide grid!' I was a few weeks into my career at Merrill Lynch and my boss Loic was urging me to produce a new set of reports that showed the risk on our options book. The need was critical because Saddam Hussein's army had just invaded Kuwait; this shocked the equity markets into free fall and made the US dollar rally hard. Trading on the Merrill Lynch options desk when I joined it was exclusively confined to regular, so-called 'plain vanilla' options. Complexity was yet to arrive. Even so, managing options risk was by no means trivial and was a very different task from trading a spot book. It is true that the jobs were not totally dissimilar. Making prices on options has a lot of the same steps as making prices on spot – check the market rate, decide on a spread, skew the price depending on your existing risk and the nature of the customer, etc. – but after dealing the jobs diverge. As a spot trader, deals come at you all day long: buy, buy, sell, buy, sell, sell, buy . . . but, even after a thousand trades, it is a simple matter to clear your risk – you can just tot up the total balance and flatten your position by buying or selling an offsetting notional.

But because FX options, like the overwhelming majority of derivatives, trade in a so-called 'over-the-counter' (OTC) market, the parameters of each deal can be tailored to a customer's requirements. A corporation needs to be able to guarantee a minimum rate for the US dollars coming from its export operations so it buys US dollar puts against the Deutschmark (the right, but not the obligation, to sell US dollars and buy Deutschmarks) at a rate of 1.3000, say, expiring on the last business day of the month. A hedge fund wants to speculate on strong economic data in the US (maybe the monthly payroll number) and buys US dollar calls at a rate of 1.3550 for the first Friday of the month after. A pension fund, thinking options are getting too expensive, sells them for expiry the Wednesday before. In short, after even a desultory day of trading, an options book is normally littered with dozens of new deals for different dates with different strikes.

One way of managing the risk would be just to call up another bank and ask for a price on each new option and do offsetting deals on all of them, but, given that the way an options desk makes money is to capture bid-offer spread, doing this is simply paying spread away to your counterparty. The salespeople might as well just call the other bank. Instead, option books are managed as a portfolio – essentially, as Black and Scholes had theorised in their work, options traders attempt to offset risk by holding and adjusting an ever-shifting collection of simpler, component products. There are numerous fascinating, exquisitely detailed and reassuringly expensive books that explain at great length how this is done. My intention now, however, is just to provide a flavour of the process.

The risks of having an option position are directly related to the pricing parameters in the Black–Scholes formula. For instance, the asset price (in FX this is the spot price) is vital. Say you sold a call on US dollars versus Deutschmarks to a fund. If the US dollar started to rally the option would become more valuable and you would start to lose money because the option would now be worth more than the premium you initially received. So, as a hedge, you would buy US dollars and sell Deutschmarks in the spot market. How many US dollars should you buy? You should buy enough so that the profit or loss on the hedge would exactly offset the loss or profit on the option for tiny moves in spot – just like Black and Scholes had assumed. The ratio of this amount to the notional of the option is called the 'delta' and buying (or selling) spot in this way is known as 'delta hedging'. For 'plain vanilla' options this ratio can be thought of as very roughly equivalent to the probability of finishing above the strike. This makes intuitive sense: if you think there's a 30 per cent chance of having to deliver US dollars to the buyer of the option you should stock up on 30 per cent of them now. But the amount you need to hold is not fixed. In the example, if the US dollar continued to rally, the delta (i.e. the approximate probability of finishing above the strike – in jargon, 'being in the money') would rise and you would need to buy more US dollars. The opposite would be true if the US dollar declined in value. This shift in delta with moves in spot is called 'gamma'. If you have sold options you have 'negative gamma' – that is, you need to buy US dollars in a rising market and sell them in one that is falling, thus locking in losses. This sounds very bad, and it is. But there is good news. If you have sold the options and have negative gamma, the passage of time is your friend, since options you have sold get less valuable as time passes (there is not so long for the US dollar to alter in value). This effect is known as 'theta' or 'time decay'. But it doesn't stop there. You are also exposed to rises and falls in volatility; if the market's prediction of the future volatility of the dollar/ mark exchange rate rises, the option you have sold will get more valuable and you will lose money. This sensitivity is called 'vega'. Your exposure to interest rates is 'rho', and so it goes on. Confused? Don't worry. Unless you are a professional derivatives trader, it is likely and understandable that you might be.

It gets worse. These risk sensitivities are not stable – they vary as the spot market moves or, even if it doesn't, as time passes. In short, the risks associated with an option are described by a large array of shifting risk measures. These are collectively termed 'the Greeks' since most of them have a Greek letter as their name. The risk of a portfolio of thousands of options is the sum of all these individual risks. Thus, the Greeks of a large option book are very complex indeed. The job of the options trader is to manage these risks by considering them at the level of the portfolio, usually with a lot of money at stake. As Loic once put it: 'It's like flying a helicopter. You need to watch dozens of dials going crazy all at once – and if you ever fuck things up? Boof! Into the mountain you will crash.'

Admittedly, in some respects running a derivatives book is a little like trading spot. For instance, let's say you are worried that you have sold too many options and that your book's exposure to a rise in the market's prediction of future volatility is getting too extreme (that is, you are too 'short vega'), then you can skew prices to customers in order to try to buy some options back or, *in extremis*, call out to buy options from another bank – just like spot traders skew prices and call out. The mechanisms by which options traders use brokers and make a market between themselves is similar to those in the pre-electronic spot market we saw earlier. Tricks and techniques of bluff and double bluff are common.

Take 'spoofing' for example. Let's imagine you are an options trader some time in the early 1990s. You want to buy $100 million notional of one-month maturity options on the exchange rate between US dollars and German marks; you are a 'buyer of a hundred one-month marks' in the lingo. The price in the brokers is 9.0/9.3 – that is, someone would buy at 9.0 per cent and someone would sell at 9.3 per cent.* But you'd rather not buy at 9.3 per cent, you'd like to buy cheaper. So, as a spoof, you show the broker an offer to sell a smaller amount – say 30 million of notional – at a price of 9.2 per cent. After a few minutes, because you are feeling brave, you improve the offer to 9.15 per cent. Your hope is that other traders, seeing the gradually lowering offers, will think that there is a seller in the market. Now is your moment to strike! You call out direct to other dealers for two-way prices. Your spoof has worked: several banks have been fooled into showing you a 9.2 per cent offer. You pay them, quickly cancel your offer (9.15 per cent) at the broker, book the deals, and accept a brief kind word from your boss – you've shown spot-dealer-like cunning.

In other ways, though, your job is very different from that of a spot dealer; in particular, risk management is utterly reliant on computers. It is possible to imagine spot traders doing without computers and simply totting up their positions manually (indeed, on occasions I have seen it done when systems have failed temporarily, albeit accompanied by a growling cacophony of weapons-grade swearing) but option traders with no computers? Never! It is simply not humanly possible to keep track of 'the Greeks' without one. This is true for derivatives in all markets, not just FX. And, as

---

* This rate, expressed in annualised volatility as a proxy for price, would be converted upon dealing to a US dollar premium using an FX variant of the Black–Scholes formula. On $100 million of notional, each 0.1 per cent in volatility is worth around $10,000 in premium and, thus, profit.

we shall see, this is why – at least in large part – derivatives in every market became more and more complex as computers grew faster.

A Better Helicopter

'Since you ask, Kevin, he was fired because he was a total idiot.' It was summer 1991 and Loic was explaining, between long drags on a Marlboro, what had happened to a recently departed senior 'quantitative analyst' (or 'quant') from the FX team. This made me nervous – I was just over a year into my career and I still felt that a feat of total idiocy was by no means beyond me – what had this harmless mathematician done while I had been away on holiday? Loic told me the story. An important hedge fund customer had believed that the Deutschmark to US dollar exchange rate would remain quiet and range-bound and wanted to bet on his view. He'd asked for a price on a contract that would pay out $1 million if, and only if, the exchange rate went neither above the recent high or below the recent low at any time in the next six months. This, at the time, was a non-standard contract and so Loic had turned to the quant for help. After a day's arduous lucubration, the quant had come back with the answer: we should charge $1.2 million. What? How on earth could it possibly cost more money to buy the contract than it could ever pay out? 'You know what he said?' spluttered Loic, getting enraged all over again in the mere telling of the tale. 'He said it was expensive because it had so much gamma!' Even I knew that this was total bullshit and so, better still, did my bosses. The quant's other recent, smaller offences against common sense had been totted up and he had been asked to leave.

In time the unfortunate chap was replaced and life went on, but the task that had tripped him up – figuring out pricing on a brand-new contract type – was, back then, at Merrill Lynch, a singularly rare occurrence. A quant's main purpose in life was trying to get 'the

Greeks' out of the computer quicker. Speed was a perpetual problem. The Greeks were unstable (yes, we made the obvious jokes) and so any big market move quickly made old risk reports useless. But churning through pricing and delta and gamma and theta and vega numbers for thousands of options was a slow process using the computers we had at the time; a full risk report might take 40 minutes or more to be ready. This often meant that we were flying blind just at the moment – the chaotic, frenzied moment – that we needed the most visibility. The quants laboured to find clever ways to make the calculations faster (for instance, why always recalculate the risks of two identical options with offsetting risks?) since even tiny improvements might make vital minutes of difference scaled up over thousands of contracts. Eventually though, Loic and his bosses realised that the old risk management system that we were using simply couldn't be hot-rodded any further and, in a move reminiscent of the change from ARM to RAPID at Deutsche Bank, a new one was built from scratch and went live in 1992. This system was called OPTICS, and was based on some very expensive and, at the time, very powerful Unix-based Sun workstations. We all thought it was great – risk reports came out in a few minutes rather than the best part of an hour! The helicopter now had better instruments; as a result, we helicopter pilots started flying faster and lower. We started taking more risk.

In part, this had the laudable effect that we were more aggressive on prices to our customers and more willing to cope with bigger deals. Soon after OPTICS went live we traded, for the first time, an option with a $1 billion notional (an exceptionally large deal back then) which had a premium with so many zeros that it couldn't be processed through our settlement systems; consequently the customer, a giant pension fund, had to pay it in pieces. But as well as making us better at handling customer requests, the comfort we got from a better and faster computer system made us more willing to take risk on the bank's behalf. We felt more in control. But this was not just 'churning' risk that comes as a natural consequence of market making. We started building up bigger positions that were on the books for days, weeks and months. In plain language, we started gambling.

In 1992, the biggest speculative game in town was the European Exchange Rate Mechanism (ERM). Early in my career, Loic had put me in charge of the ERM books. Since the currency rates were pegged within tight ranges, these were considered a harmless, boring backwater where the new kid could play around without causing too much damage. This facile assumption was shared by the whole market, which acted as if the pegs would last forever (just as it did in the Swiss franc debacle I described in the last chapter) and had invested in higher yielding currencies believing that the risk of negative currency moves had been eradicated. But by summer 1992 the ERM had become the focus of a sustained commercial and speculative attack as it became clear to most currency professionals – as a result of the tensions coming from a shock, reunification-prompted German interest rate rise – that the 'weaker' currencies (i.e. the lira, peseta and pound) might not survive within it. I had become convinced of this and, with the enthusiastic blessing of Merrill Lynch's management, I had gradually accumulated a very large option position that would pay off if either the lira or the pound de-pegged and devalued; if they didn't devalue, it would be an expensive mistake. Coming up to what was seen as a make-or-break (and achingly tight) vote in France on the EU's Maastricht Treaty on 20 September, the market's fear of a 'no' turned into a torrent of unconstrained selling that battered the very limits of the ERM – limits at which European states' central banks were treaty-bound to intervene. In the hubbub, I became an acid-stomached knot of nerves. Would my bet pay off?

I didn't have to wait for the French vote to find out. On the afternoon of Sunday 13 September I picked up the phone to hear the unexpected and eager voice of a journalist friend. 'I know you care about currencies and stuff, she said, 'so I thought you would be interested in this: I just this minute heard that the Italians are about to announce a devaluation of the lira.' My mouth went dry. The central banks had folded! I felt a surge of pure, white-hot, electric excitement. I had been right! I will never score the last-minute winning goal in a Cup Final or pump my fist as I sink the trophy-securing putt at the Ryder Cup (I am a hopeless sportsman and, besides, I'm now in my fifties) but in that instant I got a glimpse of how it would feel. It was a thousand-fold amplification of the giddy madness of backing a winner at the Grand National. I rushed straight to the office and spent the next few days and weeks in a blur of 16-hour trading sessions. The devaluation of the pound a few days after the lira on Wednesday 16 September added to the turbulence. The positions made a fortune both immediately and, with the aid of our flashy new risk system, in the weeks afterwards. In one stroke, I was no longer 'the kid'. As a result, early in 1993, my name came to the attention of some senior folk at Bankers Trust – a firm widely renowned for its expertise in derivatives – and they cajoled me into joining their bank. For the first and only time in my career I jumped ship – to a bank that, for a while in the 1990s, became synonymous with the use of computers to create complexity.

So Come Up to the Lab and See What's on the Slab . . .

Within minutes of sitting down and starting to trade at Bankers Trust I noticed something slightly shocking. Their risk systems were even faster than OPTICS had been and, probably as a result of their even greater feeling of control, my new trading colleagues took more risk than we had at Merrill. The reason for the speed was simple: because of Bankers Trust's strategic focus on derivatives (which dated back to the late 1980s), their quants had been grinding away on the speed problem for longer than those at Merrill

Lynch and their IT boffins had spent more money solving it. With this issue licked, they were free to pursue other goals. Some of them concentrated on the speed issue in interest rate products. Any derivative on interest rates is by definition more computationally intensive than one in FX because it depends not on one underlying asset (i.e. spot) but on a complex, time-based 'curve' of rates, since the cost of borrowing varies with how long you are borrowing for. Other quants got creative. In the early weeks of my time at Bankers I fell into conversation with one of them. His name was Chris. Nicknamed 'Two Brains', he sat at a desk on the trading floor piled high with teetering mathematical textbooks and littered with sheets of paper dense with equations. He was a friendly and approachable man, but with his high, domed forehead, untamed thatch of curly hair and his wire-rimmed spectacles he only needed a violently discharging Van de Graaff generator to be ready to star as an unhinged scientist in a black-and-white horror film. 'What are you working on?' I asked. 'Generalised closed-form solutions for barrier products' first- and second-order risk measures,' he replied, mildly. Then, seeing that I was genuinely interested, evidently much to his surprise, he began to explain.

Barrier products were just like regular options (the right, but not the obligation, etc.) except that they were specified to have a 'barrier level' for the life of the option. For example, with spot at 1.3100, a fund might buy a one-month maturity call on US dollars against Deutschmarks with a strike price of 1.3550 that had a so-called 'knockout' barrier at 1.2800. If, at any stage before expiry, the exchange rate fell below 1.2800, the option would cease to exist: it would 'knock out'. If it never reached that barrier level then the fund could exercise the option as normal if the final exchange rate was above 1.3550. Why would anyone want to buy such a thing? 'It's just more leverage,' Chris explained; 'it's cheaper than a plain vanilla option with the same strike' (obviously so, since it could disappear in certain circumstances) 'so if you're right in your view you get more bang for your buck of premium.' Then why would we want to sell them? His answer lay at the heart of the changes that were taking place in the markets. First up, they were more profitable than regular trades. Because they were out of the ordinary (in recognition of this, barrier options and the variants that followed them were known as 'exotic options' or 'exotics'), fewer banks could price them. This meant that the competition on prices would be less extreme and the cut-throat spread compression that was already evident in plain vanilla options, and long-established in spot, would be less intense.

Second, he said, the fact that there was more leverage shouldn't be a concern as long as we (the bank) could hedge the Greeks coming from these trades. If we could, then they would just add to, and blend in with, the risk of the thousands of other trades in the book as a whole. That was what he was working on – figuring out formulae for the Greeks that could be programmed into our risk system. Cut to its essentials, what he was saying was that the bank would offer barrier options because he had figured out how to manufacture them from simpler products. Rather like the punch line to the crude joke about why a dog licks its own testicles, we were offering these options 'because we could'.

Then Chris's eyes lit up. 'What's interesting is what we could do if computers keep getting faster,' he speculated, dreamily; 'that'd open up a world of new possibilities.' The reason it was practical to offer a relatively simple product like barrier options, he said, was that, just as was the case for the Black–Scholes formula for plain vanilla options, their price and their Greeks were solvable 'analytically' or in 'closed form'. Other more complicated potential products were not so mathematically tractable. Why did this matter? It's a little like trying to find the roots (the zero points) of quadratic equations, he told me.* This is made easy by the fact that there is

---

* You may remember from maths lessons at school that these have the form: $y = ax^2 + bx + c$, and have the solution $(-b +/- \mathrm{sqrt}\,(b^2 - 4ac))/2a$.

a simple, exact, 'analytic' formula that gives you the answer – all you need to do is to look it up and plug in the parameters from the quadratic equation you are solving. But many equations are more complicated than a quadratic and there is no simple formula. To solve these you need to use trial and error – you guess a solution and then get ever closer to the answer by improving the guess over and over again by using various rules. This is a 'numerical' solution. Performing numerical solutions by hand takes many, many times longer than merely plugging numbers into an analytic formula (all the tedious iterations of guessing take time) and, although silicon and software are hugely quicker than humans, the same relationship between analytic and numerical methods applies when computers do it. By analogy, he said, plain vanilla options and barrier options were like quadratics; more complex derivatives were like the equations that needed to be solved numerically. It could be done but, even with computers, calculating all the Greeks would be slow – this made 'mass production' of thousands of deals impossible. 'But if we can do things faster . . .' At this, Chris's daydreams were interrupted by a sudden shout as I was hollered at to sprint back to my desk to make a price; Chris returned to his textbooks and equations.

The summer of 1993 brought another assault on the ERM and we traders were caught up in long days of stressful trading. All the while, though, Chris and his quant colleagues continued to scribble and tap away. What this meant, during my first year or so at Bankers Trust, was that there was an explosion of new products coming off the production line. It was almost impossible to keep up. Some were the result of mathematical legerdemain as quants found exact analytic solutions to new 'exotic' payoffs. Some were more complex variants that required numerical solutions – these were now practical to use in limited numbers because of the tireless work the quants were doing to optimise the way they were priced and because computers were getting faster. There were 'Asian options', which paid off based on the average exchange rate during the life of the options rather than just the rate at the end. There were 'lookbacks', which paid off on the high or low. There were 'power options', which paid off not linearly, but according to the square or even cube of the final spot rate. There were 'range trades', which paid off if spot remained within a certain range for the option's life (this was exactly the same product that had caused the demise of the Merrill Lynch quant). There were 'double knockouts', which were like barrier options but had two barriers, one below and one above the current market. The list went on.

The process of innovation was an arms race with the other big banks. No sooner had a rival invented a new product than our quants would race to replicate it; the same was true in reverse. There was constant pressure to be able to offer every conceivable product since, it was feared, if we did not our competitors would gradually take over. Some products (such as range trades) came into being because clients requested them, others simply 'because we could'. The quants made things easier for the non-mathematicians on the trading floor by packaging their pricing and 'Greeks' calculations in a handy format. Called 'BTAnalytics', this huge library of computer software was accessible from traders' and from salespeople's desktops. What's more, these computer models could be plugged into ordinary spreadsheets – suddenly, everyone who could use Microsoft Excel could build their very own pricing tools. And once you had done a deal, why not simply risk-manage the thing using the same spreadsheet you had just built to price it? This was a radical departure. Prior to this, if a trader wanted to do a new type of deal he would need to go cap in hand to a quant who, if he could price the product at all, would then need to plumb the calculations into the risk management system; think of Loic with the range trade at Merrill Lynch. Risk systems were big, complex and delicate and so the burden of economic proof that it was worth changing them in order to launch a new product had always been heavy. That was no longer the case. The burden of proof had been made lighter. The ability to deal fancy products had just been democratised.

Procter and Gambling

Although the majority of clients still stuck to plain vanilla products or to just trading the underlying asset (in FX, this was spot), more and more of them began to use 'exotics'. To a large extent, this was a benign development. Most of the popular products (like barriers or range trades) were simple to understand and allowed for more flexibility in hedging or taking risk. But the sudden democratisation of product development had its dark side, too. The pace of change had been so rapid that there were very few controls put in place around what products could be sold to which client. 'What approvals do I need before I trade?' I once asked my boss as I priced up a large and complex deal. 'Are you are using BTAnalytics for pricing and risk?' he asked, sternly; I nodded. 'Fine, then, just tell the accountants when you are done so they can find the spread-sheet and put it in their profit and loss sums. But for now – you are good to go.' Things were loose, in short. This looseness led to disaster in a business that was separate from, but related to, FX. This was the interest rates desk.

Since 1989, short-term US rates had been held at 3 per cent (they had been cut hard after the stock market crash in 1987 and had remained low). But long-term bond yields had remained stubbornly high; the yields on ten-year bonds had reduced from 9 per cent at the start of the decade but were still above 6 per cent at the start of 1994.[3] There was a simple trade to take advantage of this: the carry trade. You could borrow short term and lend long term at a much higher rate by using the money to buy bonds. As well as carry, you would win if the bonds got more expensive. Since this is exactly what traders had been doing for four years or so, speculating on higher bond prices looked like a one-way bet. Everyone was at it: hedge funds, banks and even corporate treasuries. In time, as an alternative to having their clients trade physically (by actually buying bonds), enterprising banks – with Bankers Trust to the fore – allowed the same economic outcome to be achieved through derivatives. These were effectively bets on interest rates, which would simply pay out with reference to a formula based on the bond price (or an interest rate benchmark like LIBOR, the London Interbank Offered Rate) at maturity – this was known as 'cash settlement'. In certain cases, convinced of the obviousness of the trade, clients were persuaded to bet heavily by buying highly leveraged products that would win if bond prices continued to rise (or at least remained stable) but would lose many times over if they did not. To do so, the new 'exotic' option toolkit was unlocked and used to the full.

Unfortunately, on 4 February 1994, the US Federal Reserve, worried by the prospect of inflation, unexpectedly raised rates by 0.25 per cent. I was in New York at the time on a business trip and witnessed the ear-splitting, curse-laden roar of disbelief as the news hit the wires. The air grew thick with panic – the one-way ride was over! In the ensuing bond price collapse, those speculators who had bet the farm, lost the farm. Two of the biggest losers were clients of Bankers Trust. One, Gibson Greetings, was a manufacturer of, to my British eyes, somewhat cheesy birthday and anniversary cards. The other, Procter and Gamble, made familiar household goods. Away from these simple, blameless, wholesome activities their treasury departments had also been having a bash at being leveraged bond speculators. Procter and Gamble lost $157 million, a colossal sum at the time.[4] Predictably, they sued, as did Gibson. Their argument – simply put – was: 'We didn't know what we were doing; these deals were too complicated; you misled us.' The bank's reply, pointing to previous, successful deals that the firms had done, was, in essence: 'You didn't say that when you were winning.' What broke the deadlock was the fact that all conversations through the bank's telephone system were taped so that they could be referred to in the event of a dispute. This was, and is, common practice everywhere. When these tapes were handed over to the lawyers, the juicy bits of the relevant salespeople's conversations as they worked to design the offending derivatives (extracted from hour after boring hour of harmless and inconsequential chit-chat) made very ugly reading.[5] If the general tone of these sections of the tapes could be summed up in one word, that word would be a cry of 'Suckers!' – it didn't look good. Faced with this, Bankers Trust gave up the legal fight in 1996 and settled out of court.

The bank, and indeed the whole investment banking industry, learned a valuable lesson. This lesson was not, as you might be forgiven for thinking, 'don't deal complicated derivatives' but rather, 'make sure your customer knows exactly what he's buying; put legal disclaimers on everything; be careful on taped lines'. Crudely put, 'cover your ass'. Continuous stern warnings to this effect came from senior management but always with the rider that business needed to continue. There had been a setback, but the computerised creation of complexity carried on.

Spinning the Wheel in Monte Carlo

As the years wore on into the mid-1990s, the pace of product innovation slowed a little but the quants were still hard at work. The buzzword now was 'commoditisation'. How could we mass-produce derivatives that needed numerical solutions? One method was just to keep applying more and more computing power – 'throwing metal at the problem', in the slang. The quicker you could get the Greeks, the more deals you could do. This was made easy by the continued plummeting cost of computer performance. A Yale University study in 2001 calculated that the number of 'million standardised operations per second' (MSOPS) you could buy for one hour of labour – used as a measure of cost to keep things consistent – had shown a 'rate of improvement . . . [at an] annual average rate of 55 percent' since the 1950s.[6] That is, a doubling every 19 months, or, put another way, a rate which would lead to an almost 40,000 times increase in the course of my 24-year career. It became a common, almost daily sight on the trading floor to see technicians groping around under the desk of one colleague or another to install the latest, fastest, flashiest version of computer hardware. The same was happening at remote data centres, too.

Another route to 'commoditisation' was to standardise the risk management of exotic deals. Having people cook up trades on spreadsheets was a great way of spurring creativity but a nightmare for control purposes. How could the bank's management make sure that every deal was being considered when it came to do the daily accounts for profit and loss purposes? Could deals be forgotten on some trader's hard drive and then cause a massive loss without management's knowledge? Besides, even we traders started to dislike the hassle of spreadsheet deals, or, as they were dubbed, 'off system' trades. Calculating the risk on all of them became a slow, fiddly, manual, often error-strewn and deeply unpopular chore ('It's your turn to run the off system today', 'No, no, no – I did it Tuesday' etc.). So a new risk system was developed at Bankers Trust called Spreadsheet Solutions Framework (or SSF) – this acted as a central point for all spreadsheets to be stored and allowed us to calculate their Greeks automatically. Freed of most of the irritation of running the 'off system', we traders were happier to do more deals. Systems similar to SSF were developed at many of our big rival banks. The 'hassle hurdle' of dealing was being lowered across the industry. Just as had happened during the computerisation of spot FX, the easier it became to deal, the more people did so.

Last, a new pricing technique was making headway. New, that is, to banking – nuclear scientists on the Los Alamos atomic bomb project had invented it in the 1940s. Called 'Monte Carlo pricing', it opened the way to even more complex derivative structures. Chris was very excited by it and, in the mid-1990s, gave a seminar on the subject. Previously, he said, if quants couldn't figure out an exact formula to allow a derivative to have its price and its Greeks calculated analytically, the numerical technique that their models used was some variation of what was called a 'binomial tree', or just a 'tree' approach. (A colleague of mine, Paul, was once pricing up a deal and was asked by the salesman how he was going to do it. 'Are you going to use a tree?' the salesman enquired. 'No,' my friend shot back, 'I'm going to use a computer.' The quants, innocent souls, thought this was the funniest thing they had ever heard.) The precise way binomial trees work is not that important – indeed, for us traders it was safely hidden inside the code of BTAnalytics. In essence, as Chris explained it to us, a set of branching potential price paths are created for an asset – a share, say, or an FX rate – by assuming that its value can go either up or down (i.e. two ways, hence 'binomial') at each little step forward in time during the life of a derivative. The resultant bushy set of potential prices resembles a tree. The probability of getting to each of the asset prices on the tree depends primarily on the asset price now, how volatile you expect it to be in the future, and how much time elapses; that is, how far up the tree you have progressed. Once you have this tree of prices and probabilities, the value of a derivative can be calculated from them because you now can figure out how much it will pay off. This method (and some very similar variants, collectively dubbed 'lattice methods') underpinned every bank's most commonly used numerical pricing models.

But, Chris explained, the Monte Carlo method, though related, is subtly different. Monte Carlo operates in two stages. First, a potential asset price path is generated randomly; the random element is why the process was nicknamed Monte Carlo. Imagine modelling a potential path for the price of a share by tossing a coin to decide whether, each day, it moves up or down in value. Heads might mean up 1 per cent, tails down 1 per cent. If you do that for the 260 trading days in a year and plot the prices each day you will get a jagged line that rises and falls. Once you've done that, you can figure out what the derivative would be worth if that – fictitious – path actually happened. It's like doing an experiment. For example, if you had a call option on a share with a strike price of £110 and, in your modelled path, the final share price was £130, the option in that fictitious world would be worth £20 at maturity. But that's just one potential path, one 'experiment'. The next random experiment might throw up a final price of £90. What is the value of the option then? Answer: zero. If you repeat this process thousands of times, Chris said, then take the average and discount it by the interest rate, you have the price of the option now. Of course, this description is a simplification – in reality the random element is arrived at in a more sophisticated way than a coin toss since it takes account of expected volatility of the asset and of interest rates such that, repeated thousands of times, the 'experimental' results are in line with market expectations.

'So why don't we just use this method all the time?' I asked him. Monte Carlo was a simple and powerful technique, he told me, but to get sufficient accuracy you had to generate tens of thousands of paths. That's why it was only now, with fast modern computers, that the method was practical at all. Even so, it was slow compared to the 'tree', which for most purposes was still the better bet. But Monte Carlo has one massive advantage – it is better at pricing derivatives on multiple assets. Why is that? If you use a tree method to price an option that depends on the price of two shares (for example, let's say it pays off on the price difference between them, what's called a 'spread option') then, to do so, you have to generate a more complicated tree. This is because you need to figure out more than just 'share price up versus share price down' through time for one share; instead you must calculate four combinations for two shares (up/up, up/down, down/up, down/down). For three shares, you need to look at eight combinations (up/up/up, up/down/up, etc.).

In short, the computational load is proportional to two raised to the power of the number of assets. But the computational load for Monte Carlo only goes up linearly with the number of assets, since for two assets you just need two sets of paths, three sets for three assets, and so on. This meant, Chris went on, that if you looked at a derivative on ten assets, the 'tree' method would be over 500 times slower than for a single asset (i.e. 2^{10} versus 2^1) whereas the Monte Carlo would be just ten times slower. This excited Chris and his quant colleagues. They realised that, as computers continued to grow more powerful, the way had been opened to create derivatives on very large baskets of assets, whether those were shares, FX rates, government bonds . . . or mortgages. It was a path that, in time, would lead to the Great Financial Crisis.

Towards the First Near Miss

Before we go on, let me say right now that I am aware that much of this chapter may appear abstruse to you. Analytic equations; Greeks; packages of pricing models; MSOPS per dollar; spreadsheet management systems; the differentials in speed between two subtly different numerical methods – all of it may seem remote from real life or even what you imagine to be the core business of banking. But they absolutely are not remote. These obscure, computational developments allied with cut-throat banking competition led to dramatic changes in the world of derivatives and ultimately, as we shall see, to disaster.

By 1997, derivatives had already changed radically since the start of my career seven years earlier and my job was changing too. That year, I joined a newly created department in the bank that had been set up to trade emerging markets. It was from here that I was witness to the financial market's first near miss with calamity in modern times, the interlinked Asian, Russian and Long-Term Capital Management crises.

CHAPTER 5

Don't Mention the VaR

A Wake-up Call

'Hello?' I mumbled sleepily into my mobile phone. 'Mate, it's Dazza,' came the cheerful-sounding reply. It was early morning on Monday 17 August 1998 and I was on the first day of a holiday in Tuscany with my wife and toddler son, Fred. I was in bed, the sun was just rising but it was already getting warm. 'Have you seen the news?' he continued excitedly. At this, my body instantly tensed and I was suddenly fully awake. An early-morning call from my trading partner Darren while I was on holiday? News? This did not sound good. 'They've gone and done it,' he shouted, 'it's all the D's, Kev! Domestic Default, Debt Moratorium and Devaluation!' I felt bile rise. The Russians had cracked. It was not a surprise that they might do so – they had been under crippling financial pressure for months – but the timing was a shock. All our research had pointed to a decision delayed until after 14 September when a huge volume of FX contracts rolled off – contracts which would be immensely damaging to Russian banks in the event of a devaluation. So confident was I in this prediction that I had risked a holiday in the middle of market turmoil. Bad call.

'Where's the rouble?' I asked Darren. '6.3500 at 6.3550, 50 bucks up,' he replied. But that was the same rate as it had been on Friday when I had left the office! The market hadn't responded to the devaluation! 'Daz! Pay the offer! Buy dollars, sell roubles!' I shouted. There was silence on the line, then laughter. 'I was joking,' he chuckled. 'There's no fucking market, you daft git. There's nothing. Russia's a smoking crater.' I sighed. Of course, he was right. 'Ron will call in a bit,' he went on (Ron was our boss), 'but a word of advice – don't get too comfortable in your villa.' Then he hung up. A few days later I was back at my desk. I had attempted to avoid the inevitable by spending hours on the phone in Italy until I could almost feel the radiation mutating my brain, but eventually I gave up and flew back home. The next few weeks were spent sorting through the wreckage of our Russian business. Russian bonds had become next to worthless. The rouble lost 80 per cent of its value in days. An American colleague of mine who was running the Bankers Trust Moscow office at the time told a journalist from the *Financial Times* in a moment of brutal – if possibly unwise – honesty that investors, 'would rather eat nuclear waste' than invest in Russia again.[1] He left the bank shortly afterwards. One major client of ours, a hedge fund called, appropriately enough, the Triple I High Risk Opportunities Fund, which specialised in buying Russian debt, went belly up, losing its investors several hundred million dollars. Darren had to fly to the fund's headquarters in Florida to figure out what we should do. It was not pretty. What was uglier still was the knock-on effect on the rest of the markets. Equities sagged alarmingly and investors all over the world started pulling money from any risky asset. Caught up in the mayhem was a gigantic (though obscure to the general public) hedge fund called Long-Term Capital Management (LTCM). This fund, a practitioner of the most sophisticated computerised risk management techniques the world had ever seen, almost went bankrupt and looked as if it would take the banking system with it. It was a wake-up call. But it was one that the market never heeded.

Things Can Only Get Better

Eighteen months earlier, when I moved from FX to Emerging Markets at the start of 1997 it was like entering a different world. All the people who had been specialising in trading or selling European,

Middle Eastern or African (EMEA) emerging markets products in other departments – mainly FX, Interest Rates and Equities – had been lifted out and put in one place. 'Like the A-team?' I suggested when I met my new colleagues. 'More like the Dirty Dozen,' corrected Darren. He had a point; some of my new colleagues were distinctly odd. I sat next to Darren and a laconic Polish ex-tank commander called Tomasz who, one weekend, accidentally broke the leg of his three-year-old son while playing football with him in the garden. 'It was a 50-50 ball! I admit it was a hard challenge, but it was fair,' Tomasz told us, laughing. 'Now he's in a cast, poor kid, and crawling around like a cockroach. Ha! It's actually quite funny really.' Somewhat less excusably, another trader was rumoured once to have broken the nose of a salesman in a heated dispute about a price. He had been retained by the bank, it was said, after he had paid the salesman $250,000 from his bonus. This was the sort of thing I was up against.

The other big difference from my previous job was the type of business we were doing. FX is a peculiar product because it is not really an asset; rather it is a means of payment. The clients who deal FX use it to hedge cash flows coming from corporate activity or to offset the risk of holding assets in a foreign currency (like a UK investor holding US stocks) or, of course, to speculate. Although we did some business like this in Emerging Markets (I had been put into the team to be the FX specialist), the bulk of our client flow was from investors actually looking to go long – that is buy and hold on to – stocks or bonds. In this, they were simply following on from what they had been doing in Asia for a few years; the long-established Bankers Trust Asian Emerging Markets team were now our colleagues and the model for our new unit. Why did clients invest in these markets? The answer was to get much higher returns than in developed markets for – it was thought – very little extra risk. The reason they thought this was because of currency pegging. A major risk when you invest in any foreign market, but most particularly in emerging markets, is that while your investment can do well in foreign currency terms, if that currency depreciates against your own you can end up losing. You can hedge with FX products but they are costly if the market perceives a large risk and so much of the benefit of higher returns is wiped out. But if the foreign currency is pegged, as most Asian currencies were to the US dollar, then, as long as the peg holds, the currency risk disappears. Russia, the biggest of the EMEA markets, had pegged the rouble against the US dollar and so, like Asia, was beginning to see foreign investors snap up its high-yielding, short-dated rouble-denominated bonds, called GKOs. Our job was to help them do so as quickly as possible since it was widely expected – not least by the Russian government itself – that these high rates would be a temporary state of affairs and rates would fall in time.

Tomasz was the expert in the Russian market and explained how it worked on my first day in the team. The way clients invested was not by buying the bonds themselves but by buying a simple derivative that paid out the cash flows that would have come to them had they actually bought a particular GKO. Why not just buy the bond? 'It is a pain,' Tomasz told me, 'no one wants to deal with the paperwork.' Although the Russians were opening up to foreign capital with the aim of enabling them to borrow more cheaply in the long run, the bureaucracy involved was grinding: you needed a particular type of onshore bank account, a relationship with a Russian bank, special permits – the list went on. It was far easier to let Bankers Trust handle things. Tomasz went on to explain in more detail.

Step one was that a client would wire us some US dollars that we would convert to roubles by doing a spot FX deal. We would then use those roubles to buy the specific GKO that the client wanted; this would then sit in our Bankers Trust bond account. The trade was done over the phone by shouting instructions to a dealer in a Russian bank during the one, hectic hour each day – nicknamed 'the window' – that trading was permitted on the Moscow exchange (MICEX). 'That's the fun part,' Tomasz told me. A GKO was a 'zero

coupon bond"* – this meant that we would pay less than the notional of the bond when we bought it (e.g. 88 per cent of notional),
but in six months' time, say, we would get the full notional back in
roubles. Thus, in this example, we would receive approximately 30
per cent annualised interest in rouble terms. On maturity, we would
sell the roubles for US dollars and return the dollars to the client.
Assuming the rouble was still pegged to the US dollar at a rate of
around 6.0000, the US dollar yield of 30 per cent or so dwarfed any
return on a regular US-dollar-based bond where six-month yields
were running at around 6.5 to 7.0 per cent at the time.[2] All this was
documented within a 'note' that the client held; in effect it was a carbon copy of the dollar-based pay-off of a GKO. In the unlikely event
that Russia defaulted, the client would get nothing but we would be
fine because we had used the client's money to buy the bond. To use
the jargon, the deal was 'fully funded'. 'We are just a broker,' Tomasz
told me. 'We charge a fee for our work but it is risk-free.' Although,
strictly speaking, it was not agency business (the client never owned
the bond but rather a derivative 'copy' of it for which Bankers Trust
was legally a principal) the risks were 'agency-like'.

But this agency-like approach was not the way most clients wanted to deal. Most clients wanted to deal via 'total return swaps' or
TRSs. These worked in exactly the same way as a note except for one
very important difference. The client would not wire us the money
up front. Rather, we would use the bank's money to buy the bond.
At maturity we would not give all the US dollar proceeds to the client but, instead, the difference between the proceeds and the dollars
we used to buy the bonds in the first place, plus interest. In effect,
economically speaking, the TRS operated as if the client had done
two deals stapled together: one, a US dollar loan and two, a fully
funded, agency-like note bought with the borrowed money. 'This is
risky business, Kevin,' Tomasz admitted, 'but we get much more fees.'

---

* In most ways GKOs were identical to US Treasury bills. I use the term 'bond' rather than
'bill' throughout this chapter purely for simplicity and consistency.

It was risky because, if the Russians ever defaulted, the note would be worthless but the client would still owe us the principal and interest of the loan. If they didn't have the money, we would be out of pocket. To protect against this we demanded margin – some of it up front ('initial margin') and some of it later as the deal – the note – changed in value (so-called 'variation margin'). As we saw in Chapter 3, this is very much like the way prime brokerage works. The advantage to the client was that, rather than make a 30 per cent return, for example, he could make a multiple of that depending on how much initial margin he paid to us. If he could get away with initial margin of 20 per cent of the value of the bond, then his return would be around 150 per cent annualised (since on $10 million worth of bonds the client could make $3 million but only put up $2 million in margin). The lower the initial margin, the higher the return. This, then, was the other reason clients wanted to deal through Bankers Trust or our competitors – leverage. It was to become a common theme.

The first half of 1997 went by in a pleasant whirl. The weather in London was good, and business was booming. In May, a new government was elected in the UK, run by a fresh-faced Tony Blair. His campaign theme song was D:Ream's 'Things Can Only Get Better'. It became the desk's anthem, sung or hummed each time a new client request was shouted to us by a salesperson. That happened all the time, since clients were coming to us from all over the world: US hedge funds, Korean corporations, wealthy individuals in Switzerland – all chasing the exceptional yields. On the face of it what we were doing was simple, but it grew more and more complex as time went on. In the early days, in 1996, before the new team was put together, traders would fulfil client requests for particular bonds to the letter. If they couldn't get hold of the bond that a client wanted at the right price during the one-hour MICEX trading session, the client would be sent away empty-handed that day. The bonds sitting in the bank's account and the 'carbon copies' matched precisely.

By 1997, that discipline had been relaxed. The client wanted to get a 25 per cent yield over six months but the six-month bond was not for sale in sufficient size? We might just buy the five-and-a-half month bond instead but, importantly, if we did so we would fill the client on the bond he wanted. This started to create mismatches: we would be long the five-and-a-half month bond but, via the 'carbon copy' – synthetically, as it were – we'd be short the six-month bond. The natural progression from this was to just start trading for our own account. Bonds look cheap? We would buy them and hope for client demand to take us out of the risk at a profit later. Bonds too expensive? We would fill clients' orders but not buy any bonds against them. The overall effect was to create a complex tangle of risk – for some bond maturities we were long, others short. Adding to the complexity was the fact that many clients wanted to hedge against the possibility of a rouble devaluation. Thus the book was also littered with currency deals – both forwards and options. Because of currency controls (the same ones that made dealing so complicated that clients came to us) there were two distinct currency markets operating at two distinct prices: an 'onshore' market where we dealt via our Russian entity with Russian banks; and an 'offshore' market where Westerners dealt with each other and where we used our London entity. In short, our trading accounts soon began to resemble a complex derivatives book and, just as we would for any derivatives book, we needed to calculate the Greeks.

Needless to say, we relied heavily on computers. The new Spreadsheet Solutions Framework was used to keep track of thousands of deals on a hundred or so different bonds. Without the computational power of SSF the business would never have been able to grow in the way it did. Our feeling that 'Things Can Only Get Better' was boosted each day by the way our profits rose in lockstep with this growth. This was partly from fees, which at 0.50 to 1.25 per cent per annum on the notional of notes and swaps dwarfed anything I had ever seen in FX (where making 0.05 per cent on a deal was considered a notable event) and which were advertised up front on a 'take it or leave it' basis to any client wishing to deal. With yields of 25 to 30 per cent available, few quibbled. The other reason profits rose was that we were becoming investors too. Increasingly, we would simply buy lots of bonds, keep them and earn the spectacular yields for our own book – it was in this way that we quickly became visible to Bankers Trust's risk police, the Risk Management department.

Risk, and its Management

Banks that run any type of principal business take risk. This risk is handled at various levels in the organisation. At the lowest level, individual traders like Triangle Man and the other 'voice' spot traders look after their own books. Sometimes, small teams look after risk in concert: Simon's Deutsche Bank e-trading team is a good example, so too is the way Loic and I and our colleagues collaborated in Merrill Lynch. At higher levels, things become much more complex. Departmental heads always try to understand the risk their traders are taking; I certainly tried to when I ran the FX business in Deutsche Bank. But, especially in fast-moving circumstances, it was sometimes difficult to comprehend the detail of the risk fully, split as it was over multiple platoons of traders ranged over half a dozen trading centres in three continents – this despite my decades of familiarity with the market. Pity then a bank's CEO with dozens of such risk-taking departments, most of which trade products that he is not an expert in. He faces an impossibly complex task. To help him, he has a Risk Management team tasked with monitoring all the risks his bank is taking.

Risk management was not always sophisticated. In his book on the downfall of the hedge fund Long-Term Capital Management, Roger Lowenstein mentions, in passing, that in Salomon Brothers in 1979, 'the firm's capital account used to be scribbled into a little book, left outside the office of a partner'.[3] Thirteen years later, at

Merrill Lynch in September 1992 during the torrid aftermath of the Italian devaluation, the best the Risk Management guys could do was to send one of their juniors to scurry around the trading floor with a clipboard anxiously asking each team how they were doing. 'We're fine, running the numbers but I think up 25 bucks or so' – note on the pad. 'Don't ask, down five-ish' – another note. It wasn't high tech. By 1997, though, in Bankers Trust, things had moved on. Bankers Trust was an acknowledged leader in risk management.

There were two main risks that were monitored: credit risk and market risk. Credit risk is the risk that you don't get paid back if you extend a loan. Market risk is the risk you have if you own a security (a share or a bond, say) and the price falls. These risks are inextricably interlinked: if you own a bond (which is essentially just a packaged and tradable way of lending and borrowing money) the value can rise and fall because of moves in interest rates but also because the bond issuer (the borrower) looks like it might not be able to pay. Is that market risk or credit risk? Despite this linkage, for historic reasons, organisationally speaking, the Credit Risk team and the Market Risk team were separate units although they ultimately reported to the same man.

Credit Risk was represented by the formidable presence of Roselyn, known to all of us as 'Roz'. Small, cheerful, pugnacious, outspoken, as a senior woman she was a rarity on our male-dominated trading floor. She knew her stuff and was impervious to blandishment. 'That was a very nice speech,' I once heard her comment, smiling sweetly, after an impassioned plea from a salesman to increase the credit available to some low-rent hedge fund, 'but you and I both know it was total bollocks, don't we? The answer is no.' I had never really had much to do with the Credit Risk people in my previous jobs because FX is not an asset and is relatively short-dated and therefore, in the jargon, it is not 'credit intensive' (when you go to the Cambio to change money for your holiday, no one checks your credit rating). Russia was the opposite. Thus it was that I saw a lot of Roz as she went about her task of setting limits on how

much Russian business we could do. This became a critical decision because our GKO holdings started to affect the entire bank's
amount of risk-weighted assets (or RWA). Given the importance
of RWA, leverage and capital to the story of the near catastrophe in
1998 and the 2008 crash it is worth a brief detour to consider how
it all works.

Seen in slightly simplistic terms, banks accept deposits from
companies and individuals and then lend that money on. The sum
and record of all this activity is called the bank's 'balance sheet'. The
deposits are called 'liabilities' (because the bank is liable to pay them
back) and the loans are called 'assets'. Rather than making loans,
banks can also buy bonds or equities – these are called assets too.
So too is any cash. But what happens if the value of the assets falls?
How does a bank ensure its depositors can get their money back?

The answer is that it must hold capital that will act as a buffer
absorbing any loss. The bulk of capital is represented by good old-
fashioned shareholder equity – the money that the owners of the
bank have stumped up to own it – and earnings (profits) retained
from previous years. But how much capital does the bank need to
hold? Or, put another way, how many assets can it afford to have?
How big can its balance sheet be? This was (and still is) defined by a
set of rules created by the Basel Committee on Banking Supervision
called the Basel Accords. The first set of these rules, known as Basel
I, was published in 1988 and these rules were the ones Bankers Trust
were following in 1997. They stated that capital (shareholder equity
plus some other categories of equity-like stuff) needed to be 8 per
cent of the value of risk-weighted assets. Risk-weighted assets were
calculated as the value of assets multiplied by a weighting factor according to how risky they were deemed to be: the higher the risk, the
larger the weight. Basel I was a very crude set of rules and it split assets into four 'buckets' of risk. Assets like cash or gold or the bonds of
OECD governments were zero-weighted. In other words, this stuff
was thought to be so low risk that banks could hold as much of it as

they wanted without needing to back it with capital. Next, at a weight of 20 per cent, came loans to OECD banks and US government agencies; 50 per cent was applied to residential mortgages; and last, at 100 per cent, were the weightings of all other assets including corporate bonds and, importantly for us, non-OECD government debt. 'That's the bucket where all your precious Russian crap sits,' Roz berated us brightly; 'every single dollar of it feeds straight through to RWA.'

The fact that we were such RWA hogs was not a problem on one level – the returns of holding bonds for our own account were well in excess of any hurdle we faced. Simplistically stated, if we could make a return of 25 per cent on 100 million dollars' worth of bonds – which, because of its Basel weighting bucket meant 100 million of RWA with its consequent requirement for the bank to hold $8 million of capital – the percentage return on capital was unambiguously deep into triple digits ($25 million versus $8 million). By way of comparison, Bankers Trust at the time had a return on equity (a different but roughly comparable number) of around 13 to 16 per cent for the firm as a whole.[4] But what about our client business of creating notes and swaps? Here the maths was less obvious. A 1 per cent per annum fee compared to 8 per cent capital was a return that was decent (12.5 per cent) but not startling. What's more, it was much lower than the returns you could get by simply holding the bonds outright. But, we argued, that's nuts! The methodology was pushing us in what was transparently the wrong direction. The fact that the client had bought the risk from us must count for something – why were we deemed to need the same capital cushion as for holding the bonds outright? But the clients' notes were liabilities, not assets – in the crude Basel rules they didn't count. The conclusion from looking at the Basel metrics was that we should just hold bonds for ourselves and not bother with client business. We should 'go proprietary', in other words. To be fair, Roz and the other Credit Risk people realised that this was a poor idea. The arguments that went back and forth between us traders and Credit Risk were made more complicated by what the bank's market risk system said about our business. This system's methodology, called 'risk-adjusted return on capital' or RAROC, an invention of our, by this time, ex-CEO (Charlie Sanford – he of the economy plane ticket) gave very different answers.

RAROC (pronounced 'rare rock') was a revolutionary idea back in the late 1970s when it was first thought up. These days, variations of it underpin the risk management approach of virtually every bank on earth. The idea is to compare the return from any position with its risk. In the early manifestations of RAROC, the slippery concept of risk was defined as 'the maximum potential loss that could occur during a "reasonable" time required to exit positions of "normal" size'.[5] Maximum potential loss was defined by look-ing at the way prices have moved in the past. 'Let's say a trader on the bond desk owns $10 million of some corporate bond', Chris the quant once explained it to me, 'and the Market Risk guys think that it would take him three days to get rid of it.' It seemed a long time to me, used to the minute-by-minute pace of FX, but I nodded along. 'They look at what the worst three-day price decline has been since World War II and apply that loss to his 10 million – that's his required capital.' More nodding: this seemed much more logical than the Basel bucket approach. 'Then they figure out how much money the position is making, take away tax, divide by the required capital and then annualise the answer – voila! That's his RAROC,' he concluded.

It was a powerful and intuitive way of measuring risk and re-turn. But the most important thing about RAROC was that it was used to look at an entire business line including liabilities – not just a single bond or even just all assets. In our case, that meant that the fact we had parcelled off a lot of the risk of moves in Russian bond prices to clients (in notes or swaps) was taken into account. When Market Risk ran the numbers on our Russian bond business they came to much more sensible conclusions. For example, the agency-like, fully funded business was considered best since it was risk-free but still made fees. This was the opposite of the conclusion reached from looking at RWA – here the lower fees for the same amount of bonds on the balance sheet hurt the numbers.

Because of such utility, RAROC was used throughout the firm. The growing complexity of the bank's business (itself driven by a rise in computer power) made it essential that the process was automated. The risk calculations for our books and for all the others within Bankers Trust were performed daily on a gigantic computer system nicknamed 'the Engine'. This system was separate from the risk management systems that were used by the various departments and was managed centrally by the Risk Management team. One consequence of automation was that it had become necessary to alter the way that the process worked. First of all, the requirement of having separate holding periods for each instrument was dropped as being too fiddly and a uniform one-day hold was introduced to make things simpler – regardless of how long it might take to clear a position. Second, the idea of trawling back through prices recorded since World War II to find the maximum potential loss for every position, bond by bond, equity by equity, and currency by currency was not a realistic prospect. Lots of instruments had no price history; how could RAROC, as it had originally been conceived, cope with exotic derivatives for example? So a new approach had been arrived at.

Each day every department's risk system automatically sent a report to the Engine with a compendium of that department's Greeks. From all this information, which was like a risk report for the entire bank, the Engine then tried to figure out how much money the bank could potentially lose if things went wrong. The amount was called 'value at risk', or VaR, and it was used to replace the concept of 'maximum potential loss' within the RAROC process. But instead of representing maximum loss, VaR represented something subtly – but crucially – different. It was a statistical measure that was meant to show the amount that the bank could lose that would only be exceeded 1 per cent of the time. 'It's like you go to the doctor with a stubbed toe and ask him, "Doc, tell me the worst", Darren once joked, 'and he says, "Well, there's 99 per cent chance of it being better than having both your legs amputated."'

To illustrate how the Engine came up with its diagnosis, imagine that the bank only had one position, a purchase of a million units of our old friend, the share trading at £100. How much money could this position make or lose in one day? There would be a range of outcomes depending on how the share price was predicted to move. It would be most probable that the share would trade at prices somewhere in the region of £100 with a decreasing probability of bigger moves. Pictured graphically, the potential price distribution would resemble a hump, centred on £100 and tapering as you moved away to higher and lower prices. It would look, in other words, like the familiar 'normal distribution' from school maths lessons, which, when the teacher got you to plot the heights of the kids in the class, would show that the bulk of your classmates were of middling height but with a few very tall or very short outliers. And this, indeed, was how the VaR methodology assumed prices would behave – in doing so it was entirely consistent with the Black–Scholes option-pricing formula, which makes exactly the same assumption.*

What determines the 'spread' of the hump is volatility – the choppier the price action of a share, the more the potential distribution of price can smear out over time. Given this assumption, the Engine would figure out the VaR for the share position by doing the following: first it would assess the share's volatility. To do so, it would look at previous price history going back three years. If the share was newly issued and the Engine didn't have the data to hand it would be instructed by its handlers to use the volatility for a similar

---

* Technically speaking, both the VaR methodology and the Black–Scholes formula assume that the logarithms of the changes in price are normally distributed, rather than the prices themselves. This subtle tweak avoids a mathematical glitch that arises if you assume that prices are normally distributed – namely, that they can go negative.

share. It would then find, on the humped, normal distribution of prices implied by that volatility, the location corresponding to the point where there was a 99 per cent statistical chance of the price being higher. For 25 per cent volatility (typical for a single stock) this would mean a fall to a price of around £96.30 in one day, or a loss on one million shares of about £3.7 million. In the jargon, the 'one-day p99 bump' (price move over one day's trading that would only be exceeded 1 per cent of the time) gave a VaR of £3.7 million. In Darren's tasteless analogy, that was the point of double amputation.

This process, so simple for one asset position, was astonishingly complex at the level of the bank because there were thousands of separate risks, and each one had to be assessed. Derivative books would have risks resulting from their sensitivities to asset price moves (the Greeks) and these 'synthetic' positions were subjected to the same process. What made things even more complicated was that, seen at the level of the bank, it was vitally important how the risks were related. Each additional risk multiplied complexity further. For example, if, in addition to the one million shares previously mentioned, the bank had a second, long position of $100 million of US government 30-year bonds, each risk would have its own VaR. But, crucially, the VaR of the two positions combined would not equal the sum of the two risks, since bonds, historically speaking, tended not to sell off at the same time as shares. In technical terms the correlation of their price moves was not 100 per cent. If the second position tended to increase in value as the first decreased (if they were 'negatively correlated') then the risk could actually reduce. It was very much like Simon's insight when designing ARM – a basket of risks is less risky than the sum of the parts.

To figure out the risk for the bank as a whole, then, the Engine had to calculate the correlations of every single risk with all of the others. It did so by crunching through the past three years of historic data. The result was a matrix that was hundreds of columns wide by hundreds of rows deep containing hundreds of thousands of correlation numbers. This matrix would then be used, along with the long list of 'one-day p99 bumps', to calculate the VaR for each business and for the entire bank. The Engine's operators thus claimed to be able to tell Bankers Trust's management, looking at all the risks that were being taken all over the world, what was the most money the bank could lose in a day – 99 per cent of the time, that is. It was a remarkable feat and one that was only feasible because of rapidly rising computer power.

Despite the method's mathematical elegance, we traders distrusted the numbers. In Emerging Markets this was partly because, although GKOs had been trading for four years or so (and thus had a sufficiently long price history to feed the Engine), we worried about how representative the data was. This worry, though, was just a detail in our much wider philosophical difficulty with VaR: namely, it relied on the future being like the past. All the data feeding the risk numbers – data on prices, volatility and correlation – was historic. The volatility of the rouble, for example, was seen to be tiny because for the last three years it had been pegged. But what if circumstances changed like they had with the ERM? That had been calm and untroubled for years until it blew apart in a matter of a few months. Darren summed it up with his normal brevity: 'It's like jumping off the Empire State Building. The VaR model reckons things are going great because the first thousand feet are painless. But it's the last six inches that smash you to a pulp.'

Still, VaR was ubiquitous. One reason was because senior management – intermediated by the Risk Management department and desperate for some kind of easily understandable risk measure – had no other feasible way of looking at the risk for the entire bank. VaR numbers were crunched because computers were powerful enough to do so, and then they were used because they had been calculated. What else was there? Also, the Basel capital rules had been altered in 1996 to include market risk (as opposed to pure credit risk) in the calculations for RWA and capital adequacy.[6]

In an important concession to banks, the rules allowed market risk to be calculated according to a bank's own internal risk model, subject to regulatory approval. The model that regulators approved was VaR: it seemed so logical, so rational, and, besides, JPMorgan had popularised the approach by making their VaR methodology, branded 'RiskMetrics', available to other banks to use – a move greeted by dismay in Bankers Trust where our own very similar RAROC was considered to be a commercial secret. Last, we Emerging Markets traders went along with it because the Engine said our business was not particularly risky, a finding which, even if we secretly doubted it, was helpful in allowing us to argue for bigger limits despite our difficulties with RWA. The Engine was our computerised ally in taking more risk, just as OPTICS had been at Merrill Lynch a few years earlier.

Love You Long-Term

In the early summer of 1997, I was invited to attend a meeting with a couple of traders from the hedge fund Long-Term Capital Management. In light of what happened subsequently it would be convenient for the drama of my story if I could say there was something about the meeting that I could recall distinctly; that I could claim that I sensed from the clients' demeanour – from my skilful observation of their subtly hidden hubris, say – the catastrophe that would engulf them. But, in truth, I have little recollection of it, certainly no gloomy presentiments of doom. It undoubtedly followed the well-trodden path of dozens of similar meetings. Stan, our much-respected head of research, would give his rehearsed speech delivering the house view on Russia: very serviceable levels of debt; strong reserves capable of defending the rouble peg; stable oil revenues adding to those reserves; little chance of default since no country defaults on debt denominated in its own currency; the IMF would never let a nuclear power default; and so on. Conclusion? Bond yields will fall and bond prices will rise. Quod erat demonstrandum. 'Buy now while stocks last,' in other words, wrapped in the language of macroeconomics. My task was to pitch in and agree with Stan. When he'd finished, I'd explain the process of buying Russian notes or swaps and, lastly, as if it was an afterthought unworthy of the highbrow, geopolitical nature of the meeting, I would explain our eye-watering fees.

It was a practised routine. But, like all my fellow traders, I actually slightly resented these meetings. Not because I disliked customers, but rather because client meetings meant that I needed to wear a suit. The standard of dress at Bankers Trust in general, and in Emerging Markets in particular, was gradually becoming more informal. Actually, 'informal' is an understatement. The unwritten code was that the more money you were making, the more scruffily you dressed; Emerging Markets' burgeoning profits meant that our desk began to look like 3am at a student party. For all this, when we met customers, the rule was that we dressed formally – the suit had to come out of its flimsy plastic wrapper. Mine must have done that day.

But it was to no avail. To the disappointment of the salesman who had called the meeting, LTCM never dealt with us, preferring to grant its Russian business to our competitors. Not that I minded particularly. LTCM, which was dealing a lot with Bankers Trust's interest rate derivative and bond desks, had a reputation as being a pig of a customer. Its traders would argue incessantly about prices. They would chisel and chisel to get away with the least possible 'initial margin', aka 'haircut' (the bank's cushion against things going badly for the fund), so that they could enjoy the highest leverage. They would happily run a desk over with their trades in a derivative version of the FX market's hated 'drive-by'. Regardless, banks – including ours – scrambled to execute the fund's business. Partly this was because LTCM had grown to colossal proportions and, as a result, had a massive amount of business to transact. Who wanted to be the bank that missed out? But LTCM wasn't just large – it was regarded as the fund housing the smartest guys in the market. If they were doing a trade, banks wanted to know about it because the information gleaned from seeing how LTCM was dealing could help the banks' own positioning. At least, that was the theory.

LTCM had been set up in late 1993 by a man named John Meriwether who had been the head of the single most profitable trading desk in the single most profitable investment bank in the world – Salomon Brothers. The desk was called the arbitrage (or 'arb') desk and was legendary both inside and outside Salomon. My wife, who worked at Salomon for a few years prior to the arrival of our baby son Fred in 1995, recalls a trader, on a desk separate from the arb desk (and far less glamorous), telling her that he was copying one of their trades. His reasoning? 'The arb desk guys are really smart so the bet will probably pay off. And if it doesn't work and I lose, I'll lose a ton less than they do so I doubt anyone important will notice.' It was a precursor to the banks' attitude to LTCM, in miniature.

The desk's business model was to seek out inefficiencies in the markets and exploit them. Recall my finance professor's argument about how the 'share forward' should be priced. The idea was that if the forward did not trade at £110 (the price at which the forward could be 'manufactured' by borrowing at 10 per cent and buying the stock for £100) then arbitrageurs would pile into the market and eventually force the price to that level. The arbitrage desk at Salomon did just this in the bond markets, but for real, in much more sophisticated ways, and in truly enormous size. Unfortunately for Meriwether, he had been caught up in a scandal at Salomon where a trader unscrupulously attempted to rig a US government bond auction. Though personally blameless, Meriwether was ousted from the bank.[7] LTCM was his attempt to recreate the glory of the Salomon arb desk, free from the bureaucracy and politics that plague any large institution. To do so, he recruited some of his star traders from Salomon and, in a move that caught the imagination of the entire market, he persuaded two of the founding fathers of modern mathematical finance – Myron Scholes and Robert Merton (both of option-pricing fame) – to join as partners. Dazzled by this array of talent, wealthy investors provided $1.25 billion in start-up capital and, in 1994, the fund began to trade.[8]

By the time I met the fund's traders in 1997, LTCM had grown tremendously. Its initial $1.25 billion of capital had swelled to around $4.7 billion.[9] Each dollar that investors and partners had initially provided had almost quadrupled – an astonishing average annual return of around 40 per cent. These heady returns were the result of the skill of LTCM's traders in finding market inefficiencies and examples of 'mispricing' to exploit. To do so they employed massive computer power and a battery of analytic tools similar to BTAnalytics. They employed every conceivable form of derivative in huge size. But the returns were also down to the tremendous leverage that LTCM brought to bear. As we saw with GKO swaps, the smaller the amount of capital a fund needs to commit to supporting a trade, the higher the returns. Because of their size, prestige and reputation for omnipotence (they had Merton and Scholes as partners!) they were able to drive an exceptionally hard bargain on all credit terms with banks; Roz and her colleagues hated them. As a fund, LTCM was under no obligation to hold capital against RWA like a bank – it could be as leveraged as its counterparty banks would let it be. Since inception, the average ratio of LTCM's total assets to its capital had been 22.5 to 1, peaking at around 30 to 1 in 1996.[10] The blistering 40 per cent returns on capital therefore represented much more modest returns (2 per cent or so) on assets. The ratio also meant that a mere 4 to 5 per cent drop in the value of their assets would wipe them out. But looking at assets alone does not capture the true nature of LTCM's enormous books, which comprised around $1 trillion of derivatives contracts spread and split between a dozen or more banks – 'off balance sheet', in the jargon.[11] Given that the partners of the fund had most of their wealth tied up in LTCM, how could they be so confident running this risk?

The answer is that LTCM, just like Bankers Trust and its banking peers, was relying on computerised risk management and the concept of VaR. Indeed, the whole edifice of VaR was built upon theoretical foundations laid by the fund's partners Scholes and Merton. When LTCM ran their version of the Engine it gave a comforting answer. The 'one-day p99' VaR for the fund in late summer 1997 was around $100 million – a huge number, but peanuts compared to their multibillion-dollar capital.[12] It would take a 'ten sigma event' (translation – something occurring randomly once in several lifetimes of the universe) for the fund to be wiped out in a year.[13] Assuming, that is, that the future behaved itself and resembled the past. A crisis in Asia was the first sign that this assumption might not hold.

A Bit of a Drawdown

Asia's 'Tiger' economies were touted as the success story of the 1990s. Currency pegs, introduced over the previous decade, had been designed to provide reduced risk: reduced risk for foreign lenders who could rest easy that their high returns in local currency would not be devalued away, and reduced risk for local borrowers who could access the lower interest rates available in US dollars without the prospect of a stronger dollar making their repayments unaffordable in their own currency. As a result of the reassurance coming from these pegs, economies surged and debt ballooned across the region: in East and South East Asia combined, foreign debt more than doubled in the six years between 1991 ($336 billion) to 1997 ($742 billion) with Korea, Thailand and Indonesia leading the charge.[14] The IMF described the result as 'a build-up of overheating pressures, evident in large external deficits and inflated property and stock market values'.[15] Put another way, it was a monstrous asset bubble. Derivatives, the offspring of growing computer power, played an important role in this explosion of debt, which, unlike the 1980s, was no longer dominated by bank lending but rather by foreign direct investment (FDI), in large part to private firms.[16] Money was lent, often using complex variants of the total return swap, in ways that were not transparent to the rest of the market. VaR models added to the problem. Because of Asian currencies' pegs to the US dollar, which allowed only small price variations around a central rate, their volatilities, calculated by looking back over historical data series, were very low. For example, in the three years prior to June 1997 when the crisis started, the average volatility of the Thai baht to US dollar exchange rate had been around 3.7 per cent. This compares to around 10.8 per cent for the rate between the Japanese yen and the US dollar over the same period.[17] Bank after bank's version of the Engine automatically translated this fact into a simple mathematical message: 'Asia is low risk.' This encouraged even more lending and an even bigger bubble. And then the bubble burst.

Between 1995 and 1997, the US dollar had strengthened, mainly as a result of the rising interest rates that had caused such havoc with Procter and Gamble. The US dollar, which had bought around 85 Japanese yen in June 1995, bought 115 by June 1997 – a 35 per cent increase. With their currencies pegged to the dollar, this surge disadvantaged the export-led emerging Asian countries, all of which became increasingly uncompetitive. As the countries' currency reserves dwindled as a result, and the extent of the asset bubble became obvious, nervous investors began to withdraw their funds. Speculators added to the outflow, putting intolerable strain on the dollar pegs. Eventually, Thailand's was the first to snap. In an Asian replay of the ERM debacle, the Thai government was forced to devalue the baht by 20 per cent on 2 July 1997. Chaos ensued in every other country in the region. Our weekly global risk conference calls with our colleagues in Asia became dominated all summer by the spreading crisis: Malaysia, Philippines, Indonesia – even Singapore and Hong Kong came under attack. Local currencies crashed and volatility spiked.

But our Asian team was doing well. The bank's research people had been nervous about Asia's huge increase in debt and had been warning of a crisis for months. Our traders had been preparing for the worst and had bought large quantities of options from other banks. These allowed them to sell Asian currencies at, or near, the pegged rates – a right that was now immensely valuable given the currencies' precipitous declines. What made the coup even sweeter for our traders was how cheaply they had managed to do this. 'They all thought the pegs would last forever!' boasted one colleague about his counterparties as he dialled into our call from Singapore. 'They practically gave us this shit for free!' Clustered around the loudspeaker phone in London we exchanged looks – maybe we should do the same? Stan's research was still bullish on Russia, but who knew? Rouble options were cheap and it couldn't hurt. As the team's 'FX guy' I took up the task – after all, this was a similar trade to the one I'd put on in the ERM in 1992. Steadily and stealthily, all through the summer, I worked to build the position.

A few months later, the summer was definitely over; it was a dank, drizzling London morning on Monday, 27 October 1997. Tomasz had left to join my old employer Merrill Lynch a few weeks earlier and now just Darren and I were in charge of the – by now extremely large – Russian book. That day we were dreading the opening of trading. Late the previous week, the Hang Seng Index had crashed 10.4 per cent in a day as the Hong Kong authorities raised interest rates to 300 per cent in a bold – and ultimately successful – escalation of their protection of the Hong Kong dollar peg. Every indication was that the panic would now hit Russia. At 10am, within the first few seconds of trading in the one-hour MICEX 'window', our suspicions were confirmed and we knew for certain that we were in deep trouble. Prices, where they existed at all, were plummeting. Darren was trying to sell some of our long position in six-month bonds and I was attempting, unsuccessfully, to trade in the offshore FX market through brokers. All around us there was shouting as every other emerging market started to spasm. Ten minutes into the trading session I asked Darren how it was going – how much had he sold? 'Exactly 20,' came the reply. He'd sold 20 million dollars' worth of bonds? That wasn't anywhere near as bad as I'd thought it would be; the market had looked more illiquid. 'No, Kev: 20 pieces.' At that, I felt an icy chill. A 'piece' was a single GKO bond with a denomination of 1000 roubles, or about $160. He was telling me that he had sold about 3,000 dollars' worth – effectively, nothing. We were trapped. We quickly agreed to stop selling – all we were doing was driving the market against us. In the meantime, the risk system SSF was showing us a very, very ugly loss.

As if on cue, as the computers delivered their painful verdict on our morning's profitability, our boss, Ron, the Israeli ex-paratrooper, strode into view. 'How are you guys doing?' he asked, surprisingly quietly given that he must have known full well we were in big trouble. 'Not brilliantly, Ron,' we chorused airily with a tone that belied our deep unease, 'we're having a bit of a drawdown.' We pointed to the computer screen. To his credit, he maintained his complete calm and walked off, asking in mild tones to be kept updated. As it turned out, by the end of the day, despite the panic spreading to the US stock markets where the Dow Jones recorded a fall of 7 per cent – its largest since the crash in 1987 – our loss was nowhere near as bad as first we had feared. Late in the MICEX trading session, bond prices had stabilised and then bounced a bit, which had made things better. Also, in the afternoon, as the offshore rouble FX market found liquidity and prices stabilised, we found that our carefully accumulated option position had made a chunk too. We had escaped, but the lessons were obvious to us. First, if things ever really went wrong in Russia we'd never be able to get out of our risk. Second, buying rouble options was a very decent hedge. Within a week or two, the market's optimism on Russia had returned but Darren and I remained scarred by our experience. From that moment onwards, whenever we traded, we were always looking anxiously over our shoulders for the fire exits of the crowded theatre in which we had feared we would be immolated. Within a year our new-found caution was to serve us well.

Every Day I Sell the Bills

By June 1998, a year into the crisis, the Korean won had lost 35 per cent of its value; the Thai baht 40 per cent; and the Indonesian rupiah an astonishing 80 per cent;[18] but the rouble, for now, was still hanging in there, pegged at around 6.2000 per US dollar. The strains, however, were showing. Asia's economies, stunned by the sequence of events and the almost total withdrawal of foreign lending, had gone into deep recession. As a result, the price of oil, Russia's chief export and the prop for the rouble, was sagging – a barrel of benchmark West Texas Intermediate crude had dropped 35 per cent in price from June 1997 to June 1998 (from $19.3 to $13.7 a barrel).[19] Even Stan, the perpetual optimist, was worried. The market mirrored his worry: GKO yields, which had started 1997 at 30 per cent and tightened to an almost OECD-like 17 per cent by July of that year, had now ballooned to 50 per cent or more.[20]

The one thing that wasn't worried about Russia was the Engine. The rouble was still pegged and so, historically speaking, rouble volatility remained low: consequently, so did our VaR. Despite this, chastened by our October fright, Darren and I were keeping the bank's Russian risk under very tight control. We still owned GKOs but only enough for the interest we received from them to offset the carrying cost (theta) from the – by now very substantial – options position we had accumulated. We were no longer trying to make money by lending to Russia on the bank's behalf; rather, our business survived on the fees we charged the surprisingly large number of remaining investors who, in the face of everything that had happened, were still keen to pump money into GKOs. We even persuaded Ron, against the howls of protest of our Moscow office chief (the 'nuclear waste' man) to let us sell the GKOs in his jealously guarded and ring-fenced Moscow book. This position – multiple hundreds of millions of US dollars' worth – was far too large to sell quickly. Instead, a new song became popular on the desk. To the tune of Elvis Costello's 'Every Day I Write the Book', Darren and I – helped by our new recruit, a clever, young, taciturn Russian called Alex – would sing 'Every Day I Sell the Bills' as, little by little, day after day, we offloaded the risk into the market. Our plan was simple: we would hunker down and wait for the storm to pass but, if the storm were to break, we would profit from a currency devaluation just as our colleagues had done in the Asia crisis.

By July it was clear that things were getting serious. The World Cup in France acted as some distraction, but the market was in turmoil. GKO yields started to thrash around wildly, optimism on one day being replaced by black pessimism on the next as the market had its hopes of an IMF rescue package built up, then dashed. Yields topped 100 per cent. One sombre warning came when Alex told us that his parents and many of their friends had withdrawn all their money from their bank accounts and converted the roubles into US dollars – in cash. Towards the end, one baking hot day in early August, a senior official of the Russian embassy in London visited the office. He had been told all about the huge Russian business at Bankers Trust (the billions of US dollars' worth of GKOs on our balance sheet were only exceeded by those held by Credit Suisse) and was invited to meet the traders responsible. Sadly, due to a mix-up, neither Darren nor I had been informed of the visit so our suits were still at home. I was scruffy and unshaven but Darren, crop-haired, dressed in a 'Never Mind the Bollocks' T-shirt, faded jeans and flip-flops, made me look like a model from *GQ* magazine. The man from the embassy said nothing about our dress when we were introduced but I could see the light of belief die in his eyes. 'Look at the clowns who hold our bonds,' he seemed to be thinking. 'We're clearly fucked.'

As we braced for what was looking inevitable, our worries now focused on counterparty credit risk. If Russia defaulted and devalued, would our counterparties pay us? We had been very particular only to buy options from Western banks in the – more expensive – offshore market, since we realised that Russian banks would be in dire trouble if disaster struck and because we were willing to pay the small extra premium for the extra safety. But what about the hedge funds with swaps? As GKO yields had soared and their prices had fallen, the money the funds owed us swelled accordingly. Every day Roz and her team asked for variation margin to cover the shortfall but we were still concerned. We had little idea of what the biggest funds had done with other banks – how big would any fund's problem be? The lack of transparency made us fear the worst, and so to protect us against any failures resulting from the devaluation that we now thought inevitable we built an even bigger position short roubles. With the desk thus prepared for impact, but with the research team's assurances that the Russians would not act until September, I left for my ill-fated holiday in Tuscany. A few days later, I was back.

The Abyss – Take One

After the default, as we picked through the wreckage, we found that we had come out in pretty good shape. For all our efforts, we had not quite managed to sell Moscow's entire stockpile of GKOs and the few tens of millions of bonds remaining were now practically worthless. Also, we were owed money by Triple I (the 'high risk' hedge fund) that would never be returned. Against that, with the currency plummeting (a US dollar soon bought 30, not 6 roubles), our short rouble position more than made up for any losses. Others were not so fortunate.

All around us on the trading floor, as the weeks progressed, the volume of shouting began to rise to a frenzy. Shocked by the failure of Russia – the nuclear-armed power that would never be allowed to go under – every market was in meltdown. It was relentless all through the remainder of August. Over the course of the month, for example, the Dow dropped 19 per cent in several sickening plunges. Rumours then began to circulate that LTCM, the arrogant, computerised market gorilla, was in trouble. On 2 September, the rumours were confirmed. In a letter to investors that was leaked to Bloomberg, John Meriwether announced that the fund had lost 44 per cent of its capital in August alone[21] – a cool $1.9 billion. 'Jesus,' said Roz when the news hit the wires, 'I thought they were an arbitrage fund?' It was, indeed, shocking. With a VaR of $100 million, according to the maths this loss should never have happened – it was statistically impossible. But the models were at fault. The past was no guide to the present. The elaborate correlation matrix and p99 bumps were completely wrong – there was now no benefit to diversification. Every risky position was being dumped in unison, and banks, which had copied LTCM's biggest trades, were unwinding them ahead of the fund. LTCM could not get out – they were too big. On a grander and gigantically more dangerous scale, the fund was experiencing the same sick sense of being trapped that Darren and I had felt in October 1997 – they couldn't exit positions without pushing the market even more decisively against themselves. The theatre was on fire and the doors were bolted.

The size and complexity of the fund's $125 billion balance sheet and $1 trillion derivatives book, split into 20,000 trades with 75 counterparties,[22] began to panic the banks. Just like our department's concerns with counterparty credit risk over Russia, now the worries spread to LTCM. What would happen if they failed? Could they bring other banks down? The lack of transparency over where the risk was held made every bank cautious and unwilling to lend, even to each other. Banks, including ours, started to struggle for short-term funding. 'Something's going to have to change quite soon or we are going under,' a friend of mine on the money market desk warned me as the situation worsened. Our management made upbeat statements, but the stock market's assessment of the banking system was much less bullish. Bank stocks collapsed. Bankers Trust stock, which had traded over $120 in June, headed below $50. This was of more than academic interest to all of us – a substantial proportion of our pay from prior years was held in the form of shares to be delivered in the future. 'Good job you bought that house last year,' teased Darren. For once, I didn't find him quite as funny as normal. But things were worse at LTCM. All through September their losses increased until it became obvious that the fund could not survive unaided. At last, in late September, the US Federal Reserve, worried about the potential systemic risk to the banking industry of a failure of this size, arm-twisted a panel of the biggest firms to inject $4 billion of capital into LTCM. The move worked: although the partners and investors of LTCM were wiped out, the crisis gradually abated.

For us in Emerging Markets there was little rejoicing. Business had completely stalled and as a result, to reduce costs, around a third of our colleagues were laid off in October. In November, Deutsche Bank, attracted to the prospect of owning Bankers Trust's US operations, bought us for $98 a share. That was better than $50, but it also meant that even we survivors faced an uncertain future. Anticlimactically, as a reward for my part in averting a large loss in Russia (mainly for selling the Moscow book), I was promoted to managing director. I felt very little emotion. All I was certain of was that I wanted this crisis, brought on by a combination of derivative complexity, unconstrained lending and faulty, computerised, over-elaborate risk management to be my last.

It was not going to be.

CHAPTER 6

Bigger Than Iceland

Infinite Appetite

So odd were some of the requests for derivative prices we received in the first year of my stay in Deutsche Bank's Commodities department that we started to keep a list of them to provide us with light relief when business slowed. Could we hedge the Turkish hazelnut crop? Answer: no. Insure against lightning strikes? No. How about a price for some selenium-74? Uncut rubies? DRAM computer chips? No. No. No. These were strange enquiries, but some of the deals we actually transacted, or at least pursued energetically, were hardly less recondite.

For example, our well-regarded weather derivatives desk put together a deal which, in return for a premium, would pay the organisers of the 2002 Oktoberfest if it rained for more than four days during the festival fortnight: a payment would be made for each day over the four.[1] The organisers make less money when it rains and this was a hedge for them. To price the deal, the team trawled through a huge, multi-century historical database of weather measurements in order to compute statistically how many rainy days there had been during the Oktoberfest in the past. Then, using the familiar RAROC method, they worked out the amount of premium to charge the client that would give the return we wanted based on a 'maximum loss' calculated from the rainiest period the computer could find. Having dealt, there was no way for us to hedge the risk – we simply had to hope that the weather in 2002 would resemble the weather in the past. Sad to say, it didn't. The unfortunate, damp, but no doubt benumbed, stein-lifting lager fans were subjected to the wettest October fortnight in Munich's recorded history. It rained and it rained without ceasing in a way that was almost biblical. As a result, we had to pay out the maximum under the contract. It was as if God himself wanted to provide another small lesson, if one were really needed, on the perils of relying on the past to predict the future. But then another odd deal collapsed: this was a plan to buy a small, ailing UK coal-fired power station and convert it to run on coal mixed with pellets made from treated, compressed human faeces. The aim was to allow it to operate profitably as a result of claiming green subsidies. When this deal proved impossible, I quickly realised that we probably needed to get a little more mainstream in our approach.

I had moved to Commodities from FX in 2002 with the task of setting up a derivatives business from scratch. The bank was expanding aggressively in commodity trading and I'd always been fascinated by these markets, ever since my pre-City days in the oil industry. It might strike you as peculiar that a German bank would want to get involved in the commodities markets, but this move was just one symptom of rapid expansion throughout the entire investment banking arm. Just as the mantra in the FX department that 'The Big Are Getting Bigger' was the justification for our attempt to grow and automate the business, so too did it drive the behaviour of Deutsche Bank in its entirety. Deutsche was not alone – such thinking was accepted wisdom at most of our rivals. The idea was that the 'one-stop shop', able to offer every product to every customer type in every region of the world, would eventually triumph. We foresaw a future in which a tiny number of gigantic banks would be able to offer everything from retail accounts, through securities trading, all the way to M&A (mergers and acquisitions) advice. We'd be one of them. An industrial corporation, say, would be able to come to us to borrow money, issue bonds and shares, hedge its interest rate and FX risk and, when Commodities got up and running (as it had been for years at our American rivals Goldman Sachs and Morgan Stanley), insure against rises in its energy bills, all with one sophisticated, integrated behemoth – a beast dubbed by one of our most senior managers as 'the Intelligent Flow Monster'.

Within the investment bank, Rates, Equity and FX departments were all growing, but the sharpest growth was in Credit Trading.[2] It was in 2003, while having a conversation with one of this department's senior managers, a very forthright Indian, just after the faecal pellet deal fell through, that I was enlightened as to what I should be doing. 'It's all about assets, man!' he told me in his normal forceful manner. 'You're wasting your time trying to get people to do hedging.' In this he was undoubtedly right – as a new business we couldn't yet break Goldman Sachs' or Morgan Stanley's long-term stranglehold on commodity producers and consumers in traditional markets like oil, and markets in non-traditional commodities were either non-existent (hazelnuts) or tricky in the extreme (weather). 'You've got to find a way of making commodities into an asset – everyone wants alternative assets!' he roared. 'Do it and you'll kick ass, man!' He then said something that has stuck with me ever since: 'The problem for us in Credit isn't finding buyers for assets – it's finding enough assets for them to buy. They have infinite appetite.' Infinite.

The appetite for so-called 'alternative' assets (that is, not regular equities or bonds) was driven by a number of trends. First, despite the setbacks of 1997 and 1998, the continuing secular growth in the world economy created a surge in investable funds. But investors had fallen out of love with the equity market. From the start of 1998 to the end of 2003, average annual returns from the S&P 500 had been around 3.7 per cent – anaemic compared to the 17.9 per cent in the years 1988 to 1997.[3] The market was also much choppier – the big drawdowns in 1998 and in 2000 to 2002 (caused by the 1997–8 crisis, the bursting of the dot-com bubble and the after-effects of 9/11) were still fresh in investors' minds. And, by 2003, the bond markets looked unattractive too: ten-year US Treasury yields were only around 4 per cent and short-term yields of 1 per cent were at lows not seen since the 1950s. This was as a result of the Fed slashing rates in the wake of 9/11.[4] What's more, the traditional source of 'alternative' assets – emerging markets – was still looking very tarnished, though admittedly preferable to nuclear waste by this stage. All of which left the way open to new forms of investment to give investors the yields they craved. To create them, the computers were set to work.

Within Commodities, this meant creating commodity indexes. Anyone who picks up a newspaper or watches the news will be familiar with the idea of indexes. In the world of equities they have been ubiquitous for decades. The Dow Jones Industrial Average (DJIA), FTSE 100 and Nikkei 225, to name just a few, are household brands. Fundamentally, they all do the same thing. They all represent, in one number, the economics of holding a portfolio of different stocks assembled according to rules specific to that index. You can think of these rules as a sort of stock-market recipe book. There are rules about how to select the stocks that specify, for instance, on which exchange they must trade or how big the companies must be. There are weighting rules that specify whether to hold equal dollar amounts of all the stocks or weight the holdings according to market capitalisation. There are rules about how to deal with dividends. It goes on. Programmed with all these rules, computers in the companies that calculate the indexes (e.g. the DJIA is calculated by a subsidiary of McGraw Hill) whirr away to provide them to the markets, often in real time. The real importance of indexes – aside from their use as a general-purpose measure of market performance – arises from their use as the basis of 'tracker funds'. In the US alone in 2014, these funds managed around $2 trillion, 20 per cent of all mutual fund investment.[5] In tracker funds, managers do not try to pick stocks that will perform better than average but rather just attempt to give investors the returns of an index. The advantages for the investor are that the fees are low since all the fund manager needs to do is to slavishly copy the index rules (i.e. buy and sell what

the index comprises – 'manufacture' it, in other words) with no need
for expensive stock pickers who, as study after study has shown, do no
better than the average in the long run anyway.[6] My plan was to provide something similar in the world of commodities.

There already existed a commodity index called the Goldman
Sachs Commodity Index (GSCI) but I thought a Deutsche Bank
branded product would make it look more like we knew what we
were doing. To create one I hired a man named Elliot. He held a
PhD in quantum physics and was not like regular folk. For example, his CV stated that he spoke fluent Swedish. 'Why did you learn
Swedish?' I asked him at interview; 'For a laugh,' he replied. Despite
resembling a strapping off-duty policeman he was total nerd who
once commented, regarding a birthday cake that had been given to
one of the PAs: 'There's still lots left, it only has about a radian missing.' He soon set to work creating our own index. Within a couple of
months of steady work he had finished. The Deutsche Bank Liquid
Commodity Index (DBLCI) allowed investors to track a basket of
six, highly liquid commodities: WTI crude oil, heating oil, corn,
wheat, aluminium and gold. Unlike Goldman's index, ours did not
have fixed dollar weights of commodities but would vary in order to
contain more of a commodity that was trading cheap relative to its
long-run, five-year average and less if it was expensive. Because we
couldn't hold physical commodities in order to replicate it – partly
because of regulation, partly because it was utterly impractical – the
index tracked the price of financial futures on these commodities.
In effect it was a complicated side bet on the direction of commodity prices. With glossy brochures printed and trademarks applied
for, we then went out and tried to sell the product to investors.

The ways an investor could transact were, in all vital aspects,
identical to the ways they could invest in Russia – Deutsche Bank
would offer notes or swaps on the index. Just as in Russia, the draw
to investors who could, theoretically, have bought the requisite
futures themselves and cut out the middleman was convenience.

There was no need to set up brokerage accounts, or to go through the headache of deciding which commodities to choose. We packaged all that up in one easy bundle in return for running fees that were openly stated up front. The typical pitch to investors was also reminiscent, in its format and tone, of Stan's and my double act for GKOs. Michael, our head of research, an engaging and smooth-talking old-Harrovian, would lead off with the macroeconomic reasons for a fund to go long commodities: first, diversification – commodities did well when other assets crapped out; second, macro forces (growth in China and India, urbanisation, supply constraints etc.) would push prices higher so it was a good bet anyway. 'Buy now . . .' Then, I'd pitch in and explain the technicalities of index construction and how the swaps worked. I would point to how the index would have worked if it had existed in the past by whipping out graphs constructed using historic data; a so-called 'back test'. Naturally, I would be in a suit and tie, but by then, unlike at Bankers Trust, I wouldn't have put them on especially. The dress culture at Deutsche was radically different from Bankers, and I was habitually turned out in one of Savile Row's finest every day, regardless of client contact. No flip-flops at Deutsche. Whether it was my sleek turnout, Michael's well-thought-out macro arguments or the excellence of Elliot's work in index design, the deals soon started flowing.

Within a few months we had a proper business on our hands and it continued to grow year after year, eventually becoming one of the biggest contributors to the Commodities department. To illustrate its size, consider that one DBLCI tracker fund alone had assets of $6 billion by 2011.[7] But investors wanted more – not content with leverage inherent in swaps, they wanted to buy call options on the index. For technical reasons, a full explanation of which would fill a couple of very tedious chapters, this was a challenge. In essence, because the index reweighted and rebalanced itself according to Elliot's rules as commodity prices moved, you were never sure what the index would consist of in the future. Maybe, if oil prices became historically weak, the index would 'buy' more oil waiting for a rebound and thus make the index 'oil heavy'; or maybe – as actually happened – it would be weighted more towards wheat and corn. It was not possible to know and this made computing option prices analytically, or by means of a lattice, impossible.

However, help was at hand. The Monte Carlo method (the possibilities of which Chris the quant had dreamed of in Bankers Trust) was the solution. Embedded within Deutsche Bank's DBAnalytics – a fancier and much, much more powerful cousin of BTAnalytics – was the ability to run tens of thousands of simulations of the future path of any defined set of assets, including commodities. Each new simulation would show the possible path of all six commodities in the DBLCI. Then Elliot's rules would be applied to figure out how the index would look in this hypothetical future and the option price would be computed. Rinse and repeat over and over and over again and the option price – and Greeks to feed into our risk management system – would emerge. Aided by ever more powerful hardware, the Monte Carlo method's mighty computational hammer was used to crack the obdurate index option nut. Thus did advances in computer power allow investors access to leverage in a new, alternative asset class in ways that would have been impossible only a few years previously. But for all this business's growth, it was a sideshow compared to the credit markets, where similar, but much larger and more important developments were taking place.

Alphabet Soup

One such development was the headlong progress of the credit default swap or CDS market. JPMorgan had invented the CDS in the mid-1990s. We had traded a few of them on Russian debt in my time at Bankers Trust. But by 2003 they were everywhere. Deutsche Bank, a leader in the field, had seen an increase of 250 per cent in volumes from 2000 to 2002,[8] a growth which had helped the Credit department to be the biggest by revenue in the investment bank.[9] From around this time, at the annual Barcelona conference (where the Rolling Stones were the floor show in 2007), the power of the Credit department meant that presentations by its representatives were always the main event – the rest of us mere seething support acts.

A CDS is, in its most basic, vanilla form, a simple product transacted between a buyer and a seller of credit risk protection. It has a predetermined maturity – five years, say – and refers to, or 'references', a particular borrower (e.g. the Russian Federation), or sometimes one particular bond or loan of that borrower. If the referenced borrower or bond does not default, then the buyer of protection (colloquially just 'the buyer') pays a steady, usually quarterly, fixed stream of payments to the seller until the maturity of the swap. But the moment there is a default, the deal ends and the CDS buyer can simply deliver the defaulted – and by now much less valuable – bond to the seller and get the full notional in return. The risk is determined by the likelihood of default and the amount the bond would be worth subsequently (the 'recovery value' – the lower this is, the more the risk). The riskier the bond is deemed to be, the higher the fixed payments. Like any derivative, a CDS can be used in a variety of ways. For a fund that owns bonds, or a bank that has extended loans, the CDS can be used as a type of insurance. The fixed payments are like a premium and the ability to hand over a defaulted bond in return for its par value is like the recompense after a fire. The seller, on the other hand, is a little like an insurer – he gets a steady cash stream but loses on default. Naturally, as the market developed, CDSs were entered into for purely speculative reasons, too.

What is important to realise is that the CDS doesn't create any extra risk – it is a zero-sum game between two counterparties. Despite this, it has a solid economic function. It allows firms to offset risk and diversify it away to other counterparties happier to take it on. On the other hand, it also reduces transparency. Because the deals are transacted bilaterally (something which is now starting to change due to new regulation), it is difficult for anyone outside the deal to gauge exactly where the risk lies. It's a bit like the case of my horrified visitor from the Russian embassy. He knew that the scruffy kids at Bankers Trust had bought a huge number of his country's bonds, but what he could not see was the thick book of deals that passed this risk to other investors. The total return swaps on GKOs reduced our risk but smeared it over the rest of the market. CDSs, which are the first cousin to our Russian TRSs, were doing a similar thing to all the credit markets in far, far greater size.

The growth in the CDS markets really started when the product was standardised in 1999 by means of agreement between banks via their industry body ISDA (the International Swap Dealers Association). Up until then, each bank had a slightly different definition of what 'default' meant, with the consequence that superficially offsetting deals were actually incompatible. If a company (referenced in a series of CDS deals) was on the borderline of full catastrophe, it could be in default by some definitions and not by others. That meant that if you had bought protection from one bank and sold it to another, you could be in the unfortunate position of having to pay out in full on one deal and of receiving nothing in return. Standardisation reduced this so-called 'basis risk'.

Computer power then started to play a part. First, via the familiar route of allowing the product to be priced and risk-managed. At its simplest, pricing a CDS is an easy matter which relies on the same kind of arbitrage logic as my finance professor's 'share forward' example because you can replicate a CDS with a bond, an interest rate swap and a loan.* But any departure from this simplest case – a CDS

---

* Imagine a CDS referencing a single risky, fixed-coupon bond. Further, imagine that the CDS's maturity and coupon dates precisely match those of the bond. An arbitrageur can construct a risk-free portfolio by buying the CDS, buying the bond with borrowed money, and then swapping the interest rate risk. The cash flows all offset precisely. In this simple and unrealistic case, arbitrage pricing – the 'manufacturing cost' – gives an exact value to the CDS.

which doesn't match the bond maturity, for example, or one which is linked to multiple bonds because it references a borrower, not a bond – requires analytic firepower to be brought to bear. The use of DBAnalytics in Deutsche Bank and its equivalent in other rival firms directly led to the expansion of the market. Second, as was the case upon the arrival of Merrill's OPTICS system in FX, or Bankers Trust's SSF, the more convenient it became for traders to book transactions and to see their risk, the lower the barrier to dealing became. This fuelled market growth. The more the market grew and became more liquid, the more participants joined it in a spiralling virtuous cycle – or vicious cycle, depending on your viewpoint.

And how the market grew! According to ISDA, in 2001 there were $919 billion of CDS contracts outstanding; by 2007, at the start of the crisis, there were $62.2 trillion – 66 times more in six years, a growth rate of 100 per cent per year. This compares to a 33 per cent annual growth rate in the older, and even larger, interest rate derivative market in the same period.[10] The creation of a popular set of credit indexes (similar in concept to equity or commodity indexes) by a firm called iTraxx in 2004 added to the frenzy. But CDSs were only part of the massive growth in credit products.

In late 2004, I had a meeting with a man called Sunil (not his real name) from the Credit department. A slightly-built, polite, and shockingly young-looking Indian, he was a rising star in the department's 'structuring' team. He was reputedly a first-rate mathematician and was a graduate of one of India's finest universities. Structurers had a role separate from that of traders or salespeople; their job was to organise and coordinate the creation of complex derivative deals. The role's very existence was testimony to the increasingly Byzantine nature of the financial markets. When I started out in 1990 such people didn't exist – whatever would they do? Now they were commonplace and powerful. Sunil wanted to understand how commodity markets worked and what we could do with our indexes. His hope was that he could somehow use my

team to create a new market around novel commodity-based variants of a product that had taken the financial markets by storm: the
collateralised debt obligation (CDO). It was a false hope: we never
did a deal of the sort he envisioned and although one or two other
firms managed it, a market never developed.[11] While we worked on
the possibility, however, Sunil taught me a great deal about CDOs.

A CDO is a special type of bond, he explained. The buyer of
a CDO owns a part of the cash flows coming from a big pot of
interest-bearing assets like bonds and loans.* Step one to make this
happen is that a bank sets up a separate company to hold all the
assets – a so-called 'special purpose vehicle'. Then this company issues a CDO that pools together the cash flows (coupons, principal
repayments and the like) as they are received from the underlying
assets. These flows are then aggregated and paid out to the investors in regular intervals as coupons. The real twist to the whole
set-up, Sunil explained, is the creation of 'tranches'. Each 'tranche'
or 'slice' of the structure is a separate claim on the assets' cash flows
and sits in a queue for the money. The position in the queue is
known as the 'seniority' of the tranche. 'It's like standing in a queue
at school waiting to get a bowl of soup from a big pot. The older
kids right at the front should always get soup; the ones at the back
could go hungry if the soup runs out,' Sunil said, simplifying a little
patronisingly for my benefit.

The way that 'soup' becomes lacking in a CDO is if some of the
bonds start to default. Naturally, the risk of holding the 'junior'
(back of the queue) tranches is higher than the risk of holding the
senior tranches and so the reward for doing so – that is, the coupon
on the tranche – is higher too. I had to concede that the structure
was clever: investors could get access to a pool of diversified assets
while choosing the degree of risk they wanted; we, and our rivals,
got to clear risk off the books – which in the case of loans then

---

* The ones with loans in are actually called CLOs, for collateralised loan obligations, but
I will use CDO for simplicity.

freed up capacity to loan again – and managed to generate fees for all the work and brainpower expended.

When CDOs were first invented in the 1980s, Sunil told me (before you were born by the looks of it, I muttered to myself), the underlying assets were bonds issued by corporations as well as loans made to them. Over time, in the 1990s and early 2000s, more ingredients were added to create 'multi-sector CDOs' – these included emerging market bonds, student loans, loans for car purchases, mortgage-backed securities (or MBS) and many, many more. Mortgages are an interesting addition because mortgage-backed securities are, themselves, already a pool of smaller loans – the mortgages taken out by private individuals. Mortgage-backed securities work a lot like CDOs, with the same idea of tranches. What is important about this, Sunil explained, is that a CDO that contains tranches of mortgage-backed securities therefore has two levels of pooling – first from the private mortgages pooled up to the level of the MBS and then from the various tranches of these bonds into the CDO's pool; he seemed really rather proud of all this complexity. But the complexity had a price – how could customers get comfortable enough with it that they would actually buy the product? Did they need to rely solely on a bank's recommendation? If so, this was a problem because, since Procter and Gamble, banks had become a little gunshy around customers' gambit of 'I didn't understand; give me my money back' when things went wrong. The solution was ratings. Someone else – someone independent – would give the CDOs their seal of approval. That 'someone' was the ratings agencies.

Rate My Tranche!

Two huge firms dominate the ratings market: Moody's and Standard and Poor's (S&P). Fitch is a distant third. These three between them perform around 95 per cent of the ratings in the world. Their role is to assign a subjective rating, which measures the risk of default, to bonds and other bond-like stuff using a letter-based grading system (where AAA is the highest, i.e. least risky, AA the next highest and so on). For the vast majority of ordinary bonds, the process is, in essence, simple. An analyst looks at the issuer's business and its finances (how much debt does it have; how much cash; what are the firm's prospects; is it growing or shrinking; etc.) and assesses the riskiness of its outstanding bonds accordingly. These ratings are revisited regularly, which is why you will have heard of companies or governments being 'downgraded'. Given that there are many investors that are barred by law or by their own internal rules from buying bonds that are not rated, or not rated at a particular grade, the agencies are extremely important and powerful. Despite the occasional howler whereby highly rated companies suddenly go bankrupt (Enron being a classic), this part of the agencies' role is relatively uncontroversial. When the agencies began to rate the tranches of CDOs, however, they strayed into much more dangerous territory.

The difficulty with rating CDOs results from their complexity, since they aggregate the cash flows from dozens, if not hundreds, of different bonds. Some of these are, in turn, made up of hundreds of individual loans (e.g. mortgages). The problem is not just to determine the chances of default of each of the assets but also to assess the degree to which their risks are correlated. This matters a great deal. If the risks are uncorrelated, a default on one bond would not be followed by defaults on the others. The junior tranches of the CDO at the back of the queue might get hurt but the senior ones would be fine. But if the risks are correlated and bonds default in waves, the owner of every tranche, even the most senior, could get stung. The impact of even a small change in correlation can be extreme and dangerous (as it had been for LTCM: its demise had been caused by a spike in the correlations between the prices of the assets underlying their complex thicket of positions).

So in order to rate the riskiness of the various tranches, ratings agencies had to use mathematical modelling to figure out the default risk per tranche.

In doing so, they were faced with a similar problem to the one that my team encountered with commodity index options – the product was simply too complex to be priced analytically, or even by using traditional lattice techniques. The agencies' solution was identical to ours: use the brute force of Monte Carlo and lashings of chip capacity. 'The transparent and proven Monte Carlo methodology is no longer difficult to use, given today's fast PCs with superior computing power,' explained a press release from Standard and Poor's at the time of the launch of their CDO Evaluator software in 2001.[12] 'Today's PCs are fast enough to perform enough trials in a reasonable period of time. For example, it typically takes 30 seconds for 15,000 trials on a portfolio of 100 assets [and] 2.5 minutes for 100,000 trials,' it continued. All S&P needed to do was to provide their computers with the expected default probabilities and recovery values of each of the assets and a table of correlations between them. This was, in essence, very similar to the set of inputs needed by the Engine to calculate VaR, with default probabilities and recovery rates taking the place of p99 bumps. Where did this data come from? The probabilities of default and recovery rates were estimated by looking at historical data.[13] Correlations – the most critical input – were a blend of historical analysis and guesswork. Once again, the past was being used to predict the future.

As Sunil explained to me, banks had an even greater computational problem than the rating agencies. 'We would be fine if we could sell every bit of every tranche, but we can't. We have to hold parts of a CDO and the traders need to hedge them.' Hedging – which could be attempted by using CDSs or CDS indexes – requires a trader to know his Greeks. The agencies could get away with running the model once to get to a rating for each tranche. Banks had to run models again and again to allow them to understand their risk every day as the market moved. Furthermore, the agencies only needed to figure out *if* a tranche would default, the banks needed to know *when*; this would allow them to put on hedges with the right maturity. All in all, it was a much bigger version of what had happened to Darren's and my Russian book – risk management was trivial when we traded every GKO back-to-back with a client via a swap; the computers needed to fire up once we didn't and once the book became a mess of different positions. But even with the most powerful computers banks found it tricky to calculate the required Greeks in adequate time, so massive was the task. An 'overnight' risk run at one bank took 40 hours so it needed to be done at the weekend.[14] One solution to this problem was the introduction by banks' quants of a simplifying mathematical technique called the Gaussian copula.[15] Borrowed from the world of actuaries, where it is used to look at the correlation between death rates, it allowed the complexities of the correlation matrix to be boiled down significantly – this made calculations easier and quicker. Rather like the idea of VaR (another 'boiled down' risk approach), it quickly took hold in banks and, latterly, in ratings agencies, partly due to the sponsorship of JPMorgan, a massive presence in the credit markets. The other familiar solution was simply to 'throw metal' at the problem. Either way, the market for CDOs, like that for CDSs, grew exponentially.

Sub-Prime Numbers

From around this time onwards there was a strong feeling in Deutsche's investment bank, in common with most of our rivals, that complexity was good and that the cleverness needed to create it would be rewarded. Naturally, this resulted in some behavioural change. In one small but emblematic symptom of this change, the more complicated end of my old FX options business was rechristened 'complex risk' by my former colleagues in what looked like a transparent attempt to make the FX department seem a little less dull. The FX team's bread-and-butter business of transacting spot and forwards in huge size, with tiny spreads, and at increasingly astonishing speeds was not considered exciting – 'transport and haulage' was the dismissive term used by some. The modish title 'complex risk' (which I confess I retained with no debate at all when I eventually returned to FX and took over this business in combination with commodities derivatives in late 2005) suggested a more cerebral gloss. It was as if a manufacturer of reliable, fuel-efficient but workaday family cars had decided to sponsor a Formula One team and call its least boring model the Testosterone.

We all grew used to attending presentations where people from Credit would explain the latest variant of the CDO. Some meetings were internal and used as a chance to show off the department's brilliance. Some, like the Barcelona conferences, were for clients and attempted the same thing. The expression 'boxes and arrows' began to be used to describe the inevitable charts showing the web of entities (boxes) and cash flows (arrows) involved in these increasingly convoluted deals. 'Did you go to the Credit presentation?' 'Yeah,' (weary sigh) 'an hour of boxes and arrows.' All the variations – which were promoted with equal vigour by our rivals – were designed to continue to feed the 'infinite appetite' of the investing community, which, just as was the case with Russian GKOs, spanned every conceivable type of investor. Tranches were held by the unlikeliest of firms based all over the globe: a small industrial bank in Germany, a hedge fund in France, an insurer in Japan and so on. Many of these investors were buying tranches with borrowed money, thus tying the banking system to the risk.

From 2004 or so, in order to spruce up the yields that the market still craved, US sub-prime mortgages began to be introduced into the CDO mix. Sub-prime mortgages are those granted to borrowers who – let's put this kindly – aren't quite from the top drawer in terms of credit quality. As a result, they pay more interest. The good thing about mortgages is that they are backed by the value of the property they fund. This makes them less risky in theory since the 'recovery value' in the case of default is what the lender can get for the repossessed house – if house prices keep rising (as they had been) then the lender won't lose out. For the agencies that were rating CDOs, concerned as they were by the correlation of risks, the fact that house prices in the US had never before declined in all parts of the country at the same time meant that a geographically dispersed pool of mortgages was therefore diversified and safe. Thus it was that tens of thousands of individual loans, each of which was risky and definitely 'sub-investment grade' (a rating lower than BBB, or, less kindly, 'junk'), were transformed by the power of combination, blending and high-speed computerised mathematics into securities where, according to S&P's definition of AAA, 'the obligor . . . has extremely strong capacity to meet its financial commitments'.[16] Designing the deals was made easier by the credit agencies' helpful practice of making their evaluation software available to banks – this allowed the desired ratings to be built into structures right from the drawing board. It was computer-aided design for CDOs.

Through 2005, 2006 and 2007 the variants kept coming. In July 2006, to great internal fanfare, Deutsche acquired MortgageIT, a US mortgage originator, for $429 million. 'It is a key element of the Bank's build-out of a vertically integrated mortgage origination and securitization platform [and] will provide significant competitive advantages, such as access to a steady source of product for distribution into the mortgage capital markets', said the press release in the rather bland manner of such things.[17] What it meant was that the one-stop shop was getting yet another aisle and growing still further as a result. The 'steady source of product' was more loans to be packaged into CDOs for eager investors, thus solving the perennial problem of finding enough assets for them to buy. In truth, we at Deutsche were a little late to this particular party; our rivals at the big US banks had already bought other originators. Lehman Brothers – a giant in the mortgage market – had bought five. This vertical integration was an attempt to simplify, or at least internalise, the complex chain of deals behind any CDO: a broker would persuade a borrower to take out a loan from the originator; that loan would be sold from the originator to a bank (or, rather, to a bank-owned special purpose vehicle); it would then be repackaged and sold on to the end investor. But if integration was a simplification – albeit one that increased banks' risk since loans would now be sitting on banks' balance sheets prior to being sold on – in other ways the market grew ever more complex.

I recall one lecture about the 'CDO-squared'; I sat in an auditorium squinting, yet again, at slides showing tangles of boxes and arrows. The product came about, the lecturer explained, because, even when a CDO starts to sell, parts of it might not sell as fast as others. In particular, what are known as the 'mezzanine' tranches (halfway down the soup queue) often proved difficult to shift. One solution to this problem was to repackage the unsold pieces of an old CDO into a brand-new bond known as a CDO-squared (a CDO made up of CDOs), whereupon the unloved tranches were reborn via the rating agencies' computers as highly rated new investments. The other solution was for banks simply to hold on to any unsold tranches and become investors themselves. Banks began to eat their own cooking.

What were bankers' motivations in all of this? There is, I believe, a widely held view that the primary, overwhelming driver of all of this was pay. While I think the outright level of pay was certainly an important factor, the picture is more complex than that because what drives people's actions in banks is more nuanced than the popular cartoonish view of bankers all being amoral, wealth-maximising automata.

I managed a lot of bankers over the years and, in the course of doing so, paid out a lot of bonuses and decided a lot of promotions. To be even passably successful at my job it was vital to understand what motivated the people who reported to me. While it is true that some people were very focused on the absolute amount they earned, they were strongly outnumbered by those who cared more about their relative pay and its perceived fairness. A former colleague summed up this attitude best in almost Dickensian terms: 'You get paid three and your buddy gets two. Result: happiness. You get paid three and your buddy gets four. Result: misery.' When pressed as to what units he was referring to, his response was typically terse: 'It doesn't matter. It could be millions; it could be bowls of rice.'

And, while this may surprise you, many people weren't even primarily concerned about money. Some were motivated by promotions and the prospect of running things; that is, power. Others focused on doing interesting work or even just a quiet life. Many had a blend of these motivations. I'd put myself in this category. Running behind all this, for many, was fear: fear of being made redundant or even just fear of being thought bad at their job. And do not underestimate the force of convention and peer pressure as drivers as well. As one academic study of traders found: 'Overall, traders are *more* risk averse than other groups. In particular they are noticeably less inclined to take social *or career risks* [my emphasis].'[18] Deals get done, in part, because it is a lonely and disagreeable task to stop them being done. I have on occasion in my career aborted deals that I considered to be overly risky late in the day, and the stress and ill feeling it causes are immense. Trust me, it is not a quick route to popularity. Any risks in a deal are always a matter of opinion. You can never be certain that a deal is really too risky, and besides, if the deal does go wrong it will go wrong in the future. In contrast, the happy customer, the congratulatory emails, the celebratory dinner – the glory – happen right now.

In short, even without considering absolute levels of pay, there have always been numerous motivational forces driving bank employees to get new clients, or to do new deals, or to create new technology. Driving them to compete, in other words. In all this they are little different from other corporate employees. I think this explains why there is a quite weak correlation between pay and failure in the 2007–8 crisis.[19] Some firms paid extravagantly well and blew up (e.g. Lehman); some paid equally well and were in good enough shape to be called on as a buyer of last resort for other failing banks (e.g. JPMorgan). Others, like the UK's Northern Rock, paid their staff really rather poorly in banking terms but were first over the cliff. The other things that motivate individuals – trying to get paid well relatively speaking or trying to get promoted – spurred the gradual move to immoderate risk-taking, independent of the lure of instant riches.

Regardless of the causes of the spiral of financial change, in the real world a property bubble began to form: the Case–Schiller index, the most authoritative measure of US house prices, which had hovered near 100 for most of the 20th century, reached 195.35 in 2005 – up 58 per cent from 2000.[20] This drew in more buyers, many speculative by now, and so the rise carried on all over the US. Agencies' Monte Carlo models, fed with these comfortingly correlated inputs, continued to spit out comforting outputs in the form of ratings. Lending skyrocketed as a result: from 2000 to 2007, around $1.4 trillion of cash CDOs were issued, the bulk in the last three years of that period.[21] To put it in perspective, the total notional of all Russian domestic debt that had caused such difficulties in 1998 was about $41 billion, around 3 per cent of the CDO lending figure.[22]

The market's complexity continued to multiply in lockstep with its size. In the last years before the Great Financial Crisis broke, yet another astonishing CDO variant was born – the synthetic CDO. Here, instead of a CDO being made of actual bonds made up from real loans, the bonds were replicated by hundreds of CDSs (hence, 'synthetic'). It was a side bet on the performance of bonds – just as Elliot's commodity indexes had been a way of taking side bets on the value of commodities without having to own any of them. Investors wagered that the bonds would perform by selling protection on them via CDSs (and getting regular payments, just like coupons from a real bond); hedge funds shorted (i.e. bet against) the bonds by buying CDSs. The funds were, in effect, paying premiums for the chance to get a big payout in the event of a wave of defaults that they now thought likely, if not imminent, despite the solid ratings these synthetic products were receiving from the ratings agencies. Funds were buying insurance on a theatre they didn't own against a fire they expected in the future. Without the tedious and expensive need to find real borrowers (they'd been replaced by the hedge funds' short positions), the volume of these deals exploded too – by some accounts to trillions of dollars' worth.[23]

If the advent of microwave communications in the world of electronic FX marks a point at which technological competition can be said to have tipped into the absurd, synthetic CDOs marked a similar point in the steady rise of derivative complexity. Extravagantly convoluted, their creation utterly reliant on massive computational power, dogged by accusations that they embodied inherent conflicts of interest (for whose benefit were banks constructing these deals – buyer or seller?), completely removed from any real-world purpose other than speculation, these exemplars of the zero-sum game stand as a kind of ornate spire on top of a cathedral of complexity dedicated to the mischievous god of 'because we can'. In retrospect, their advent was a sign that the end was in sight.

Citi's FIFA Ranking

For my part, aside from feeling the general pressure within the bank to do deals that were clever and having to attend the occasional box and arrow show, most of these developments passed me by. But what was obvious by the end of 2006 or so was that the bank was changing very rapidly. In the FX department (which I had re-joined when Commodities had been paired with it in a combined business called Global Currencies and Commodities a couple of years earlier), the transformative latency battle in spot FX that I described earlier was picking up pace. Complexity was increasing every month in the credit markets. Similar, if less dramatic, change was occurring in rates and equities. To cope with it all, employees were joining the investment bank in a steady stream. The annual graduate recruitment drive had become a frenzy to get the top can-didates from the world's leading universities in competition with our banking rivals. Every large bank had a graduate programme; we at Deutsche Bank were very proud of ours. Competition to join it was intense. Candidates were selected for interview from the thousands of CVs that flooded the HR department every year. Despite the numbers, it was a rare event to take a candidate from outside the most prestigious of schools. The lucky ones entered an interview process that was long and occasionally brutal.

I was once assigned to conduct interviews along with Sunil, the credit structurer. The first candidate was a confident young phys-ics student from Cambridge. 'What characteristics do you think you need to succeed on a trading floor?' I opened up, gently. It was my cus-tomary first question designed to relax candidates, to check whether they knew even the least bit about the realities of banking, and to test whether they could sell themselves. 'You need to be numerate and good under pressure,' he replied, perfectly reasonably, after a few seconds' thought. 'And how could you persuade me that you are nu-merate?' I probed. He proceeded to list an impressive array of qualifi-cations and prizes, but he was suddenly interrupted by Sunil – silent up until now – who barked a question without warning: 'What's 19 times 17?' I saw complete consternation flicker over the features of the Cambridge man. 'Quick!' Sunil urged. The interviewee began to sweat visibly. I felt bad for him but he was on his own. At last, he mumbled an answer: 'Three hundred and twenty-one.' 'What?' Sunil almost shrieked in mock outrage. 'How the *hell* can it end in a one?' There then followed an excruciating 20 seconds of utter silence. Oh dear, I thought, maybe not so great under pressure. The poor candidate eventually corrected himself but the confident air had completely evaporated and after another 15 minutes I wrapped up the interview a bit early – never a good sign.

Despite the difficulties of the process, graduates joined in ever-increasing numbers. When we managing directors lectured them about our businesses (and, in not-so-subtle terms, tried to make them come and work for us) we did so in huge auditoriums, so large was the programme. Maybe as a result of the hurdles they had overcome to join the bank, their ambition levels were high. Credit was the first choice for the majority of them. 'You people in FX seem like nice chaps,' said one drawling young Harvard graduate to me almost pityingly at a graduate drinks event, 'but it's all about assets and you aren't an asset business.'

He was right – it *was* all about assets and Deutsche's balance sheet reflected that. In 2004, the total assets in the investment bank (called the Corporate and Investment Banking or CIB division) had been €729 billion; this was roughly in line with where assets had been, on average, since 2000 when the numbers begin to reflect the integration of Bankers Trust.[24] By 2006, though, assets had grown to €1,012 billion, an increase of €283 billion (or 40 per cent) in just two years. By 2007, the investment bank's assets had increased by another 29 per cent in one year. Risk-weighted assets (which, as you may recall, are calculated under the Basel rules to assess a bank's capital adequacy) increased by 70 per cent in the investment bank between 2004 and 2007, from €139 billion to €237 billion. By 2007, the investment bank held 72 per cent of the RWA for the bank as a whole. Deutsche stayed within the Basel capital rules because profits were strong (pre-tax returns on equity of 20 to 30 per cent) and so the capital base was growing. Regardless, it was a truly gigantic step change. But, according to Deutsche

Bank's version of the Engine, the bank was not much riskier – the investment bank's one-day p99 risk (which made up virtually the entirety of the risk for the whole bank) had only gone from €90 million to €105 million between 2004 and 2007, up just 16 per cent and representing only a small fraction of our capital. According to the computers the growth was safe, at least when seen in mathematical market-risk terms. Greater profits coupled with the perception of stable risk boosted the bank's share price, which doubled from €48 per share at the start of 2004 to €96 early in 2007.[25]

Deutsche Bank was not alone in this epic growth. All our major rivals – Lehman Brothers, Merrill Lynch, UBS, Barclays and others – were growing rapidly. Even Citigroup, a firm that most of my colleagues in Deutsche's investment bank regarded as unutterably stodgy, increased the size of its already huge balance sheet by 48 per cent from 2004 to 2007.[26] Indeed, everything about Citi was large. By 2007, Citigroup employed 368,000 people worldwide.[27] 'That's bigger than Iceland,' Elliot the index man once pointed out to the rest of us. It was true – Citigroup had more employees than the population of a sovereign nation which boasts its own currency, army and internationally ranked football team. The last point delighted us. Iceland has a respectably able football team (they are ranked 37th by FIFA as I write this, just below Poland and above Sweden) and we amused ourselves by arguing about whether a Citi team would be better or worse than Iceland's. In Citi's favour: a lower proportion of old people and children than lived in Iceland and, we guessed, a higher proportion of males, many of whom came from Brazil and Germany. Against: lots of Americans who would want to run the show bureaucratically. It was a tricky call.

Citigroup was an extreme example of a trend. During my career the growth in banks and the increase in market concentration had been dramatic. One illustrative statistic: in 1990, when I started out, the ten biggest banks in the US had a share of around 27 per cent of all US banks' assets, slightly up from around 22 per cent in

1960, a growth of 5 per cent in 30 years. By 2005, only 15 years later, the top ten banks' share had more than doubled to around 60 per cent.[28] Growth in share of employee numbers and deposits shows a similar picture. How had it happened? In the main, it had occurred as a result of mergers. For example, sitting next to Loic in 1990, back in my days at Merrill Lynch, I could deal FX options with Chase Manhattan, Manufacturers Hanover, Chemical Bank, First Chicago and J. P. Morgan – all banks of significant size. By 2006, these five had been merged in a succession of deals until there was only one: JPMorgan Chase, a bank with $1.35 trillion of assets and 174,000 employees.[29] My own bank, Deutsche, was an amalgam of Bankers Trust, Deutsche Bank and an old British merchant bank called Morgan Grenfell. Most other large banks were similar patchworks.

Why had this happened? Certainly in the US, the immediate trigger was regulatory change. The Riegle–Neal Interstate Banking and Branching Efficiency Act of 1994 permitted bank holding companies to acquire banks in any state and allowed interstate bank mergers from 1997. The Gramm–Leach–Bliley Act of 1999 allowed banks to engage in non-banking financial activities such as insurance – in effect repealing the Glass–Steagall Act of 1933 which had, in the aftermath of the crash of 1929 and subsequent Depression, forcibly separated commercial and investment banking. But regulatory change explains why mergers were no longer impossible, not why they were done. Looking through the press releases of some of the mergers that occurred in the 1990s and 2000s, two dominant publicly expressed motivations keep recurring: the idea of the one-stop shop and the idea of efficiency gains. For example, here is William Harrison (CEO of Chase Manhattan) speaking to analysts after his bank's acquisition of J. P. Morgan in 2000: 'I think there will be less than a handful of end-game winners in this space. This gives us platform to be one of those winners.'[30] A one-stop shop, in other words. On the other hand, the motivation for the earlier merger of Chase Manhattan Bank and Chemical Bank in 1995 was couched in terms of efficiency: 'The merger, which brings together $300bn assets and $20bn of shareholders' equity, is designed to achieve annual cost savings of $1.5bn.'[31] Computer technology was central to the idea of efficiency improvements. The costs of building and running a computer system (whether that be a trading system like Deutsche's ARM FX spot system, a VaR system like the Engine at Bankers Trust or a system to provide retail banking services) are similar regardless of whether the technology is used to support a large market share or a small one, especially in the face of rapidly and continually improving computer performance per dollar spent. This was certainly true in every business I ever ran. Given that banks these days amount to not much more than a lot of people using and tending a collection of computer systems, the importance of computer technology in mergers should not surprise us. But the influence of information technology in terms of economies of scale was not the only way it encouraged increasing bank size. Rapid advances in the ability to communicate also played a strong part.

Back in 1990, at the start of my career at Merrill Lynch, mobile phones were still an expensive, heavy novelty; Loic and I and the rest of his team did not have one. Email was not available. Our risk system was slow and not global. The best way to update our colleagues in New York with a new position was to phone them on a landline or to send a fax of the printed sheet. Risk management, at the level of the firm, was rudimentary. By 2006, however, every single employee in my team had a mobile phone – mostly Deutsche-Bank-issued BlackBerries that allowed us all to be contacted at any hour of the day or night, either by being called or, more often, by email. The use of emails was all-pervasive; I would regularly receive 400 or 500 a day and I would send multiple dozens. This allowed me to be kept informed of everything (deals, gossip, problems and gripes) from every corner of a global business. The same was true of all my managerial colleagues. Risk management, at the level of each desk and at the level of the bank, was a sophisticated, automated process. Our CEO could be told every single day the most money the bank could lose (99 per cent of the time) with great precision, if not, as it turned out, with great accuracy. All of this was the same at all of our rivals. In short, the huge advances in computer and communications technology made it seem as if we collectively knew what was going on and that we were in control. This feeling (which turned out to be an illusion) facilitated the growth of banks. Just as the transparency that Merrill Lynch's OPTICS system gave me about risk back in the early 1990s meant that I took more of it, so, on almost inconceivably greater scale, did the illusion of control prompt risk-taking in the banking system. It was all so easy. A boiled-down risk number like VaR, for example, could be understood by a CEO and his board whether the bank had $300 billion of assets or $2 trillion. That it would turn out to be catastrophically wrong was beside the point.

I'm Forever Bursting Bubbles

From late 2006 onwards the going in the CDO market got tougher. The headwinds came from two, related, problems. Property prices stopped rising (after years of straight increases, the Case–Schiller index declined by 1.5 per cent between 2005 and 2006[32]) and, more seriously, mortgage 'delinquencies' (i.e. the anteroom to default) were on the up. A *Businessweek* cover story – 'Nightmare Mortgages' – on 10 September 2006 placed the blame squarely on mortgages granted in 2004 and 2005, which, after their initial 'teaser' interest rates had finished, were now resetting at much higher, and often unaffordable, levels.[33] The article quoted a housing economist's description of these mortgages as 'like the neutron bomb'. By late 2006, various people in the market were starting to get nervous. One was my colleague Greg (the mortgage man from the Rolling Stones night), whose pre-existing bearishness was growing. Others could be found in the management of Goldman Sachs, who instructed their mortgage desk to 'get smaller, reduce risks and get closer to home'.[34] Numerous hedge funds also scented blood. The result, as the months wore on into 2007 and the numbers of mortgage delinquencies jumped alarmingly all over the US, was that the prices of CDO tranches started to slide. They did so because the comforting assumption of diversification that had been built into the Monte Carlo runs of ratings agencies and banks began to look false. The past was not repeating itself. Correlations were rising, disastrously. The front of the soup queue looked as though it might go hungry – an unthinkable prospect when the deals were structured.

As the crisis spread in summer and autumn 2007, the main focus was the funding markets. Banks relied on short-term funding, which needed to be rolled (that is, renewed) every day, or at best every three months. Imagine buying a house, not with a long-term mortgage but with a one-week loan that, every Monday, you needed to repay or renew by getting another. Fine as long as you look capable of paying the interest and as long as the house looks as if it's worth more than the money you borrowed. But if your lenders ever doubt you, then the loans dry up and you will need to sell your house in a hurry to get the money by Monday. Banks had done the equivalent of this to the tune of trillions of dollars. This reliance happened as a result of a trend in the US for individuals to choose to put their cash in money market funds rather than in bank deposits (whereupon the funds would promptly lend short-term to the banks) as well as a growth in the 'repo' (repurchase) markets where banks could pledge assets like bonds or CDOs to each other in return for short-term funding. Why had the managers of banks felt comfortable with this precarious situation? Because, armed with sophisticated systems, which naturally extended to managing funding, they had felt in control. Once again, computer modelling similar to VaR was implicated. 'Most of our funding was – contractually speaking – just overnight,' I was told by a friend of mine who worked in a competitor's treasury department (where funding is managed) at the time. 'But we thought we were fine because our predictions on future funding levels were based on how counterparties had behaved in the past.' That behaviour was to change.

When the sub-prime bubble started to pop in summer 2007, lenders no longer felt safe because they no longer felt confident about the value of the assets that had been pledged. They withdrew liquidity and wouldn't lend. Some banks were left begging for funding and the price of short-term money rocketed – exactly as my pessimistic Canadian friend David had predicted on the night of the Rolling Stones' gig. To raise cash, banks needed to sell assets like CDOs, but this drove their prices lower and made the banks' problems worse. The entire market was now feeling the same sense of trapped panic – multiplied 10,000-fold – that Darren and I had felt in the first warning tremor of the Russian crisis. It was LTCM revisited. In an extreme echo of 1998, the complexity of the global interconnections between banks, money market funds, insurance companies and the like, combined with the obscurity of many of the assets that were being funded, meant that lenders were not clear where problems were hiding and so they withdrew funding through fear of the unknown.

All of this would never have happened if not for the real underlying weakness in the system: banks were just too leveraged. Lehman Brothers, at the end of 2007, had $691 billion of assets and $22.5 billion of shareholders' equity – a leverage ratio of 30:1.[35] That meant that only a 3 per cent decline in the value of the assets on Lehman's balance sheet would be enough to wipe them out – they were more leveraged than LTCM had been. The bank Bear Stearns had a leverage ratio of 30:1, too.[36] But these were not even outliers: the average leverage across the banking system was in excess of 40:1. As Andrew Haldane, a bigwig at the Bank of England, described it in a speech in August 2011, 'At the height of the boom, every $1 of bank assets was financed with $98 cents of debt. The global banking system was financing itself with a 98 per cent loan-to-value mortgage.'[37] Why such leverage? The motivation was to enhance returns on equity. The more that a bank is financed with borrowing relative to the amount of capital, the easier it is to make fat returns for shareholders. It's the same bet as investors made when they bought Russian GKOs via swaps – put a small amount of money down but get the gain on the full notional. My own bank, Deutsche, had set a hugely ambitious target of 25 per cent pre-tax returns on equity and even went as far as to buy its own shares back to achieve this.[38] It was another arms race – all the senior folk at big banks were looking over their shoulders at their rivals and attempting to deliver returns that were not out of line with them. It is possible, to put it gently, that the increasing use of shares to pay senior people in order to 'align them with shareholders' played some part in this. Whatever the motivation, the bank's computers and the ones inside ratings agencies said the leverage was safe. The computers were wrong.

As the crisis progressed wearyingly throughout 2008, it gradually became clear how wrong. The news just kept getting worse month after month. At last, in September, the climax came as Lehman Brothers was allowed to fail. So it goes. I heard the news that it would almost certainly happen during a conference call I was obliged to attend while I was sitting, in balmy, late summer heat, in a restaurant in Lisbon. It was the evening of Saturday 13 September, a couple of days before the bankruptcy became official, and I was at a celebration for a close friend's 50th birthday. Everyone else around the table, none of whom were connected with finance, was eating, drinking and chatting cheerfully while I tried to juggle a phone in one hand and a fork in the other. At last, when the call was over, I put the phone away with a heavy heart. My friends were curious, what was the call about? Why the furrowed brow? 'Lehman is going bankrupt,' I explained. 'Remember this date – it will be one that is taught in history lessons for a century to come.' They looked at me uncomprehendingly, but I knew what was coming. The next day I flew back to London to face the inevitable chaos.

A month later, Lehman was gone, my old firm Merrill Lynch had been merged with Bank of America to prevent its demise, and the massive insurance firm AIG (which had destroyed itself by supplying tens of billions of dollars of insurance on high-rated tranches of CDOs to one and all) had been bailed out by the US government. Ironically, both Citigroup and Iceland were on their knees. The introduction of the Troubled Asset Relief Program (TARP) halted the panic by effectively guaranteeing US banks, but the damage had been done. Although it did not need direct support from any government and by so doing joined the ranks of the world's best-run banks, Deutsche Bank lost €8.5 billion in its trading businesses in 2008 having 'recorded significant losses in credit trading, equity derivatives, and equities proprietary trading' despite 'strong results in more liquid, "flow" trading businesses including foreign exchange, money markets and commodities'.[39] The performance of the businesses I was associated with gave me some sense of pride, but it was not a lot of comfort. Deutsche Bank's stock price, which had been as high as €89.80 earlier in 2008, plummeted to a low of €18.59.[40] The scale of the losses was in sharp contrast to the bank's still reasonable-looking VaR (the loss figure that should only be exceeded one day in a hundred, remember), which averaged €122 million during the year.[41] I asked one senior risk manager if his department was still going to calculate VaR despite its obvious and complete failure. 'We have to,' he said sadly, 'the regulators want it; it's baked into the way the bank runs.' He paused, then: 'But it's just a lot of nonsense, Kevin. It's the 1 per cent event that kills you and the method doesn't tell you how big it will be.'

In the wake of the disaster, to save costs, large programmes of redundancies were put in place at Deutsche Bank and at our competitors. Pitifully, a few of the people on the graduate programme who had chosen to go to Credit now started phoning me wondering if there were any positions in FX or Commodities. There was nothing I could do. Tough as it was for those who were affected, few people outside banking mourned for the employees who were made redundant; the world had entered a recession from which it is still gradually recovering and public anger with banks was burning intensely. My colleague in Risk Management summed up my feelings exactly when he remarked, around the time of the TARP, 'We've seen it all before, haven't we? But we never learned the lesson of '98. You and I will be retired or dead before anyone ever trusts banks again.'

In that, I am sad to say, I am sure he was correct.

PART THREE

Making and Mending

CHAPTER 7

Ethics and the Panopticon

Dinner and Slavery

The extent of people's anger with bankers was brought home to me by an incident at a dinner party in October 2008. It was a few weeks after the Lehman bankruptcy and there was a real fear that the entire financial system could come to pieces. So frenzied did things become that it seemed strange, leaving the office at night, to see people going about their normal business in the streets, unhurried and untroubled. The air of utter chaos inside the bank had subconsciously prepared me to see burning cars, corpses, rivers of blood and flesh-crazed zombies on my exit. As a result of this frenzy, I was a little tired.

At the dinner, I was seated next to the wife of a friend of the person whose house we were dining in. I didn't know her and she didn't know me. After a few minutes of preliminary chit-chat (how we knew the host; weather; kids) came the question I had been dreading: 'Anyway, what do you do?' For a second I considered just coming out with the truth but, maybe unwisely, and since I was not at my best, I decided to dissemble. 'It's a bit embarrassing and controversial.' Her eyes widened slightly. 'I . . .' (I paused; her face now started to show genuine curiosity) 'I run a company which is involved in . . . the child slave trade,' I lied. Her face was immobile, her smile frozen. After a few moments of obvious confusion she asked, hesitantly, 'The child slave trade? Do you mean the legal kind?' At this I thought it best to confess that I was, in fact, a banker and that I worked on a trading floor. Her response surprised me.

'A banker?' she hissed, clearly furious. 'That's even worse! All you people should be jailed!' It was then that I knew for sure how far my profession's reputation had fallen. In the mind of this educated and – previously – charming lady, being a banker was worse than being a (legal sort of) child slave dealer, and possibly, although I never determined this for sure, even a little worse than the much more common illegal sort. My suspicions about the fall in my status were confirmed a few weeks later when an article was published in the German press reporting the result of a social attitudes survey. People had been asked to rate various professions according to whether they would like to have a friend who did that job. Bankers came third last, beating only convicted criminals and prostitutes.[1] A disappointing result, if I'm honest, although I suppose that it's at least something that we weren't at rock bottom.

In the face of this overwhelming public anger and scorn there was little that I could do but to try to get on with my job. The same was true for my colleagues. There was seemingly endless administrative and legal mopping up to do as a result of the default of Lehman. The volatility of the markets, although declining from its previous torturous level as the months wore on, was still high enough and unpredictable enough to cause me constant anxiety. In time, in FX, the high-frequency trading firms came back and the race for speed became a worry all over again. In a way, I welcomed these concerns as comfortingly familiar. I suppose I was simply hoping that everything would return to normal, even if 'normal' meant ever more brutal competition. I looked back on this collection of old headaches with the same retrospective fondness with which I might have remembered petty family squabbles after some tremendous natural disaster. To be sure, I knew in my heart that change was coming. Listening to the politicians, there was no doubt that stricter regulation was on its way and it seemed difficult to deny that stricter regulation was exactly what was needed. But nothing prepared me, or any of my colleagues, for the changes that resulted from the string of scandals that now hit banking. If the public had simply thought we were incompetent before, they now thought we were all crooks. It was hard to take. For me, two scandals in particular were the most personally troubling: LIBOR and the FX-fixing affair.

Crime of the Century?

The LIBOR scandal has been described, a little hyperbolically, as 'the crime of the century'.[2] Even if it is not quite that, it has generated acres of newspaper coverage, billions in fines, and, as I write this, a number of current court cases both civil and criminal. You will forgive me, I hope, if I tread a little warily in what I say on this subject and on the related issue of the FX-fixing scandal since both are in effect, *sub judice*. Nonetheless, it is important to understand what happened and why, if only to illustrate some of the complexities of modern banking and the dilemmas bankers face.

All through my career, LIBOR was a familiar concept to me because, although trading it or setting it was never a responsibility of mine, it touched virtually every market I had been involved in. Despite that, I could not have told you the details of how it was arrived at or even why it had come to exist at all. I had never really given either topic a moment's thought. As the scandal broke, I became educated very quickly. Like so many financial innovations, LIBOR came into being as a way of solving a particular, one-off problem. Back in 1969, a group of banks wanted to make a syndicated (that is, 'shared') US$80 million loan to the Shah of Iran. The loan, which was a large one for the time, was part of a growing business in 'offshore' dollars that arose because of the capital flows resulting from the costs of funding the Vietnam War. The Shah's financiers wanted to pay a floating rate on the loan – but what rate? There was no existing reference. Minos Zombanakis, a Greek banker who ran the London branch of Manufacturers Hanover (later subsumed in

JPMorgan) came up with a solution: LIBOR, or the London Interbank Offered Rate. Every quarter, to determine the interest rate for the quarter to come, the banks in the syndicate would submit how much it cost them to borrow dollars in the London market. The average would be taken and that reference (dubbed LIBOR) would be used as the rate for the loan – plus a spread to offset the risk of default and to create profit. In the gentlemanly world of 1960s banking the penalty for trying to 'game' the reference by submitting a very high borrowing cost was ostracism from a lucrative club.[3]

The idea caught on. More and more loans started to use the rate. Eventually, in 1986, to ensure some kind of credible control over LIBOR, the British Bankers Association (a trade body established in 1919), loosely supervised by the Bank of England, took over the rate's administration. Then, in the years that followed, LIBOR's importance was magnified a thousandfold as the computer-led derivatives explosion of the 1990s took place. Interest rate swaps – in which, most often, fixed payments are swapped for floating payments – needed a reference to calculate the cash flows for the floating leg. LIBOR was the natural place to turn. Other derivatives, such as forward rate agreements (FRAs) and interest rate futures (both sets of contracts settling on what an interest rate will be in the future) also used LIBOR. In the world of interest rate references, it became winner takes all. Within a big portfolio of derivatives it made sense for rate fixings to be consistent so they could offset each other, like Lego bricks snapping together.* The LIBOR fixing became one of the most important Greeks in any interest rate derivative book. The market in these derivatives, made easier to transact and risk-manage by virtue of rapidly expanding computer power, reached enormous size. Between 1990 and 1997, the

---

* There were actually rival fixings, arrived at through almost identical processes (e.g. EURIBOR in continental Europe, TIBOR in Tokyo), but LIBOR was by far the most important and is used as shorthand for all fixings in this chapter.

total notional of swaps outstanding rocketed from $2.3 trillion to $23 trillion. By 2008, the year of the crisis, the notional was $400 trillion.[4] But LIBOR had barely moved on from its roots in the distant past. Just as it had been since 1986, it was still calculated from the 11am London time submissions of a panel of 18 banks with little more to deter gaming than the way the four highest and four lowest quotes were discarded before averaging the remaining ten.* It was as if a gigantic steel and glass skyscraper of risk was resting on ancient, rickety, wooden foundations.

You might be wondering why the benchmark was never updated. Two reasons dominated. The first was simply sloth. Getting anything done or changed in the banking industry takes a great deal of effort from lots of people if multiple banks are involved. Even within banks, changing behaviour is not straightforward and often requires threats or the use of low cunning. Changing the LIBOR process would have probably have needed a similarly intense effort to the one I needed to go through to get options traders to update their prices electronically (and which I described earlier in this book). It would be a pain, in short. Why bother wasting time that could be expended on more exciting and lucrative activities if LIBOR did not appear broken? The second reason was LIBOR's huge legal momentum. With trillions of dollars of outstanding derivatives based on the reference, any change to the fixing mechanism, no matter how sensible or superficially trivial in effect, could potentially alter the economics of deals transacted under the previous regime but which still had cash flows left to fix. Any firm that believed it would be worse off could cry foul and then resort to the courts as a result. This would inevitably gum up the markets. Outcome: nothing changed and the system remained vulnerable. On the face of it, then, the LIBOR scandal is easy to understand and easier to condemn. Banks' traders purposely exploited the system's vulnerabilities by submitting incorrect rates. They did so in order

---

* The number of panel banks varied by currency – 18 is for US dollars.

to influence LIBOR so that fixings in their derivative books made more money than they should. But there was a little more to it than this simple picture shows.

In discussions of LIBOR I often get the impression that people believe there is always a simple, unambiguous answer to the question of what rate to submit. It is as if they think that submitting rates is the equivalent of being asked, 'How many fingers do you have?' The correct submission should be ten, but, in a transparent lie and because the desk is long a few finger futures, the number gets bumped up to eleven to try to make money. That impression is incorrect. First off, LIBOR isn't just one number but 150: 15 different tenors – that is to say, maturity dates (from overnight to one year) – for 10 different currencies. What's more, the question that submitters are asked is not entirely precise: 'At what rate could you borrow funds, were you to do so by asking for and then accepting inter-bank offers in a reasonable market size just prior to 11am?'[5] The problem is that the cash market for borrowing and lending funds (the deposit, as opposed to the derivatives market) is, and was, often patchy and rather illiquid, even in calm times. In periods of turmoil it was worse. You can get some idea of just how patchy by considering some data from 2011, a year that was a relatively quiet period in the funding markets. The intensity of market activity in 'Unsecured deposit transactions by LIBOR contributing banks' – the trading that allows banks on the LIBOR panel to answer the submission question directly – was considered by the authors of the 2012 Wheatley report into LIBOR to be 'medium-low' or 'low' in almost 90 per cent of the 150 required rates. These thin markets were not just in the obscure tenors of fringe currencies: their number included three-month and six-month US dollar, sterling, and yen rates – mainstays of the market.[6]

Imagine yourself in the place of the person working on the cash desk of a money markets business whose job it is to submit rates. It's coming up to 11am and you need to decide what to submit.

You look at the US dollar sheet first of all. Maybe you have not traded three-month US dollar deposits trade for a while but you might have just seen the six-month trade at a higher rate than yesterday. You guess that three months is probably higher, too, but your submitted rate must – by necessity – be an estimate. Maybe, in another currency, you might have observed some small offers in the broker market but you would be unsure if they were 'in a reasonable market size' or not. Maybe the reasonably sized offer should be a little higher? In another currency, say New Zealand dollars, you might not have seen a single deal. All in all, the decision on what rates to submit is, and always was, as much art and guesswork as science. As one trader I spoke to (under conditions of strict anonymity – nervousness about saying anything on this topic is still supremely high) explained to me: 'You'd be getting ready to submit and you'd know you could quite legitimately type in either 3.26 per cent or 3.27 per cent for three-month dollars. It was kind of a coin toss. It happened a lot. And in 2007 and 2008 it got way, way worse – things got so stressed that the range of possibilities was huge.' This ambiguous state of affairs, which emerged because a gigantic computerised derivatives market had coalesced around a relatively small and illiquid cash market, created the environment in which the scandal took root and grew.

The first type of manipulation that went on was, if ethically wrong, at least partly understandable. Derivative traders (whose profits stood to gain if LIBOR moved even fractionally their way, so large was their risk) cajoled their cash trading colleagues to exploit any ambiguity in the derivatives book's favour when submitting rates. I suspect that doing this didn't feel particularly dishonest to a submitter. Faced with deciding 'on a coin toss' whether to submit 3.26 per cent or 3.27 per cent, why not go higher if it would help? It's only one number in 150, the submitter might have thought, and if my submission is too high it will be discarded. Besides, LIBOR is an averaged number anyway – my submission will have only a

small effect. Further, he might have thought, some other bank must
have the opposite position to us – what happens if that bank's desk
submits a low rate? My bank may lose out if I don't go high. It was
another minor version of the Prisoners' Dilemma. Certainly, none
of those involved seemed to take much care to cover their tracks. At
Barclays alone, 'between January 2005 and May 2009, at least 173
requests for US dollar LIBOR submissions were made to Barclays'
Submitters'[7] – that is, on around one day in six someone tried to
coax a submitter into helping out. Each request was made on some
form of permanent electronic medium. The insouciance that was
displayed no doubt reflected a feeling that what was happening was
not really harming anyone. Maybe this feeling was correct. What I
say now may shock you, but if LIBOR manipulation had stopped at
simply tweaking rates within the bounds of the legitimate and plausible – possibly to be cancelled out by other banks' biases, possibly
to be discarded or, if not, definitely to be averaged – the real impact
on banks' customers would, in my view, have been extremely mild.

But that is not where it stopped. First, it is perfectly possible
(though difficult to prove in retrospect) that rates were submitted
that were outside what was a reasonable and valid range – they
were outright lies, in other words. Worse still, a few traders are alleged to have colluded with their rivals at other banks with the result that 'the risk of manipulation increased materially'.[8] By doing
this, a line was definitely crossed. Nobody could have believed that
this was a legitimate thing to do after even a moment's thought.
The swamp of ambiguity at the intersection of the new computerised world of derivatives and the clubby old world of cash lending
had thrown up behaviour that had mutated into downright deceit.
Most disturbing of all, there were allegations that, during the crisis,
several banks systematically entered LIBOR submissions that were
too low with the tacit – or even explicit – encouragement of banking regulators. Since LIBOR submissions measure borrowing costs
and higher than average borrowing costs could have signalled that

a bank was in difficulty, it is easy to see what the motivation could have been. Regulators have strenuously denied this, although staff (and, later, senior management) at the Federal Reserve were made aware of under-reporting by traders from Barclays in a phone call on 11 April 2008: 'There was um, an article in the *Financial Times*, charting our LIBOR contributions and comparing it with other banks and inferring that this meant that we had a problem raising cash in the interbank market,' the trader told the Fed. The consequence? According to the trader, submissions were made 'so we just fit in with the rest of the crowd, if you like . . . so, we know that we're not posting um, an honest LIBOR'.[9] It led to some questions being asked, but no action. Maybe because the fact that the LIBOR process was handled by a trade body like the BBA meant that submissions were – astonishingly – not officially a regulated activity at that time, or maybe because there were much more critical things for regulators and central bankers to worry about (like the potential collapse of the financial system), full investigation of LIBOR only really gathered pace after the crisis was over. Even in the future, after all the civil and criminal cases are complete, it is possible that we will never know the full story of what happened.

No Quick Fix

The fact that regulators had been distracted when doubts emerged about LIBOR seemed to make them even keener to act quickly when the next scandal broke. On 12 June 2013, Bloomberg reported that FX traders had been manipulating a widely used fixing called the WM/R.[10] When I read the article, sitting alone in my office on a cloudless summer's day, I felt physically ill. First, because I worried that, without my knowledge, the traders in my business had been involved. Second, because I knew what was coming – months of intensive and excruciating internal and regulatory investigation.

The article implicitly linked the allegations on FX fixings with the LIBOR scandal, but this ignored some very major differences between the two. The biggest difference is that, unlike LIBOR, the WM/R FX fix (calculated and published by the WM company and Reuters) is not arrived at on the basis of subjective submissions but rather by observing real deals in the FX spot market. Every hour, in the one-minute period straddling the hour mark (called 'the window'), the company automatically observes all the myriad of deals happening on EBS and a couple of other dealing venues and then takes the median of the prices at which it sees deals happening. Among all the fixings that are published, the 4pm London fixing (WMR11), has become the de facto market standard. When the Wheatley inquiry into LIBOR considered the question of how to improve LIBOR, the WMR11 FX fixing was, I am told, held up as an ideal of how it should be done.

But why have fixings at all? Like LIBOR, the answer lies in the market's desire for a standard. Back in the 1990s, pension funds and the like started holding much larger proportions of their assets in foreign bonds and stocks (indeed, this trend was the initial spur for the growth of the FX markets before the automation surge in the early years of this century). They needed to mark these foreign holdings to market and so required reliable FX rates at which to do so. But because FX markets are open 24 hours a day, there is no natural cut-off price to use as a reference. In this respect FX is like the money markets that spawned LIBOR and unlike equity markets that have an official close. Thus, the fixings were born. But they only really took off in importance when they were incorporated into global equity and bond indexes which – naturally enough, since they are global – track assets in multiple currencies. Once that happened, the fixings had a real impact on index-tracking funds since any FX deal that they did – but which was not done at the same rate as the FX fixings built into the index – would show up as 'slippage' away from their benchmark. Slippage was something to be avoided at all costs. And so, as a result, funds started to leave 'fixing orders' with banks' FX desks.

A fixing order is an order to buy or sell an amount of a currency pair at a published fixing rate. So, for example, a fund could call up a salesperson at 3pm and ask to buy €100 million versus US dollars at the 4pm fix. A few minutes past 4pm, when the fixing gets published, the salesperson would call back and tell the client at what rate he transacted. In the early days of fixings (mid to late 1990s) banks charged for the service. But, with increasing competition, and because the funds were important clients, the charge was gradually dropped and these days the service is provided free as a loss-leader. The funds love it – it costs them nothing and avoids slippage since they deal at the exact fixing rate. The spot trader who has to handle the flow, on the other hand, is put in a difficult position – what should he do with the order? He knows he is obliged to sell €100 million at the fixing rate, but when should he buy the euros back? If he buys them as soon as gets the order at 3pm he is at risk – if the euro weakens versus the US dollar in the hour before the 4pm fixing he will lose money on this purchase which he will then lock in by selling euros to the customer more cheaply. (Of course, if he is lucky he could win.) If he waits and buys the euros at 4pm in 'the window', so as to get his purchases as closely aligned to the fixing rate as possible, he will pay away bid-offer spread and get no spread in return from the client – an almost sure loss. In truth, because of this, industry-wide, spot traders and their managers generally dislike the fixing order business. It makes up a tiny proportion of any desk's total flow, takes time and care to process and makes little, if any, money. Nor, in contrast to LIBOR, do fixings facilitate a huge derivatives business. FX derivatives based on fixings are, and always were, a fringe product.

Despite all this, the Bloomberg article made a massive splash. Its accusations were stark. 'By concentrating orders in the moments before and during the 60-second window, traders can push the rate up or down, a process known as "banging the close", was one claim. 'Employees have been front-running client orders,' was another.[11] My colleagues greeted these charges with consternation. 'But that's total bullshit,' one trader told me angrily, 'if I hedge orders before the fix they'll say I'm front-running and if I hedge during the fix they'll say I'm "banging the close". What do they want? I can't win.' He had a point. But another accusation in the article made my blood run cold: 'Dealers colluded with counterparts to boost chances of moving the rates.'[12] Just like with LIBOR, there was no ethical grey area here – everyone knew that collusion was flat out wrong. Wrong, but potentially profitable, since it is easier to make money when you have more information about flows. And so, as a result of the article, at every major FX bank the dreaded process of investigation – familiar by now from years of LIBOR – ground into action: tens of millions of emails and electronic chat messages were scanned by arrays of powerful computers; teams of lawyers interpreted the suspicious ones then interviewed the authors; taped phone conversations were analysed. At last, in November 2014, the fines started coming. 'Traders at different Banks formed tight knit groups in which information was shared about client activity . . . [they then used] the information obtained through these groups to help them work out their trading strategies,' explained the UK's Financial Conduct Authority (the FCA) when announcing punishments.[13] The FCA was just the first to issue fines. To date, banks have paid out more than $10 billion for FX violations.[14]*

What part did computers play? In a very tangential sense, the environment of indexes, index tracking and FX fixes in which the misconduct took place would not have come into being without massive computer power. Certainly computers allowed a record to be kept of misbehaviour that may have gone on unnoticed in the past. But in my view the real part they played in this scandal was

---

* At the time of writing, Deutsche Bank has not been fined for FX misconduct by any of the authorities involved.

as a means of allowing traders to collude. Traders did so in art-lessly named multi-trader electronic chat rooms like 'The Cartel' or '1 Team, 1 Dream' hosted by data providers like Bloomberg. The transcripts of their conversations released by regulators are star-tling. Here is one excerpt as traders discuss whether to let a fourth trader into their three-man, three-bank club. Trader One: 'I trust you implicitly and your judgement, you know him. Will he tell the rest of his desk stuff or God forbid his New York?' Trader Two: 'Yes, that's a really important question. Don't want other [idiots] in market to know, but not only that – is he going to protect us like we protect each other against our own branches?'[15] My reaction to this, apart from a cold fury that these people traduced an industry where I spent much of my adult life, is shock that they were so contemptuous of their own teammates and that their real loyalty seems to be to their little 'cartel'. But perhaps the way they com-municated made it easier to think like that. In the past, communi-cating with people at other banks was a distinctly different activity from conversing with your colleagues. To speak to another bank you needed to pick up the phone. As a consequence, it was really rather impractical to get a group of three or four together during the working day; even now, arranging conference calls is an an-noying chore. That changed once multiparty chat rooms became commonplace. What's more, if you are used to communicating by electronic means all the time – and it was routine in the latter years of my career for people sitting within view of each other to email or send a chat message rather than actually speak – the differenti-ating boundaries between who is really on your team (your work-mates) and who is not (your cartel) become blurred. It is plain to see how this shift made collusion easier in practice. Did it also make wrongdoing easier to contemplate? It is certainly tempting to think that the anonymised, specialised, transactional nature of the entire banking system lowered the barriers to some people's wrongful or harmful behaviour. If the customers you harm are an abstraction (whether because they are hidden by layers of CDO complexity or by means of screen-based communications), does the harm you cause feel as bad? Has anonymity created a behavioural cousin of the baleful modern Internet-enabled phenomenon of trolling – abuse that would be impossible face to face? It seems to me that it has.

Ethics of Automation

The regulators' focus on the ethics at play in the still-human world of money markets and FX traders has now shifted to the world of computerised trading – naturally enough, since, as we have seen, the way algorithms work in various heavily automated markets like FX or equities grew out of the pre-electronic methods of human traders. But what was once considered acceptable – or even laudable – behaviour for human traders has become frowned upon. What's more, it is now thought even more problematic when machines do it. For example, take the practice of 'spoofing', which I described earlier in this book, whereby real bids or offers are held out by a trader in the broker market in order to mislead other traders as to the state of supply and demand when asking for a price. When I first started trading, the technique of the 'spoof' was taught to me as a basic skill – like signalling 'yours' or 'mine', dealing with an angry salesman, or getting brokers to buy you drinks. As long as I was prepared to honour the offer if someone called my bluff and paid it in the broker market, then all was fine. I was at risk. All's fair in love and trading.

These days, however, many (although by no means all) traders would feel uncomfortable and consider spoofing to be market manipulation since the intention is clearly to mislead. But, importantly, at no point has there been an actual regulatory change – it's just that trading culture has moved on. The ambiguity is even more pronounced in electronic markets. What is acceptable? The blistering speed and algorithmic nature of electronic trading allows a lot of strategies – like spoofing – that inhabit an ethical grey area. They may be permitted by the rules of the exchange or ECN but still feel scuzzy and benefit only those with the computational speed to post, and then cancel, spoof bids and offers before they can be traded on. The fact that computers are using these techniques to trick other computers is irrelevant. What's more, as markets become more automated the question is becoming of more than theoretical interest.

Currently, Navinder Singh Sarao, a 36-year-old British stock trader, is fighting extradition to the US where he is accused of causing the 6 May 2010 'Flash Crash' in which billions of dollars were temporarily wiped off equity markets. What is extraordinary is that he is alleged to have done so by spoofing the market using commercially available trading software from his bedroom in his parents' home in Hounslow, a West London suburb.[16] Somewhat belatedly, as a result of cases like this, exchanges and regulators are moving to clarify what is and is not allowed. The Chicago Mercantile Exchange (CME)*, for instance, issued 'Rule 575 – Disruptive Practices Prohibited' in September 2014. It specifically bans the practice of entering 'an order with the intent, at the time of order entry, to cancel the order before execution' and also 'messages with intent to mislead other market participants'.[17] No spoofing, in other words. Also banned is the practice of 'quote stuffing', in which thousands of bids or offers are submitted and cancelled in order to overload a trading site to the advantage of the stuffer. There are potential problems with what the CME has done – how 'intent' is defined, for instance – but at least they are trying.

Other regulators and central bankers are considering a bigger, longer-term and much more ambitious question: how should all electronic markets be designed to make them fairer? In 2013, the Federal Reserve Bank of Chicago (home of the CME) released an influential paper exploring the details of how this could be done.[18]

---

* Along with the Chicago Board of Trade, NYMEX and COMEX.

Its nine recommendations, although technical, amount to a manifesto to bring balance back to the markets so that traders willing to hold out bids and offers for a long time (tellingly, in the brave new automated world this means a second or so) are not disadvantaged by the microsecond speed advantage of computers. Most controversially, recommendation number five suggests that, instead of running continuous matching (where there is no constraint on the advantage offered by computer speed), trading venues 'should divide their trading sessions into discrete periods of one half second', whereupon, 'at a completely random time within each half-second period . . . the trade allocation algorithms should be run once'. This would mark a true counter-revolution in the way electronic markets work – microsecond tick-to-trade technology would be made almost worthless at a stroke. Needless to say, HFTs hate the idea. I have to say I rather like it since it will allow a much greater diversity of market participants – not just those with deep enough pockets to afford ultra-fast computers. What is certain, however, is that if regulators have concerns about electronic markets they will need to think at this level of detail when they set limits to banking activity. Fluffy 'principles' simply won't cut it in the face of exponentially increasing computer power and the brutal competition for survival it creates. Whatever rules are decided on in electronic markets, regulators will need to monitor them – the only practical way of doing so will be with computer power. But the changes in the banking industry mean that it is not just algorithms that will be continuously monitored by computers. People will be too.

Automating Ethics

It was Friday, 13 June 2014, my last day in the banking industry, and I was feeling a little below par. My retirement party had been held the previous night and a couple of hundred of my colleagues, former colleagues and friends had turned up at a nightclub that I had hired for the evening, close to the Deutsche Bank offices. A number of them, knowing of my love for the art of the 1960s and 1970s, had clubbed together to buy me a leaving present of a lovely aquatint by Howard Hodgkin – a gesture so touching that it brought tears to my eyes. The last of the stragglers left in the early hours of the morning; I was one of them. I confess that I struggled to focus on the administration I needed to do on my last day. The very last task I completed, aside from handing in my security pass, was dutifully to perform my daily check of my subordinates' emails.

The selection I needed to monitor was not random – a computer had picked out those emails and electronic chats that, based on secret algorithms and keywords programmed into it by our Compliance department, looked as though they could be suspicious. The idea was to stop further scandals but, although I knew it was necessary, it was a job I disliked intensely. It always felt like I was prying. Despite the fact that personal use of company email was discouraged, a decade or more of us all answering work emails on smartphones outside office hours and of shopping online during them had blurred the boundaries between the personal and the corporate to such an extent that people still did it routinely. I got to read all sorts of stuff. The surprise (but not the pleasure) I had shown when presented with the Hodgkin print had been entirely simulated; the system had been showing me the emails in which my friends had discussed what to give me for weeks beforehand. No doubt the computer felt that 'clubbing together' smacked too much of collusion. That day, as on all other previous days I had done the check in the months since the system's introduction, I saw nothing suspicious. After pressing the button to say I'd looked at that day's batch, I logged off my computer for the last time, then left to watch football on TV in a pub with my colleagues. The Brazil 2014 World Cup had just started; my career was over.

It is the central theme of this book that – because banks consist of very little other than people and computer systems, and because computers have grown, and are growing, exponentially in power – banking has been transformed. The pressures of competition have resulted in a gradual but inexorable and uncontrollable change wherever computer power has been able to upset the competitive balance: whether that is in a race to microsecond reaction times in FX or in the creation of the baroque derivative complexity that lay behind the Great Financial Crisis. Similar forces, set in gear by the scandals and their aftermath, are now driving the development of electronic surveillance in banks.

Although targeted email-checking by supervisors was a relatively new phenomenon as my career came to a close, having Compliance do it was not. Deutsche Bank started ramping up its electronic monitoring in 2006 since, in the words of a senior compliance officer at the time, 'we see it as prudent to monitor our risk to reduce the risk of breaches'.[19] In this, Deutsche was by no means alone. Traders had always been monitored – from the first day of my career at Merrill Lynch my telephone calls at work had been taped. The idea was to refer to them in the event of a dispute over the details of a deal. But the current work on surveillance is on a very different level of sophistication. Banks' motivation for all this is clear: they want to avoid more fines and to cut the gigantic legal bills that have been presented to them as a consequence of investigations. The size of the regulatory fines, which banks have little opportunity to diminish or appeal, has led to desperation to avoid more. As a senior manager of one of Deutsche Bank's rivals told me: 'We can't fight the fines – they're being imposed on us like reparations after a war. All we can do is stop another problem. We're blitzing it.' Worryingly, there is one aspect of the way fines are levied that could trigger a spiralling electronic surveillance arms race: it matters greatly how fast a bank discovers a problem because, in the EU and US (the major centres of finance), the bank that is the first to confess can have its fine reduced or set aside. UBS and Barclays both benefited from this in the LIBOR investigation.[20] It is the familiar Prisoners' Dilemma with billions of dollars at stake. The competition to be fastest is already under way.

Message surveillance has been the first big area for banks' efforts. I have heard it said that managers in banks tarnished by a scandal like LIBOR either knew what was going on – in which case they were criminals – or did not, which meant they were fools. But that ignores the difficulty of knowing about activities that happen over electronic channels, as was the case for most of the LIBOR manipulation. Even a manager of a relatively small business (30 people, for instance) would need to be monitoring tens of thousands of emails and chat messages each week and potentially a million or more in a year. A bank with tens of thousands of employees may have billions of messages. Among these, just one email can be fatal. This fact has prompted the use of automated checking that picks out suspicious-looking messages to be passed on to humans, much like the system I used on my last day at work. Making these filters quicker and more accurate is a goal of virtually every bank's Compliance department these days. But the search for speed hasn't stopped there.

JPMorgan, for example, following painfully large fines triggered by (among other things) its sales of mortgage bonds and FX misconduct, has invested heavily in surveillance technology that takes things one step further. Its goal? To catch offenders before they even do anything. The bank is proud of its advances and has boasted about them to Bloomberg. The system will take 'dozens of inputs, including whether workers skip compliance classes, violate personal trading rules or breach market-risk limits' and then, in the words of Sally Dewar, a very senior compliance staffer in JPMorgan, it will 'start to draw any themes about a particular desk or trader – the idea is to refine those data points to help predict patterns of behaviour'.[21] And it isn't just JPMorgan – the same Bloomberg article quotes the CEO of Digital Reasoning Systems

Inc. (a firm that includes Goldman Sachs and Credit Suisse in its customer list), whose company has a similar goal: 'If you want to be proactive, you have to get people before they act.' He goes on to explain, rather chillingly: 'We're taking technology that was built for counter-terrorism and using it against human language, because that's where intentions are shown.'[22]

It's very likely, though, that banks are getting sucked into a battle that they simply cannot win. Bankers' misconduct has been of two sorts. First, activities where the individuals involved didn't think they were doing anything unethical because there was a lack of clarity in the rules or because the practice was widespread. The self-serving but almost casual 'biasing' of plausible LIBOR submissions within a reasonable range would be an example. The second type is where the traders must have known that they had crossed an ethical boundary and went on regardless. This is characterised by much more furtive behaviour – for example, in the FX collusion conversation I quoted earlier, the concern about whether a new member would, 'protect us like we protect each other'. In making this distinction I am not saying that the first type of infraction is acceptable – just that the best means of eradicating it is not the use of increasingly high-tech 'counter-terrorism'-style surveillance but rather clarity and education. Clarity: what exactly are the rules and how are they meant to work? Not in principle but in detail. This is a job for regulators and for banks and it is a job that is being tackled. The process around LIBOR, for instance, has been overhauled: following the Wheatley report, submission is now a regulated activity; banks are segregating submitters from their derivatives staff; a massive process of education for all traders is under way. Similar clarity is being pursued in FX where – for decades – the rules of what was acceptable were vague and globally inconsistent. In doing all this, banks will be working with the grain for, despite a widely held view to the contrary, the overwhelming majority of bank staff, like the general public they are drawn from, are fundamentally honest and certainly do not want to engage in any activity that may lose them their jobs. I make this statement having managed hundreds of bankers over the years.

But, having also sat on disciplinary panels during that time, I accept that there will always be a small minority of bank employees who are less scrupulous. The problem that banks face is this: any employee who knows that an activity is wrong and believes that he is under surveillance will simply resort to greater and greater subterfuge. Company phone is being monitored? Use private phones or meet in person. Company email? Use private email or some other private messaging service. And then what should banks do? Should the banks' response be to insist on monitoring all employees' private phones and private emails? At some point, the regulators need to make it plain when a bank has done enough surveillance and when the burden of responsibility has passed to the employee alone who, if he insists on acting criminally, must be punished severely if caught. If regulators do not do this, and if the arms race in surveillance matches that in FX spot trading, the descent to absurdity will have started. In the course of the coming years it would not surprise me to see voice recognition applied to employees' phone calls; monitoring of their speech patterns for stress; even facial recognition built into the omnipresent rows of monitoring cameras suspended over every trading floor. Like inmates in a modern-day version of Jeremy Bentham's Panopticon, bank employees could become some of the most watched human beings on earth. As a Russian quant in his mid-twenties who worked with me in Deutsche Bank's London office put it: 'It's great. I was too young to be spied on under Communism, but now I have the chance to experience it under Capitalism. I guess you could say that's progress.'

CHAPTER 8

Das Ende! Das Ende!

The Death of Nuance

I have often heard it claimed that pre-crisis banking was, effectively, 'unregulated'. It is not true and it certainly did not feel true at the time. Finding out that the BaFin (Bundesanstalt für Finanzdienstleistungsaufsicht, Deutsche's regulator) was due to perform an audit on any business that I was running inevitably made me groan out loud. BaFin staff would descend in great numbers and were entitled to ask – and did ask – any question that they wanted to about the business. They could ask for organisational charts, profit and loss reports, balance sheet statements or computer system schematics. They could look in detail at analytic pricing models or at the minutes of meetings. Nothing was off-limits. My job, aided by a team of internal accountants from the finance department and of business managers (administrators dedicated to a business like FX), was to answer their questions as promptly, accurately and cheerfully as I could. It was nerve-racking. If I didn't answer adequately, or if the BaFin didn't like what I told them, a poor audit report was a potentially career-limiting event. All regulators, whether in Germany, the US, the UK or elsewhere, had similar powers and could, if they chose to, look at any aspect of a bank's operations. It was also no secret where the biggest changes in those operations were occurring: the massive growth in balance sheets and in the complexity of financial products prior to 2007 was a matter of public knowledge, not least because banks actually boasted about them. Much of the risk these changes caused was systemic and a consequence of the (computer-enabled) linkages between firms. To manage risk it wasn't enough for a bank to look at its credit exposure to another counterparty – it needed to figure out how that counterparty would fare if its counterparties failed, and so on. Practically speaking, this was (and is) a phenomenally difficult problem to solve, not least because the information needed is not available to any one firm. But it is available, or could have been, to banking regulators. Regulators, should they have wished to, collectively had the powers to understand the danger threatening the banking industry and the powers to alleviate it. Why didn't they?

I described in the first three chapters of this book how the competitive pressures within spot FX resulted in an arms race of computer speed. Once started, the race dragged market participants – both banks and funds – some willingly, some unwillingly, towards a new and very different world. It was a form of Prisoners' Dilemma – act or lose out. Something similar happened to regulation. Throughout the 1980s and 1990s, there was a gradual relaxation of banking regulation in the US – the world's biggest and most important financial market – culminating, in 1999, in the Gramm–Leach–Bliley Act that ended the separation of investment and commercial banking brought in by Glass–Steagall in 1933. As I have discussed before, this relaxation was accompanied by a merger wave in US banking. In a similar spirit, the Conservative government in the UK deregulated the City of London in 1986 in a series of measures dubbed 'Big Bang'. Later, in 1997, the incoming Labour administration created a new regulatory regime, the philosophy of which was principles-based regulation (PBR) or 'light touch'. The idea was that firms could best manage themselves within a regime based on principles, not detailed rules. But what was the underlying reason for all these changes? In a word: competition. As one expert commentator put it: 'Beyond the official rhetoric, there is also a clear subtext to much of the political debate. In the US–UK context, and to an extent in the EU–UK context, PBR is intimately

embroiled in a competition between regulators (and their governments) for business. There is no doubt that, at least at the rhetorical level, PBR is a weapon in the fierce battle for business between
London and New York.'[1] In other words, in terms of regulation, it
was an 'arms race to the bottom'. The concept of 'regulatory capture' is often invoked to explain this. The idea is that regulators,
dazzled by banks' brilliance or hoping for lucrative rewards in the
industry after they are all done with regulating, skew things in
banks' favour. There might be some truth to this, although I have
to say that I never got the impression that I had 'captured' the dozens of unsmiling visitors from the BaFin. To me it felt like the exact
opposite had happened. Instead I think there is ample evidence
that, at the time, regulators believed that 'light touch' was the right
course to take as matter of principle.

The chief intellectual architect of the US's all-important regulatory approach was Federal Reserve chairman Alan Greenspan,
whose unprecedented five-term tenure at the Fed between 1987 and
2006 corresponded almost exactly with the period of most frantic
change in the financial industry. Greenspan's view on regulation
was underpinned by a sweeping vision of the power of markets and
of enlightened self-interest – a vision revealed to him in his youth
by his 'objectivist', libertarian intellectual guru and friend, the author Ayn Rand, to whom Greenspan responded with 'the fervor of
a young acolyte drawn to a whole new set of ideas'.[2] It made him
profoundly suspicious of governmental interference with markets.
In July 1998, just weeks before the Russian default and the collapse
of LTCM, he gave testimony to Congress arguing against the attempt by the Commodity Futures Trading Commission (CFTC)
to impose regulations on over-the-counter (i.e. bilaterally, not
exchange-traded) derivatives: 'The Federal Reserve Board sees no
reason why these markets should be encumbered with a regulatory
structure devised for a wholly different type of market process.'
His reasoning? 'Professional counterparties to privately negotiated

contracts ... have demonstrated their ability to protect themselves from losses from fraud and counterparty insolvencies. They have managed credit risks quite effectively through careful evaluation of counterparties, the setting of internal credit limits, and judicious use of netting and collateral agreements.'[3] The market would sort things out, in other words.

Greenspan's faith in markets was widely shared. The idea that 'the market knows best' had been deeply embedded in the prevailing political orthodoxy in the UK and US and, to a lesser extent, the EU since the early 1980s. It was certainly a cornerstone of financial economics. In my time at business school, in the late 1980s, I was taught the rather elegant theory of efficient markets as gospel in finance classes. Built upon the decades-old observation that it was impossible to beat the stock market consistently and that past price activity gave no clue about future prices, efficient market theory held that asset prices embodied all available information – that they were, in a sense, 'right'.[*] The idea was that, if they were not, informed market participants would push prices to where they 'should' be in the face of uninformed 'noise traders'. In a way, it was an expansion of the idea underpinning the law of one price. But, instead of simply claiming that asset prices were correct if they were in conformity with other assets so that there were no arbitrages, it claimed that asset prices were right in and of themselves. Markets were self-correcting. Individuals may be klutzes, but the crowd was wise and rational. The people acted, en masse, as if they were perfectly informed and all-knowing: *vox populi, vox Dei*. The theory was taught as orthodoxy in every business school and economics faculty despite numerous worrying weaknesses in it: why were stock prices more volatile than you would expect based on the data that the market would use to derive them? How could the US

---

* To be precise, there are three 'flavours' of efficiency: 'weak' is when all past price information is embodied in prices; 'semi-strong' is when all publicly quoted information is reflected; 'strong' is when all information, public and private, is included.

stock market be correct at one price at the start of trading before the crash on 19 October 1987 and still be correct 20 per cent lower at the end of the day, in the absence of any significant new data?[4]

In a strange way, the fall of the Berlin Wall and the collapse of the Soviet Union at the beginning of my career reinforced the general faith in markets. One American colleague of mine at Merrill Lynch even went so far as to claim, on the subject of rational markets, that 'markets must be efficient because without them society fails – just look at Russia'. His leap of logic seems absurd but was, emotionally speaking, in tune with the widespread triumphalism of the time: Western free-market economies had just won the Cold War; the argument between state control and 'freedom' was thus seen to have been conclusively settled; and a popular and influential book even explained that we might be 'at the end of history'.[5] This, then, was the background to the regulatory environment that emerged. A widespread faith in the efficacy and inexorable 'rightness' of markets led, first from changes in the US, and then via inter-country rivalry, to a regulatory framework embodying the belief that professionals had, in Alan Greenspan's words, '[the] ability to protect themselves'. What is ironic is that the banking industry, in a reverse of the idea of 'the wisdom of crowds' that lay at the foundation of the theory of efficient markets, took a lot of extremely clever people and, collectively, as a mass, contrived to have us act like idiots. A simplifying idea (markets are right, rational and self-correcting) had been draped comfortably over the complex reality of an entire industry in much the same way as simplifications like VaR or credit ratings obscured the complex reality of risk. Maybe such thinking was just part of the zeitgeist? Is it a coincidence that the other great attempted simplification of unsimplifiable complexity – the euro – was implemented around the same time, with similar unpredicted and catastrophic results?

Shortly after the peak of the crisis, in October 2008, a humbled Alan Greenspan realised his error: 'Those of us who have looked to the self-interest of lending institutions to protect shareholders' equity . . . are in a state of shocked disbelief. . . . [The] modern risk management paradigm held sway for decades. The whole intellectual edifice, however, collapsed in the summer of last year.'[6] Watching a broadcast of him testifying to Congress on one of the TVs on the trading floor, it made me sad to see an old man publicly confront the death of his youthful faith, his life's work mocked by events. Then the chaos of business intervened and the moment was lost in a confusion of phone calls and a blur of numbers.

The dominant view of markets as self-correcting, inherently wise, inherently rational and, thus, ultimately stable (a view still held to this day, I would guess, by a large number of financial theorists and market professionals despite Greenspan's Damascene moment) is at odds with the somewhat messier picture of reality that I have set out. In the rational markets view, there is little room for the consideration of the effects of innovation (other than assuming innovation's contribution to greater 'efficiency'); little room for the feedback loops inherent in hiring policy or risk modelling; little room, or none at all, for the contemplation of bubbles or their collapse. But bubbles and collapse are what concern us here! The financial system is clearly *not* self-correcting and stable. I feel this viscerally: having lived through several so-called 'hundred-year storms' in the course of my career I should be as old as Yoda.

Banking is unstable and some economists, outside the mainstream, agree that it is inherently so. One of their inspirations for this view is the work of a maverick American economist, Professor Hyman Minsky (1919–96), whose 'financial instability hypothesis', built on the work of Keynes, states the heretical notion that modern economies financed by a modern banking system will inevitably experience bubbles and crashes without needing an external ('exogenous') shock.[7] Over a protracted period of 'good times', he asserts, capitalist economies naturally move from stability into a regime of speculative, 'Ponzi', pyramid scheme finance that

eventually collapses in on itself in a 'Minsky moment'. Although
he never lived to see it, the credit implosion of 2008 is the exem-
plar of such a collapse. Central to his argument is that bankers 'are
merchants of debt who *strive to innovate in the assets they acquire
and the liabilities they market*' [my emphasis], thus increasing the
stock of 'money' for speculation.[8] The process of innovation is
continuous. The one that I have described at length in this book,
where increasing computer power has destabilised parts of banking and driven it to the point defined by regulatory, or sometimes
even physical, limits is merely its most modern and most virulent
manifestation. Indeed, the Minsky pattern was clear as long ago as
the late 1850s. As one contemporary commentator put it: 'Within
the last 60 years, at comparatively short intervals, the commercial
world has been disturbed by a succession of those terrible convulsions that are now but too familiar to every ear by the expressive
name "panic". Each separate panic has its own distinctive features,
but all have resembled each other in occurring immediately after a
period of apparent prosperity, the hollowness of which it has exposed.'[9]

Whatever modern day regulators' views on the exogenous or
endogenous nature of financial crisis, like Greenspan they had all
been shocked by the panic of 2008 and by the chasm of hollowness
that it had exposed so painfully. Thus chastened, they set to work
to make sure such a crisis never happened again.

Regulatory Shock and Awe

'The good news is that your business is making money,' the young,
keen graduate recruit to the Risk Management department was
telling me at our regular, official weekly risk meeting in the autumn of 2013. 'But look,' he said as he pointed to a number on the
risk report I was holding, helpfully printed on a big sheet of A3 as

a gesture to my middle-aged eyesight, 'the bad news is that your Stress VaR has gone right up.' What? 'Well, if the books had looked like they do right now back in 2008 your guys would have lost a ton of money.' This was undeniably true, but it was not 2008; did we need to do anything? 'No,' he replied, 'we have to produce the number and I just thought it was interesting.' The meeting moved on. Stress VaR was the new computerised tool on banks' risk workbench. Its use was made mandatory under the third iteration of the Basel capital adequacy rules – Basel III. The idea, since regular VaR had failed so dismally, was to supplement it with this new technique. Stress VaR takes banks' risk positions on a trip back through time to see how they would have coped in prior meltdowns. It is hoped that this will make up for the acknowledged blind spot in VaR: it doesn't say what happens in the 1 per cent of times outside its methodology.

The roll call of historic scenarios that banks are required to test positions against is like a track list from the greatest hits album of the band Banking Chaos: 'the 1987 equity crash, ERM crises of 1992 and 1993, fall in bond markets in Q1 1994, 1998 Russian financial crisis, 2000 technology bubble burst, 2007/2008 subprime turbulence'.[10] It almost makes me nostalgic to write them all down. Whether or not the new technique will be any more effective than the old is open to debate. As one cynical colleague of mine observed: 'Running Stress VaR based on World War I is what the French did in the 1920s before they built the Maginot line.' Stress VaR, in other words, still relies on the future resembling the past. But Stress VaR is just one detail in Basel III, which, along with reams of new legislation in the US, EU and other OECD countries, is attempting to make the global banking system safer and more robust.

The core of Basel III, unveiled in 2010, is the requirement for banks to hold more capital against the risks they run. It replaces Basel II (designed in 2004 and partially implemented in 2008), which was made redundant by the crisis like so many employees of the banks it regulated. In gradual stages, until 2019, banks that comply (because their home government has made compliance with Basel III – technically a voluntary code – obligatory in law) will require total capital of 10.5 per cent of RWA. This is a rise from the 8 per cent of Basel I and II. That doesn't sound like much, but the rules are much stricter on what qualifies as 'capital', and the requirement to hold the most solid form of capital of all – common equity – goes from 2 per cent under Basel II to 7 per cent.* It is a genuine step change and banks have already responded. According to the BIS: 'Weighted average capital ratios for large, internationally active banks have risen from 5.7 per cent at the end of 2009 to 9.2 per cent at end-2012.'[11] What's more, 'retained earnings account for the bulk of their higher . . . ratios'. That is, not reduced lending, selling down assets or altering the balance of riskiness of the assets. Put simply, banks have been increasing their capital and behaving the way that regulators want them to.

But Basel III goes further than higher capital ratios. It also mandates a cap on leverage. This is another big step. Neither Basel I nor II said anything about leverage – the ratio of total assets to capital – but only about the ratio of capital to risk-weighted assets (RWA). By this measure, as long as the risk weighting of their assets was low, banks could load up on them to their hearts' content. Indeed, under the ancient and crude Basel I, some sovereign bonds had a risk weighting of zero, which technically could have meant infinite leverage if these had been banks' only assets. The problem – as was obvious in the crisis – is that sometimes the assessment of the riskiness of assets is incorrect: AAA tranches of CDOs turned out to be anything but low risk, for example. Now, under Basel III, the ratio of total assets to capital will not be able to exceed 33:1, regardless of the other, traditional, capital ratios. It is meant to act as a sort of risk backstop. In a similar way, Basel III introduces

---

* 7 per cent includes a 2.5 per cent 'capital conservation buffer' which is meant to be in place to prevent the real, absolute minimum of 4.5 per cent ever being reached.

minimum requirements for liquidity, so that banks must have sufficient funding in times of stress. One measure tests banks' ability to fund themselves for 30 days in an unpleasant scenario of severe funding pressure. Another specifies the minimum proportion of 'stable' funding that a bank holds; for example, retail deposits that tend not to be withdrawn in times of stress.

Regulators' efforts were not just confined to Basel III. In 2009, in Pittsburgh, the leadership of the G20 made a commitment to kill the bilateral web of derivative complexity that had spawned the crisis. Transparency would be assured by mandating that standardised OTC derivatives contracts must be traded electronically on exchanges and by forcing banks to report everything they were doing to a central 'trade repository'. What's more, they announced, these contracts must be centrally 'cleared' – that is, all the cash flows, and thus credit risk, should be washed through a so-called clearing house or Central Counterparty (CCP); for example, the CME or the London Clearing House. The CCP would stand between the two sides of every deal in a supersized version of prime brokerage. And what would happen to those deals that were not standardised and centralised? Higher capital charges and more margin would be needed in an attempt to make them uneconomic.[12] In 2012, the EU's European Market Infrastructure Regulation (EMIR) came into force to stamp the G20's commitment into law. In the US, in 2010, a part of the gigantic and sprawling Dodd–Frank Wall Street Reform and Consumer Protection Act did the same thing. It was regulatory shock and awe.

All of this set off a frenzy in banks. Desperate to avoid angering their regulators by failing to comply with the new rules, banks scrambled to make the necessary changes to their businesses. For most of the changes, that meant building new IT systems: the solution to a crisis created by computerisation was more computers. At Deutsche Bank, as at all of our rivals, many of our computer systems needed to be altered to talk to exchanges and to CCPs, and our risk and settlement systems needed to be able to report deals within minutes to the newly created 'trade repositories' – a task made more complex by the (maddening) fact that requirements in Europe and the US were incompatibly different. It was not a fun job. For the last few years of my career, for hours every week, I chaired meetings overseeing the process of change for the FX department. It was tedious stuff, and I wasn't even the one doing the real work. Hundreds of people worked full time on the project, which, as well as taking up huge quantities of IT department time, also altered the work patterns of every trading floor employee: how they talked to clients, made prices, booked deals. Happily, the bank was ready for the regulators' deadlines right on schedule, despite numerous scares.

The regulatory changes, however, did not stop at controls on capital adequacy, limits on leverage and decrees on liquidity, nor at the stricter rules on dealing, clearing and reporting of derivatives. Regulations were also introduced regarding employee pay. Based on the thesis that bankers' pay – in particular bonus pay – was kerosene on the fire of the crisis, restrictions were placed upon it. In the US, the emphasis was on deferring the payments for years and allowing it to be reclaimed ('clawed back') in the event of losses. In the EU, a cap was placed on the proportion of compensation that could be in the form of a bonus. This was either equal to an employee's salary or double his salary if the shareholders agreed. As a final salvo to show intent, the UK introduced a new offence of 'reckless management of a bank' – in section 36 of the Financial Services (Banking Reform) Act 2013 – punishable by up to seven years in jail. The message? The regulators meant business. No more crises.

A Trillion-Dollar Question

Are the new regulations sufficiently strict? It is clearly a step towards further safety that banks are being mandated to equip themselves with more capital as a buffer against loss. Ditto the cap on leverage.

But are these new minima enough? Regulators in many countries clearly think not, since 'Singapore imposes a 2 per cent surcharge over Basel; the Vickers proposals in the UK call for a 3 per cent surcharge; and Switzerland requires that its international banks hold an extra 6 per cent capital'.[13] One IMF economist calculates that 18 per cent capital to RWA is the right number, with a leverage of 9:1 – not 33:1[14]. A book by economists Anat Admati of Stanford and Martin Hellwig of the Max Planck Institute goes even further and suggests that banks move to a leverage of around 4:1 – which would mean a massive increase in the equity capital required for the industry.[15] In response to the expected objection from banks that this is impossible because equity is 'expensive' (since the returns it offers must be much higher than those on debt), the book's authors point out, quite reasonably, that this is a result of equity being risky. Furthermore, equity is particularly risky in highly leveraged banks because only a small decrease in the value of banks' assets would wipe it out. If banks had more equity, they say, it would be safer and thus the returns investors demand would be dramatically lower. It is a powerful argument and a bold policy prescription. Bold, but unlikely to be implemented, given the still considerable influence of the banking lobby and the daunting practical difficulties of implementation: trillions of dollars of extra capital would need to be raised or decades of earnings retained. If a radical step change in the amount of banking capital is unlikely, how safe are the current limits?

The method that is being used by banking regulators to answer this question is the annual stress test. These tests are first cousins to Basel III's Stress VaR but, instead of taking positions back through time, the regulators launch a made-up scenario at banks' overall risks and see how the banks would cope. In Europe, the tests are conducted by a small flotilla of regulators, with the European Banking Authority (EBA) taking the lead. The 2014 'adverse scenario' included the following: an increase in global bond yields; a deterioration of credit quality in countries with feeble demand; stalling confidence in public finances; and an increase in the bank's funding costs. Of 123 banks tested (70 per cent of European banking by assets), 24 failed by showing a predicted reduction in capital below the threshold set by the EBA.[16] In the US, a similar process, called the Comprehensive Capital Analysis and Review (CCAR) is carried out under the supervision of the Federal Reserve. So swimmingly did this process go in 2015 that banks were given the go-ahead to pay bigger dividends and to use cash to repurchase shares – up to 50 billion dollars' worth – thus slightly reducing, rather than increasing, their capital.[17] Although I think that doing stress tests is undoubtedly a 'good thing' since at least the right questions are being asked, I am profoundly unconvinced that, even if every bank passed every test, we can all sleep easy. The essence of financial crisis is that it is inherently unpredictable. We don't know what will cause the next one, or how it will spread. Nor do we know what type of panic will make the perception of banks' health, rather than the reality, the defining force of the new crisis (as it has been in all past crises). But what we do know is that complexity and its associated lack of transparency in the banking system allows this panic to spread. How effective, then, are the regulations aimed at reducing complexity and increasing transparency? The report card is mixed.

On trade reporting, even the Financial Stability Board (the body tasked by the G20 after the crisis with monitoring and making recommendations about the financial system) seems to have its doubts. As they admit in their 2014 update: 'While a majority of jurisdictions have introduced trade reporting obligations, the usefulness of this data in supporting monitoring of financial stability risks is limited by data quality issues'.[18] It's all a bit of a mess, in other words. Partly, this is because the various reporting regimes are incompatible. What data is needed in Europe is different from what is needed in the US – even for exactly the same deal. Partly, it's because the amount of data that needs to be submitted is ludicrous. Early in the process of making sure that Deutsche was ready to report on its FX deals, I was challenged by one of the senior people in charge of the IT project to guess how many data fields were needed to describe a trade of a regular, simple, plain vanilla FX option, the product where I started my career. 'Fifteen? Twenty?' I estimated after a bit of thought, trying to aim high. 'How about close to 140,' she told me as my mouth fell open. All told, what trade reporting will undoubtedly generate is a truly gigantic quantity of data. Whether it will lead to any useful information or, more crucially, any useful insight into systemic risk is less certain. In my view, trade reporting is a technological comfort blanket. It gives the appearance of something being done, but unless the right questions are asked of the data it will be worthless. Bear in mind that the information needed to diagnose the growing risk to the financial system prior to 2007 was readily available to regulators without the need for terabytes of minutely detailed trade information supplied by elaborate computer systems; all they needed to do was to ask banks the right questions.

Besides, the emphasis on technology might have another, subtle, but unintended consequence. The cost of complying with the new regulatory demands will, at the margins, make it less feasible for smaller firms to compete. As I pointed out when looking at the role of computers in the economics of banking mergers, the cost of a computer system is only weakly related to the size of business it supports. By imposing a fixed cost on all firms, elaborate regulatory requirements could easily lead to increased market share concentration; that is, fewer, bigger banks.

Concentration risk is also an unintended consequence of the requirement to clear trades. On the face of it, central clearing through CCPs looks like an unambiguously positive step. In place of the thicket of bilateral trades, central clearing ensures that all mandated trades are routed through a few easy-to-monitor locations. Although legal implementation of mandatory clearing rules is a little spotty around the world, in certain very important products it is becoming dominant. For example, in the largest derivative market of all – interest rate products – $169 trillion notional of trades is cleared. This is around half of all the notional of such trades.[19] In smaller markets, like credit products, the proportion is smaller but growing. But worries are starting to multiply about the effects of all of this. What would happen if a CCP failed? They face the same problem as a prime broker – if the counterparty on one side of a trade goes under, the CCP is still exposed to the other leg. CCPs collect margin in the form of collateral to offset the risk but that does not guarantee safety. The backstop for any losses they might suffer is provided by the banks that act as 'clearing members' – hence failure could propagate outwards into the banking system.

Research by Froukelien Wendt, a senior financial markets specialist at the IMF, addresses the issue that CCPs may become 'too important to fail' by virtue of their critical importance to a network of other institutions. The report on this controversial topic, which is prominently emblazoned with the warning that it 'should not be reported as representing the views of the IMF', concludes: 'Existing and planned measures reduce the probability of a CCP's default, but have yet to address risks arising from interdependencies and interconnections . . . [which] may pose a significant threat to financial stability.'[20] Put another way, the attempt to transfer risk to CCPs could simply have moved the problem of systemic risk to another location. It's as if a monstrous balloon has been squeezed in the middle only to bulge at the ends. This image shouldn't be thought of as applying just to clearing houses. If CCPs are one of the bulges in the balloon, another is the 'shadow banking' sector, which is made up of firms (like insurance companies, money market funds or hedge funds) that extend credit but are not banks and are not covered by banking regulations. This sector is extraordinarily large. According to the Financial Stability Board, 'shadow banking' assets globally reached $75 trillion in 2013 – about half as big as the entire global banking sector. Not only that, but the shadow sector grew at 7 per cent in 2013 whereas traditional banks' assets were unchanged.[21] This is leading some regulators to worry. 'There's a lot of pressure to regulate the shadow banking industry. It's a very difficult issue to figure out,' fretted Mark Flannery, the Securities and Exchange Commission's chief economist at a conference in April 2015. 'It's not clear at all to me that making the banks safer has made the economy safer.'[22]

So what else can be done? A huge amount of effort has gone into the current, well-intentioned if backward-looking and still incomplete regulatory framework; how can it be improved? I am not a regulator and I do not envy them their Herculean task, but here are a couple of suggestions for some extra measures aside from the already recognised need to focus extra attention on CCPs and shadow banking.

First off, establish a global team of regulatory 'cops on the beat'. Each trading floor or major office of each important enough bank or other financial player would have two or three or four regulators permanently stationed there. Their task would be to poke around in the belly of their institutions. They would be mandated to be informed of every meeting – from board level downwards – and have the automatic right to attend, to observe, and to ask questions at any of them. They could follow and monitor whatever they felt was interesting and call in reinforcements if something struck them as being amiss. Although they might be hired from the population of ex-bankers, banks would be forbidden from hiring them back to avoid any possibility of compromising their independence. The aim would not be to supplant the work done by other regulators, but rather to act as an early warning system. One of my eccentricities while doing my old job was that I insisted on sitting out on the trading floor rather than isolated in my comfortable glass office. My theory was that by walking around and hearing and observing what was going on, I'd have a better clue about the reality of the business than by reading reports. This is an amplified global version of the same theory. Human interaction would be substituted, in part, for the simplification of boiled-down risk measures and 'trade reports'.

How practical would it be? At least half of the regulators would need to be experienced (15 years or more, say) and could therefore be quite expensive. Globally, there would need to be a few hundred of them. If, for a start, the most important banks from the FSB's list of 'globally systemically important banks' (G-SIBs) were covered – a list that would include JPMorgan, Deutsche Bank, Goldman Sachs and other mega-institutions – it would amount to 11 banks.[23] I'd estimate 30 'cops' could cover Deutsche Bank, taking into account the number of major trading locations and offices in the bank. Maybe more would be needed for the behemoths of Citibank, HSBC or JPMorgan, maybe fewer for slightly smaller institutions. All told, let's say 400 would be needed for a first wave. Hired within the FSB to ensure a global coverage, the cost would be single-digit billions of dollars – expensive on the face of it but cheap relative to the huge costs of financial meltdown and relative to the gigantic combined resources of the multitude of governments that sponsor the FSB.

Second: a suggestion on the 'bank tax'. In 2010, the IMF, at the prompting of the G20, suggested that banks make a 'financial stability contribution' (dubbed the 'bank tax') to ensure that 'the financial sector could make a fair and substantial contribution toward paying for any burden associated with government interventions to repair the banking system'.[24] Subsequently the emphasis shifted towards measures that would fund the cost of any future intervention. Numerous schemes have been implemented or proposed: charges related to balance sheet size; 'bonus taxes' levied in proportion to discretionary pay levels; extra taxes on profits; a 'financial transactions tax' or 'Tobin tax' (after the 1972 suggestion by Nobel Prize-winning economist James Tobin) on every transaction.

In my view these levies all have a critical drawback in that they are only tangentially related to the risk, and therefore the real economic cost, created by the bank being levied. Charges based on balance sheet size ignore the capital strength of the bank. Transaction taxes either penalise institutions with large flows (but which may not be risky) or, ultimately, would be paid for by the public as end users of the service. Instead, I propose an 'option-based recapitalisation charge' (OBRC). The idea is this: the most common real backstop preventing a bank's failure is its home government's willingness to recapitalise it – that is, buy shares in it – in the event that the bank's share price collapses because the market believes failure is imminent. This is precisely what happened in 2007 and 2008 in numerous instances. The UK government's takeover of RBS is a classic example. Seen through the eyes of a derivatives trader, each bank that is 'too big to fail' is long a huge put option on its own equity granted by its own government. But there are two problems with this statement. First, the option is not explicit. In a crisis the government may step in (RBS) or may not (Lehman). This creates uncertainty and extra panic in a crisis. Second, the potential beneficiary of the option – the bank – pays no premium. The implicit option is free and therefore the unpaid premium is an undeclared subsidy from the taxpayer to the bank.

My OBRC proposal is to transact the option for real. Each year, a bank's home government would sell it an actual equity option. Banks under a certain size could be exempted. The strike of the option would be at a (low) share price determined in advance: maybe somewhere below the historic low or some small fraction of the previous year's average price. The notional of the option (that is, the amount of money the government would be on the hook for) would be calculated to be enough to recapitalise the bank to a minimum Basel III standard given the size of the bank's balance sheet and RWA at time of trade. The premium of the OBRC option would be calculated from observed mid-market prices for options with the same strike and tenor, albeit much smaller notional. The benefits of this scheme would be various. Since it would legally commit governments to recapitalise banks at a certain very low share price, it would make explicit and transparent what is currently implicit and murky, and it would raise money in direct proportion to the risk (or at least the market's best estimate of the risk) posed by each bank. It would also encourage banks to reduce their riskiness. As discussed earlier, the more heavily capitalised and safer a bank is, the lower its share price volatility should be.[25] Since option prices move in lockstep with volatility, this would feed through to a lower OBRC payment. There is also precedent for a scheme like this since it is a close cousin to the common practice of deposit insurance, via which governments guarantee small depositors' savings, a guarantee that is also charged for. Naturally, the more creditworthy the government is, the more valuable and credible the OBRC put option would be perceived by the market – which is precisely as it should be. At the very least, the amount of annual premium that should be charged under OBRC could serve as a useful benchmark for how much banks are paying via other levies. My own calculations show it to be similar in magnitude.

With or without my suggestions being followed (a low-probability outcome, I will concede), the essential structure of the new regulations is clear and is being implemented – but what about the banks themselves? Have they changed? To what extent are the forces that pushed them to the regulatory limits still in operation?

Marvellous Minsky Machines

I have argued in this book that the combination of rapidly increasing computer power and tooth-and-claw competition were central to the development of modern banking and were tied up inextricably with the developments that led to the 2007–8 crisis. Let me reiterate my argument.

During the 1990s and 2000s, as computers became steadily faster and cheaper, banks, under commercial pressure to maintain profitability, developed a vast array of more and more complex derivative products. Freed from the need to solve the problems of pricing and the calculation of Greeks by means of exact analytical solutions (exemplified by the brilliance of Black–Scholes), each incremental advance in computer power allowed a corresponding increase in complexity. The process of invention of derivatives was 'democratised' by the widespread use of analytic packages available from within spreadsheets on salespeople's and, latterly, structurers' desktops. At the level of a business within a bank (like FX, or mortgages, say), sophisticated risk management systems allowed traders to see their risk more quickly and more clearly and, just as better seat belts and crumple zones in cars encourage drivers to increase their speed, this made traders more comfortable taking risk. At the level of the bank, powerful computers allowed techniques like RAROC and VaR to summarise risk in ways that seemed scientific and rational and which had a similar risk-enhancing effect on bank size and leverage. Very similar methods were also used by ratings agencies – again utilising rising computer power – to assign ratings to literally incomprehensible products. At the level of the market, computers' ability to handle the routine bookkeeping of hundreds of thousands of deals split between multiple counterparties allowed risk to be cut and diced and smeared over the entire globe, destroying transparency. Advances in telecommunications, on the other hand, made the world seem smaller and the task of managing complexity seem easier.

Overall, then, the use of computers did two dangerously contradictory things: it made the underlying reality of financial markets much more complex, risky, fragile, interconnected and intractable to analysis and yet, at the same time, it made markets seem simpler and more amenable to control to the people within banks. It was this widening chasm – a 'risk perception gap' – between the reality of growing, uncontrollable, unfathomable complexity and banks' illusion of control that ultimately ended in disaster.

I admit that this argument is a simplification. Naturally, the effect of the usual suspects – economic growth, central bank rate policy, compensation structures and the like – was also important. So too was a regulatory environment that set limits to this process that were not strict enough. But the role of technology was vital. I have asked colleagues of mine who doubt this to consider a thought experiment: imagine that computer technology had never moved on from its state in 1990. Would the 2007–8 crisis have been possible? I believe the answer is no. The complexity, leverage and size of the banking industry that caused such problems in 2008 would not have been possible with the computers of 1990. I concede that some other, different, probably less severe and less computationally intensive crisis might have happened instead, but the crisis of 2008 needed the computers of 2008.

What is really interesting about this story is what we humans were up to, especially when it comes to understanding how banking may evolve in the future. How did the gulf, born of technology, between reality and illusion come about? Why did bankers believe the illusion? What behaviours changed? How did banking culture contribute? I have already explained my suspicion that the anonymity of banking might have altered the industry's ethics – how about its attitude to risk? One ex-colleague, when I interviewed him for this book, remarked sadly that 'we all started to believe the computers'. I understood what he meant. When I was at university, a fellow student had, as part of a project to design an oil refinery, submitted a design for a distillation column 300 metres high and about 2 centimetres in diameter. When asked why he had not questioned something so blatantly absurd, he responded querulously that he had used the design software provided and that was the answer it had given him. It was my colleague's view that similar behaviour was commonplace in finance. But when I pressed him on whether he, himself, had blindly trusted the output of his models and risk systems he hotly denied it. He had been in the markets for years and knew better. Rather like Darren and I knowing full well that the real risk of our Russian business could not be as low as it had been calculated, he was experienced enough to appreciate the truth, he said. His claim was that others had been naive and trusting, not him.

The pejorative name used in the markets for a trader who acts in this way is 'model dope' or 'F9 monkey' (after the command in Microsoft Excel used to recalculate a spreadsheet). Some academic studies into the culture of finance dispute the existence of such traders: 'Model dopes are invoked routinely in public discussion of financial markets . . . However, empirically it is far from clear that model dopes do exist: the contributions to the nascent social-studies-of-finance literature on modelling that have addressed the issue have all failed to find them.'[26] But I am not quite sure how academics hope to capture so illusory a quarry since it is impossible to find out what people believe simply by observing their actions. Maybe they attempt to find model dopes by interviewing traders? 'Are you a naive user of computer models who believes everything they spit out at you?' 'Yes, I am' (researcher smiles meaningfully and scribbles a note on a pad). It's an unlikely scenario, in my view. In the same way that virtually all drivers believe that they drive a car with a better than average level of skill, I suspect virtually every trader believes that he appreciates the reality of risk better than his computer models and, even if he thought otherwise, he would be loath to admit it. Indeed, the evidence of my own career leads me to think that my colleague was onto something. Not only was there naivety, but there also existed a mechanism to concentrate it where complexity was highest.

As a trader, I got better with age. This is also true of every trader I have managed. The reason is simple and obvious – the more you trade (assuming that you don't blow up and get fired) the more you learn both about markets and about the limitations of models. By reverse logic, the less time under fire that the traders on a particular desk have, the greater the chance of the 'model dope' problem occurring. A general pattern in the businesses that I ran was that the more heavily mathematical the product, the younger and less experienced the traders. There were a couple of reasons for this. The first was that, paradoxically, the simpler the product, the trickier it was for a new trader to pick it up. Back in my time at Merrill Lynch, I was a passably competent FX options trader almost from the very start, but I struggled in the – superficially simpler – world of spot. No theoretical knowledge could help much in voice spot trading; success was pretty much down to pure cunning. This cunning was expensive to acquire while competing with hardened veterans. At Deutsche Bank, years later, I similarly found it very difficult to find and train graduate spot traders whereas, at the other end of the complexity spectrum, the Complex Risk team was more or less exclusively staffed by people from the graduate pool. In the middle ground (in terms of complexity) of vanilla options or forwards, the staffing was a mix of new blood and old veterans. The other reason that more complex products were the responsibility of less experienced traders is that the products were newer. For any manager trying to build a new business, bright young graduates were the quickest – and cheapest – way to assemble or grow a team. Do not imagine, though, that this was a process started in the mid-2000s or one that was unique to that period; in a milder form, the pressure had always been there. For example, I had been part of the same trend when, years earlier, in my first trading job, I was hired (with absolutely no experience whatsoever) to trade FX options at Merrill Lynch. Back then the product was hot and new and the few already knowledgeable people in the market who could conceivably be hired in my place were unavailable or very expensive. As a result, Loic and his bosses had decided to 'make their own' and my career got under way.

Due to the extravagant intensity of the interview process, the graduates we bankers hired in the build-up to the crisis were all extremely bright and capable but were, in some vital ways, surprisingly uniform. An awful lot of them were from technical, numerical subjects: physics, engineering, maths, computer science, economics and the like. Many were specialists in mathematical finance. Historians, philosophers and English graduates were rare beasts. The prospect of seeing a new version of someone like Bev, the FX saleswoman I met early in my career who ascended to seniority on the trading floor from a starting point in the back office, was practically zero. What had happened was that within the banking industry a powerful cultural feedback loop had been created. Finance, fuelled by computational power, grew more complex and mathematical. Therefore, technical people were needed and were duly hired through a process weighted in their favour by virtue of the type of people interviewing them. Having been hired, they, in turn, whether by force of commercial pressures or expectations, or simply because – being a bit geeky – they thought it was cool, dreamed up yet more complexity. Thus the feedback continued. And where was the hottest place for these graduates to end up? They fought to go to the asset businesses that became the centre of the crisis. (To avoid any accusation of hypocrisy at this point, I fully admit that in my own way I was an enthusiastic part of all this – whether pressing ahead with automation in FX, creating new products in FX or Commodities, or hiring technical graduates. The culture was all-pervasive.) But if the process of hiring and assigning graduates tended to mean that the least practically experienced and intellectually most uniform traders ended up in the most complex product areas – thus widening the gap between real and perceived complexity at the lowest level of seniority on banks' trading floors – what of management?

Chain of Command

Managers are, almost by definition, more experienced than the people who report to them. It seems reasonable to think that they should not have been fooled by the perception gap. But what if the managers in complex products were, themselves, lacking enough experience? There is an obvious way that this could have come about, industry-wide. Fast-growing businesses built around new products very often rely on managers promoted from within. If the pool of traders to choose from is inexperienced, their managers will be too. Indeed, it seemed to me that when I met my manage-rial peers from the fastest growing businesses they were very often significantly younger than me. Sunil was a good example. I was a representative of the relatively staid world of FX where greybeards in their forties could be found; he came from the rocketing, shiny new world of credit trading. 'I am going up for a meeting with Credit,' one of my FX colleagues once told me, wearily, 'Land of Boy Wonders.'

The real problem, however, was not youth, as such. The benefit of having experienced managers is that they have lived through more economic cycles, crashes and disasters (or near disasters) than their teams. At Deutsche Bank, in the managerial years of my career, I was cautious about my teams' risk because of my brush with Russian catastrophe in 1998 and because of my vivid memories, from the ERM crisis in 1992, of how shockingly quickly markets can explode into chaos from positions of tranquillity. As I scanned risk reports, I was always figuratively looking for the escape routes. My colleagues occasionally teased me for this tendency: 'Not bashing on about Russia and LTCM again are you, Kev?' But the world of CDOs and structured credit had developed so quickly (a curiosity in 2000; gigantic and dominant by 2007) that – some wobbles aside – no one in it, trader or manager, had seen the market really crater. The collective memory of past crises was not available to contradict the computers' optimistic output. There was a blind spot. As an aside, a worryingly similar trend could be occurring right now in the markets where 30 per cent of all traders on Wall Street (average age: 30) have joined the industry since 2008 and have known nothing but zero interest rates.[27] I am keeping my fingers crossed.

Besides all this, there was another, subtle way that computerisation allowed an increasing gap between real and perceived complexity and risk. As banks grew, there was increased specialisation within them. For example, any trader within Deutsche Bank who wished to transact FX (an equity trader using FX to hedge a stock position held in a foreign currency, say) was obliged to deal internally with the Deutsche Bank FX department. The entirely plausible idea behind this was that we specialists would do a better job of managing the risk and that by 'internalising' the flow (which might match off against trades from another part of the company), the bank, as a whole, would pay less bid-offer spread to the outside market and thus make more profit overall. This approach was made much easier by computerisation – in this specific case, giving Autobahn, the FX trading system, to anyone in the bank who needed it. Identical rules were common practice among our rival banks, too. In a similar way, when we in the FX department wished to reduce the credit exposure that we had to a particular client, a specialist desk within FX, set up for this purpose, would buy protection via a CDS on that name from the bank's credit derivatives people. Our risk systems had been altered to make this possible. We in FX were now hedged and expected an internal 'insurance' payment in the event that the client defaulted. What the credit people did afterwards with the risk they had assumed on our behalf was not our concern. Once again, this was a common strategy at all our main rivals. The net effect of all of this was to make banks more efficient as they scaled up, but also more fragmented. Each business could concentrate on its own risk specialism and, by hedging internally, more or less ignore all other risk. Psychologically speaking, each desk became an island, entire of itself.

In theory this didn't matter, for at the apex of each bank sat the board and CEO aided by the Risk Management department with its array of computerised risk measurements. They could see every risk. The problem was that, given the growing size and complexity of banks, senior management necessarily saw everything through a distorting mirror of simplified, boiled-down abstractions like VaR. Despite most banks' board members' wealth of experience (Dick Fuld, for instance, CEO of the doomed bank Lehman Brothers, had started trading in the late 1960s), they were cut off from the day-to-day reality. In my entire time at Deutsche Bank, I can recall only one visit to our trading floor from CEO Josef Ackermann. It was as tightly organised as a visit by royalty and, as I imagine would be the case with a member of royalty, a burly and unsmiling bodyguard was at his side at all times.* Herr Ackermann was charming, engaged and curious about the FX business but, naturally, could only glean a superficial gloss on things. This is absolutely not a criticism of him: given the complexity of Deutsche Bank (dozens upon dozens of countries, business units and trading floors, staffed by tens of thousands of employees) what else was feasible for one man? At our bigger rivals like Citigroup, say, the problem was doubtless even more acute. Size created remoteness; remoteness made abstraction and simplification necessary. In turn, the comfort provided by abstraction was the gateway to more growth and to ballooning size across the banking industry.

---

* This was by no means a vanity or extravagance: in November 1989 a previous Deutsche Bank CEO, Alfred Herrhausen, had been murdered in his car by a roadside bomb. No one has ever been convicted of this crime although the terrorist group the Red Army Faction was the prime suspect for some time.

But you should not get the impression that a simplified measure like VaR was accepted naively. Everyone knew its theoretical limitations. Indeed, Deutsche Bank's annual report for 2007 contained a lengthy section entitled 'Limitations of our proprietary risk models' which could be used as the basis for the prosecution case against VaR.[28] As well as warning investors of the potential unreliability of using the past to predict the future and of a host of other technical weaknesses, it included the observation, soon to be demonstrated in deadly earnest: 'The use of a 99 per cent confidence level does not take account of, nor makes any statement about, any losses that might occur beyond this level of confidence.' But what good did this theoretical understanding really do? Similar statements were included in the annual reports of all our competitors. Certainly they were in those issued by UBS, a bank which nevertheless contrived to lose $42.8 billion in sub-prime by September 2008 and which was described by its regulator as 'not aware of the extent and the nature of its exposure to the Subprime and related markets until August 2007, and . . . thus unable to take appropriate measures in a timely manner'.[29] Those two words, 'not aware', are the most chilling. For, despite honourable exceptions (my Deutsche Bank colleague and mortgage expert Greg, for one), the entire banking industry seemed 'not aware' of the danger it was in. From my vantage point on the island of FX, I confess that I certainly was not. At all levels of their huge organisations, the computerised, specialised, technocratic nature of banks blinded them to the peril.

In my view, then, it is clear what the path to the next crisis would have been for the banking industry if it had been allowed to return to business as usual following the convulsions of 2008; just as it had been – albeit with some minor tweaks to the rules – after the near miss in 1998. In a hypothetical world after 2008 where regulators, despite having a nagging feeling that this was a foolish course of action, simply allowed banks to carry on as before, it is overwhelmingly likely that in time we would have experienced some form of 'Super-2008'.

At first, following the crisis, banks would have licked their wounds, but sooner or later the old machinery would have creaked into operation. No doubt there would have been widespread up-grades to risk models to incorporate the lessons of the crisis (all the lessons, of course, bar the eternal one that the future doesn't necessarily resemble the past). Banks' lending policies may have been altered at the margin. But I am sure that, after an interruption, the rise in product and market complexity would have continued as before, spurred by a steadily rising level of computer power. (As one ready-to-hand example of this continuing rise, my iPhone, if linked to the Internet, has the ability – without laborious 'training' – to parse human speech almost completely accurately in real time. This is a trick requiring such computational intensity that it would have seemed almost magical as little as five years ago. The same rapid improvement is happening in corporate computing.) A flood of new recruits would have arrived – no doubt in the most complex areas. Leverage, driven by competition, would, I'm sure, have been taken to the limit again. Where the eventual trigger for the next Minsky moment would have occurred, and how many years it would have taken to get to it, is a matter of pure speculation. Would it have been another property-related crash? It is tempting to think so, since property is a gigantically important asset class. If you are lucky enough to have accumulated any wealth in your lifetime it is likely that a large part of it is stored in the value of your home: the total market value of housing in the US in 2014 was around $22–4 trillion, the same order of magnitude as the value of all privately held paper financial assets, or approximately 150 per cent of GDP.[30] Ratios are higher in other countries, such as the UK. Or maybe it would have been another emerging market crisis like Asia in 1997 or Russia in 1998?

Although the shape of a potential future crisis would have been relatively easy to predict if the banks had gone back to business as usual, in the new world created by the regulatory step change after 2008, it is much less apparent. Could the next 'banking crisis' instead be a CCP crisis, or a hedge fund crisis, or an insurance company crisis? Will it be triggered by property prices or by emerging markets or some new risk? For my own part, I worry about geopolitical strife causing problems – especially if they arise from tensions with the nascent economic superpower of China. But, if I'm honest, I will admit that I really have no idea. But nor, I am absolutely sure, does anyone else: not regulators, not politicians, not senior bankers. One prediction I am willing to commit to paper is this: when the next crisis comes it will come – shockingly – from some part of the financial machinery that, although obviously risky in retrospect, was not thought so in the build-up to the crisis because 'this time it is different'. The search for extra yield will no doubt be to the fore. Needless to say, given the message of this book, I am sure that complexity caused by computer power will also be heavily implicated.

'Waiting for the End of Banking'

If Minsky was right and if, as I claim, the forces propelling the finance sector to greater riskiness are still present, there is one possible course of action that some have proposed and which is still open to society. Should banks be broken up and made smaller? This is a controversial issue. In part it is controversial because there is no very clear relationship between size and failure. In the 2007–8 crisis, some large banks failed (Citigroup) while others (JPMorgan Chase, HSBC) did not. The related issue of whether to allow banks to combine investment banking with retail banking is also cloudy for the same reason: the three large banks just mentioned all have this 'universal banking' model. Similarly, some 'pure play' investment banks went under but others survived (Lehman and Bear Stearns versus Goldman Sachs, say). Ultimately success or failure seems to have come down to managerial competence or plain luck rather than the banks' business models. Regardless, regulators have made a somewhat half-hearted attempt to mandate more separation of investment and retail banking without resorting to a 21st-century version of Glass–Steagall. Within the Dodd–Frank bill in the US the 'Volker rule' bans proprietary trading by deposit-taking banks. In the UK, the Vickers report recommended that banks' retail activities be 'ring-fenced' from any investment banking. Similar proposals are included in the 2012 Liikanen report into EU banking. My own view is that a full separation would be a good thing and that banks should be smaller. As an IMF report (once again hedged with disclaimers that it 'does not necessarily represent IMF views or IMF policy') puts it: 'Large banks tend to have lower capital, less-stable funding, more market-based activities, and be more organisationally complex than small banks. This suggests that large banks may have a distinct, possibly more fragile, business model.'[31] To me the key is organisational complexity as banks become 'too big to understand'. If banks are relying on managerial competence to close the risk perception gap and keep them safe, it will be easier to find such competence if the task of running a bank is less complex because it is smaller. The same goes for the combination of retail and investment banking, since few CEOs will have had long experience of both these aspects of the business; normally, they will have come up through the ranks in one of them. Simpler, smaller banks may have fewer economies of scale (a fact that prompts the IMF report to observe that '"optimal" bank size is uncertain') but they would be easier to run and would create a smaller crater if they blew up.

In recent years, banks appear to have begun to agree, at least in part. The commitment to the idea of the one-stop shop has waned and bank after bank has attempted the difficult task of simplifying its business. JPMorgan, for example, has ceased to provide student loans or identity theft insurance and has sold its physical commodities business.[32] HSBC's CEO Stuart Gulliver has 'told colleagues he will redouble efforts to make Europe's biggest bank "simpler and smaller"' – including a retreat from Brazil and Turkey, two growth areas under the previous CEO.[33] My own ex-employer, Deutsche Bank, has carried out similar moves.

One of these moves was to close down the biggest part of its Commodities unit, just as JPMorgan had done. I was tangentially involved in this decision because – despite the fact I was no longer in Commodities – my advice had been sought on certain details of the closure since I had spent a chunk of my career building the business years earlier. Like so many of the divestment decisions announced by banks, the motivation was primarily economic. Under the new regulatory regime, especially under the new Basel capital requirements, the returns from being involved in commodities simply didn't stack up – a fact that was publicly acknowledged by Deutsche Bank at the time.[34] The day of the closure announcement, a gloomy, freezing, grey Thursday in December 2013, was one of the most painful of my career. Apart from the obvious numb disappointment I felt that a business I had helped to build was to be dismantled (all those thousands of hours of meetings, now worthless), what hurt most was that a number of friends were laid off: while some appeared resigned to what had happened, some were angry, others in tears. But the story didn't end on that day. In the months that followed, I began to realise that it wasn't just the human cost of closing businesses that made it difficult to do – it was just difficult to do, full stop. Closing down a business is a complex matter. Books of deals need to be sold off but, if they cannot be (maybe because of their peculiar legal structure or some other wrinkle), they must be held and run to maturity. For long-dated derivative deals this means that the computer systems and support staff needed to administer them must be kept in place, sometimes for years. As an operations manager joked to me about one complex set of deals that he would need to look after (echoing the words of Slade's Noddy Holder about his band's perennial Christmas number one): 'To you it's just a derivatives book; to me it's a pension plan.'

Actually, Commodities is a relatively easy place for a bank to trim its size since the unit usually stands apart from more mainstream activities. Core businesses, on the other hand, especially those that have existed for some time, become almost inextricably linked into the rest of the bank. You cannot just turn off their supporting computer infrastructure because other remaining businesses rely on it, often in surprisingly subtle ways. Computer systems, ironically enough, regularly seem to put up more of a fight for their career survival than the people who use them. As a result, costs are hard to kill in banks. For all their efforts and talk of simplification, banks' progress towards a more streamlined model has been slow. Take, for example, the number of legal subsidiaries that banks have. According to official filings, banks in the US have made very little progress in reducing the number of their subsidiaries, which, for the biggest banks, amount to thousands of entities. JPMorgan, for instance, has 3,400. Often they exist in multiple layers of legal interconnections.[35] What this all means is that, in the event of a bank's failure, just as was the case for Lehman Brothers, it would be immensely difficult to figure out who was owed what – how to 'resolve' the bank, in technical-speak. Computers have made it easy to create complexity in banks; they have also made it difficult to eradicate.

But, ultimately, banks may be forced to change not by dint of regulation but by the predatory intentions of a swarm of new, computer-powered competitors that are attacking the most vulnerable and the most profitable parts of the banking business. Stripped to the essentials, banks provide society with five main services: they keep people's and companies' assets safe; they allow these assets to be transferred to others; they transform risk (lending long term versus borrowing short term, say); they provide liquidity; and they provide advice for a fee (M&A advisory, for example). Each aspect of this quintet is under threat. In my old field of FX, for instance, where banks have completely dominated the provision of spot liquidity for decades, the beginning of the rise of a new breed of competitor can be discerned. Coming in at number 34 in the 2015 *Euromoney* FX poll was the market-making spin-off (called XTX) of hedge fund GSA – the first time a hedge fund has become visible in the rankings.[36] Hedge funds were always customers of banks and took proprietary risk, but they have now turned into outright competitors in the realm of market making. Many of these firms are staffed by ex-bankers who have either been laid off or who have deliberately left banks to pursue potentially lucrative new careers – an unintended consequence of the tight regulation of banking pay.

In retail banking, too, new competitors are emerging. In the UK, in June 2015, the Bank of England approved Atom Bank as the first ever purely digital lender. Based on a mobile smartphone app, with no branch network at all, its aim is to let consumers 'have a bank in their pocket that is ready whenever and wherever they need it'.[37] In the lucrative field of payment services, new competitors like PayPal are nibbling at one of the banking industry's biggest revenue pools – around 43 per cent of all its revenues according to management consultancy firm McKinsey.[38] In all these cases, the new competitors have one critical advantage – they are not shackled to a vast, fragile network of ageing legacy systems which are difficult and expensive to upgrade and are thus becoming unreliable. Banks often do have these shackles: one very visible sign of this is that embarrassing failures of retail banking systems are becoming more and more common. One such failure (RBS/Ulster Bank in 2012) prompted a Bank of England regulator to observe: 'I feel we are a very long away from being able to sit here with confidence and say that the UK banks' IT systems are robust.'[39] Banks are vulnerable and some of their potential competitors are no longer tiny start-ups but gigantic technology firms like Google or Apple with huge resources. '[Banks] did create online banking,' observed Philip Bruno, a senior partner in McKinsey's Global Payments Practice in the *Forbes* article about payments referenced above, 'but they did it at banking speed. Now they have to operate at Silicon Valley speed.' This is supremely worrying to the most thoughtful senior bankers.

These worries were made plain to me when I had drinks with Mike (not his real name), a senior technologist in a large bank, in the course of researching this book. 'Banks used to be at the cutting edge of technology,' he said quietly in his understated Californian way, 'but we simply aren't any more.' If banks are just 'people plus computers' and if the computer systems are becoming more important, it is no longer the banks that are the best at creating them. There are bigger and better technology players. He smiled conspiratorially: 'Secretly, inside banks, what we are planning for is the collapse of the banks. We're waiting for the end of banking.' At this, an image of the god Wotan, slumped and resigned to his demise surrounded by the flaming ruins of Valhalla, popped un-bidden into my opera-lover's mind. Mike was most likely being as melodramatic as my mental image; I think banks will still have a long run yet.

But what is true is that the same technologies that are under-mining the traditional roles of banks could have a more radical and profound effect. Using computer power, the new competitors are not just limiting themselves to doing what banks have always done in better, faster and more convenient ways – they are also striking at the very heart of what banking means. Innovations like the virtual computer-generated currency Bitcoin are taking the monopoly of the creation of money away from governments and, with them, the banks that serve them. Online peer-to-peer funding initiatives like Prosper, LendingClub or Zopa enable individuals to lend directly to other individuals without going through the intermediation of a bank. Similar technological efforts – dubbed crowd-funding – are democratising the raising of equity capital for start-ups. The break-up of a traditional banking model clearly comes with risks. Who will regulate the new world and how will they do it (since leaving systemic safety purely to the market is an idea which, it seems, is definitely past its time)? On the other hand, the transition provides the opportunity to migrate to a more decentralised and possibly more robust banking model. It is early days for all of this, but it seems to me that competition and computers, the very forces that helped create the innovative but dangerously concentrated and fragile state of the banking industry in the late 20th and early 21st centuries, may well turn out to be the cause of its gradual, benign destruction in the future.

If this happens, computers will have eaten banking once again.

Appendix 1: *Euromoney* FX Survey – Market Shares 1996–2015

Ranking 1996	Ranking 1995	Bank	1996 Estimated share (%)
1	1	Citibank	9.10
2	N/A	Chase	9.04
3	3	HSBC/Midland	6.50
4	7	NatWest	4.90
5	8	J. P. Morgan & Co.	4.22
6	5	Union Bank of Switzerland	3.53
7	11	Barclays Bank	2.98
8	6	Bank of America	2.81
9	**22**	**Deutsche Morgan Grenfell**	**2.78**
10	9	SBC	2.59
11	18	ABN Amro	2.28
12	16	Credit Suisse	2.02
13	10	Standard Chartered	1.83
14	27	Goldman Sachs	1.79
15	15	Indosuez	1.74
16	14	SE Banken	1.71
17	19	Royal Bank of Canada	1.66
18	N/A	National Australia Bank	1.58
19	N/A	Tokyo-Mitsubishi Bank	1.44
20	13	BNP	1.37

		1997	
Ranking 1997	Ranking 1996	Bank	Estimated share (%)
1	1	Citibank	8.30
2	4	NatWest	5.62
3	24	Merrill Lynch	5.18
4	**9**	**Deutsche Morgan Grenfell**	**4.79**
5	2	Chase	4.65
6	10	SBC Warburg	4.43
7	5	J. P. Morgan & Co.	4.40
8	14	Goldman Sachs	3.82
9	3	HSBC/Midland	3.24
10	7	BZW	3.14
11	8	Bank of America	2.56
12	12	Credit Suisse First Boston	2.39
13	19	Bank of Tokyo-Mitsubishi	2.14
14	6	Union Bank of Switzerland	1.87
15	11	ABN Amro Hoare Govett	1.82
16	28	Commerzbank	1.78
17	N/A	Sumitomo Bank	1.69
18	N/A	Dai-Ichi Kangyo Bank	1.68
19	17	Royal Bank of Canada	1.64
20	13	Standard Chartered	1.60

	1998		
Ranking 1998	Ranking 1997	Bank	Estimated share (%)
1	1	Citibank	8.54
2	**4**	**Deutsche Bank**	**5.57**
3	5	Chase Manhattan	4.78
4	8	Goldman Sachs	4.04
5	9	HSBC	4.00
6	7	J. P. Morgan & Co.	3.05
7	6	SBC Warburg Dillon Read	2.69
8	3	Merrill Lynch	2.65
9	2	NatWest	2.60
10	35	Industrial Bank of Japan	2.53
11	15	ABN Amro	2.41
12	11	Bank of America	2.29
13	21	Morgan Stanley Dean Witter	1.93
14	23	AIG	1.91
15	28	S-E-Banken	1.83
16	19	Royal Bank of Canada	1.72
17	20	Standard Chartered Bank	1.65
18	91	Bear Stearns	1.40
19	14	Union Bank of Switzerland	1.33
20	10	Barclays Capital	1.11

		1999	
Ranking 1999	**Ranking 1998**	**Bank**	**Estimated share (%)**
1	1	Citibank/Salomon	7.75
2	**2**	**Deutsche Bank**	**7.12**
3	3	Chase Manhattan Bank	7.09
4	N/A	Warburg Dillon Read	6.44
5	4	Goldman Sachs	4.86
6	12	Bank of America	4.39
7	6	J. P. Morgan & Co.	4.00
8	5	HSBC	3.75
9	11	ABN Amro	3.37
10	8	Merrill Lynch	3.27
11	21	Credit Suisse First Boston	3.11
12	15	SEB	2.68
13	9	NatWest Global Financial Markets	2.63
14	16	Royal Bank of Canada	2.60
15	13	Morgan Stanley Dean Witter	2.29
16	20	Barclays Capital	1.88
17	39	Svenska Handelsbanken	1.74
18	17	Standard Chartered Bank	1.59
19	62	MeritaNordbanken	1.48
20	44	Bankers Trust	1.45

		2000	
Ranking 2000	Ranking 1999	Bank	Estimated share (%)
1	2	**Deutsche Bank**	**12.53**
2	3	Chase Manhattan Bank	8.26
3	1	Citigroup	8.07
4	4	Warburg Dillon Read	5.02
5	8	HSBC	4.55
6	5	Goldman Sachs	4.38
7	7	J. P. Morgan & Co.	3.94
8	10	Merrill Lynch	3.27
9	11	Credit Suisse First Boston	2.89
10	15	Morgan Stanley Dean Witter	2.87
11	13	NatWest Global Financial	2.71
12	16	Barclays Capital	2.07
13	14	Royal Bank of Canada	1.96
14	44	State Street Bank & Trust	1.95
15	6	Bank of America	1.86
16	9	ABN Amro	1.72
17	43	Bank of New York	1.24
18	186	Lehman Brothers	1.22
19	22	Crédit Agricole Indosuez	1.02
20	79	Brown Brothers Harriman	0.74

			2001	
Ranking 2001	**Ranking 2000**	**Bank**	**Estimated share (%)**
1	3	Citigroup	9.74
2	**1**	**Deutsche Bank**	**9.08**
3	6	Goldman Sachs	7.09
4	7	J. P. Morgan & Co.	5.22
5	2	Chase Manhattan Bank	4.69
6	9	Credit Suisse First Boston	4.10
7	N/A	UBS Warburg	3.55
8	14	State Street Bank & Trust	2.99
9	15	Bank of America	2.99
10	10	Morgan Stanley Dean Witter	2.87
11	12	Barclays Capital	2.46
12	5	HSBC	2.44
13	16	ABN Amro	1.86
14	48	BNP Paribas	1.81
15	28	Bank of Nova Scotia	1.58
16	26	CIBC Wood Gundy	1.55
17	43	Bank of Montreal	1.52
18	37	Toronto Dominion Bank	1.48
19	8	Merrill Lynch	1.44
20	N/A	Royal Bank of Scotland	1.32

2002

Ranking 2002	Ranking 2001	Bank	Estimated share (%)
1	1	Citigroup	11.17
2	7	UBS Warburg	10.96
3	**2**	**Deutsche Bank**	**9.79**
4	3	Goldman Sachs	6.69
5	N/A	JPMorgan Chase & Co.	5.86
6	6	Credit Suisse First Boston	4.62
7	10	Morgan Stanley Dean Witter	3.70
8	13	ABN Amro	3.40
9	35	SEB	2.76
10	11	Barclays Capital	2.61
11	9	Bank of America	2.45
12	12	HSBC	2.37
13	20	Royal Bank of Scotland	2.30
14	25	Dresdner Kleinwort W'stein	2.24
15	23	Royal Bank of Canada	2.09
16	14	BNP Paribas	2.01
17	37	Nordea	1.64
18	N/A	Bank One	1.46
19	N/A	Svenska Handelsbanken	1.43
20	8	State Street Bank & Trust	1.31

| | | | 2003 |
Ranking 2003	Ranking 2002	Bank	Estimated share (%)
1	2	UBS	11.53
2	1	Citigroup	9.87
3	**3**	**Deutsche Bank**	**9.79**
4	5	JPMorgan Chase & Co.	6.79
5	4	Goldman Sachs	5.56
6	6	Credit Suisse First Boston	4.23
7	12	HSBC	3.89
8	7	Morgan Stanley	3.87
9	10	Barclays Capital	3.84
10	8	ABN Amro	3.63
11	24	Merrill Lynch	2.98
12	13	Royal Bank of Scotland	2.85
13	16	BNP Paribas	2.72
14	11	Bank of America	2.42
15	14	Dresdner Kleinwort W'stein	2.01
16	20	State Street Bank Trust	1.97
17	15	Royal Bank of Canada	1.87
18	23	Lehman Brothers	1.84
19	9	SEB	1.82
20	27	Crédit Agricole Indosuez	1.54

		2004	
Ranking 2004	Ranking 2003	Bank	Estimated share (%)
1	1	UBS	12.36
2	3	**Deutsche Bank**	**12.18**
3	2	Citigroup	9.37
4	4	JPMorgan Chase & Co.	5.78
5	7	HSBC	4.89
6	5	Goldman Sachs	4.54
7	9	Barclays Capital	4.08
8	6	CSFB / Credit Suisse Group	3.79
9	12	RBS	3.51
10	11	Merrill Lynch	3.49
11	10	ABN Amro	3.19
12	15	Dresdner Kleinwort W'stein	2.92
13	8	Morgan Stanley	2.92
14	18	Lehman Brothers	2.09
15	14	Bank of America	2.09
16	16	State Street Bank & Trust	1.86
17	17	Royal Bank of Canada	1.49
18	13	BNP Paribas	1.43
19	19	SEB	1.22
20	23	Société Générale	1.16

| | | 2005 | |
Ranking 2005	Ranking 2004	Bank	Estimated share (%)
1	2	**Deutsche Bank**	**16.72**
2	1	UBS	12.47
3	3	Citigroup	7.50
4	5	HSBC	6.37
5	7	Barclays	5.85
6	10	Merrill Lynch	5.69
7	4	JPMorgan Chase & Co.	5.29
8	6	Goldman Sachs	4.39
9	11	ABN Amro	4.19
10	13	Morgan Stanley	3.92
11	9	RBS	3.62
12	14	Lehman Brothers	2.46
13	12	Dresdner Kleinwort W'stein	2.37
14	8	CSFB / Credit Suisse Group	2.36
15	17	Royal Bank of Canada	1.77
16	15	Bank of America	1.60
17	16	State Street	1.35
18	21	Calyon	1.15
19	18	BNP Paribas	1.09
20	20	Société Générale	0.80

	2006		
Ranking 2006	Ranking 2005	Bank	Estimated share (%)
1	**1**	**Deutsche Bank**	**19.26**
2	2	UBS	11.86
3	3	Citigroup	10.39
4	5	Barclays	6.61
5	11	RBS	6.43
6	8	Goldman Sachs	5.25
7	4	HSBC	5.04
8	16	Bank of America	3.97
9	7	JPMorgan Chase & Co.	3.89
10	6	Merrill Lynch	3.68
11	9	ABN Amro	2.93
12	10	Morgan Stanley	2.55
13	12	Lehman Brothers	1.84
14	13	Dresdner Kleinwort W'stein	1.66
15	14	Credit Suisse	1.61
16	18	Calyon	1.40
17	19	BNP Paribas	1.10
18	17	State Street	1.06
19	15	RBC Capital Markets	0.88
20	20	Société Générale	0.61

2007			
Ranking 2007	**Ranking 2006**	**Bank**	**Estimated share (%)**
1	1	**Deutsche Bank**	19.30
2	2	UBS	14.85
3	3	Citigroup	9.00
4	5	RBS	8.90
5	4	Barclays	8.80
6	8	Bank of America	5.29
7	7	HSBC	4.36
8	6	Goldman Sachs	4.14
9	9	JPMorgan Chase & Co.	3.33
10	12	Morgan Stanley	2.86

Banks 11–20 removed due to changes in *Euromoney* data presentation

2008			
Ranking 2008	**Ranking 2007**	**Bank**	**Estimated share (%)**
1	1	**Deutsche Bank**	21.70
2	2	UBS	15.80
3	5	Barclays	9.12
4	3	Citibank	7.49
5	4	RBS	7.30
6	9	JPMorgan Chase & Co.	4.19
7	7	HSBC	4.10
8	8	Goldman Sachs	3.47
9	10	Morgan Stanley	2.56
10	6	BAML	2.23

2009

Ranking 2009	Ranking 2008	Bank	Estimated share (%)
1	1	**Deutsche Bank**	20.96
2	2	UBS	14.58
3	3	Barclays	10.45
4	5	RBS	8.19
5	4	Citibank	7.32
6	6	JPMorgan Chase & Co.	5.43
7	7	HSBC	4.09
8	8	Goldman Sachs	3.35
9	N/A	Credit Suisse	3.05
10	N/A	BNP Paribas	2.26

2010

Ranking 2010	Ranking 2009	Bank	Estimated share (%)
1	1	**Deutsche Bank**	18.07
2	2	UBS	11.30
3	3	Barclays	11.09
4	5	Citibank	7.69
5	4	RBS	6.51
6	6	JPMorgan Chase & Co.	6.35
7	7	HSBC	4.55
8	9	Credit Suisse	4.44
9	8	Goldman Sachs	4.28
10	N/A	Morgan Stanley	2.92

2011

Ranking 2011	Ranking 2010	Bank	Estimated share (%)
1	1	**Deutsche Bank**	15.65
2	3	Barclays	10.76
3	2	UBS	10.60
4	4	Citigroup	8.86
5	6	JPMorgan Chase & Co.	6.44
6	7	HSBC	6.27
7	5	RBS	6.20
8	8	Credit Suisse	4.80
9	9	Goldman Sachs	4.13
10	10	Morgan Stanley	3.65

2012

Ranking 2012	Ranking 2011	Bank	Estimated share (%)
1	1	**Deutsche Bank**	14.57
2	4	Citigroup	12.26
3	2	Barclays	10.95
4	3	UBS	10.48
5	6	HSBC	6.72
6	5	JPMorgan Chase & Co.	6.60
7	7	RBS	5.86
8	8	Credit Suisse	4.68
9	10	Morgan Stanley	3.52
10	9	Goldman Sachs	3.12

2013

Ranking 2013	Ranking 2012	Bank	Estimated share (%)
1	1	**Deutsche Bank**	**15.18**
2	2	Citigroup	14.90
3	3	Barclays	10.24
4	4	UBS	10.11
5	5	HSBC	6.93
6	6	JPMorgan Chase & Co.	6.07
7	7	RBS	5.62
8	8	Credit Suisse	3.70
9	9	Morgan Stanley	3.15
10	N/A	BAML	3.08

2014

Ranking 2014	Ranking 2013	Bank	Estimated share (%)
1	2	Citigroup	16.04
2	1	**Deutsche Bank**	**15.67**
3	3	Barclays	10.91
4	4	UBS	10.88
5	5	HSBC	7.12
6	6	JPMorgan Chase & Co.	5.55
7	10	BAML	4.38
8	7	RBS	3.25
9	N/A	BNP Paribas	3.10
10	N/A	Goldman Sachs	2.53

		2015	
Ranking 2015	Ranking 2014	Bank	Estimated share (%)
1	1	Citigroup	16.11
2	**2**	**Deutsche Bank**	**14.54**
3	3	Barclays	8.11
4	6	JPMorgan Chase & Co.	7.65
5	4	UBS	7.30
6	7	BAML	6.22
7	5	HSBC	5.40
8	9	BNP Paribas	3.65
9	10	Goldman Sachs	3.40
10	8	RBS	3.38

Appendix 2: A Timeline of Events Mentioned in the Text

Date	Event
1973, May	Black and Scholes option-pricing paper
1986, October	'Big Bang' regulatory regime in the UK
1987, October	Stock market crash
1990, August	Iraq invades Kuwait
1992, September	ERM crisis, 'Black Wednesday'
1993, Summer	Second ERM crisis
1993, Autumn	Hedge fund LTCM set up
1994, February	Federal Reserve unexpected rate rise; bond crash
1995	Deutsche Bank investment banking build-out starts
1996, May	Bankers Trust settles with Procter and Gamble
1997, May	Election of Tony Blair's New Labour government in UK
1997, July	Thailand devalues the baht
1997, October	First big sell-off in Russian bonds
1998, August	Russia defaults and devalues
1998, September	Failure of LTCM
1998, November	Deutsche Bank bids for Bankers Trust
1999, January	Creation of the euro
1999	Merger of Prebon Yamane and Marshalls
1999, June	Bankers Trust taken over by Deutsche Bank
1999, November	Gramm–Leach–Bliley Act in the US repeals Glass–Steagall
2000, Spring	Deutsche Bank wins *Euromoney* FX poll for first time

2001, September	9/11 attacks on World Trade Center and Pentagon
2003, Autumn	EBS launches dealing API
2004, Spring	Launch of EBS Prime
2005, May	Deutsche Bank wins 2004 *Euromoney* poll
2005, Summer	Barclays launch Precision Pricing; EBS opens to funds
2006, April	EBS bought by ICAP
2006, July	Deutsche Bank buys MortgageIT
2007, July	Ratings agencies begin to downgrade CDOs
2007, September	Run on Northern Rock
2008, September	Collapse of Lehman Brothers
2008, October	Introduction of the TARP; start of global recession
2010, May	Flash Crash
2012, August	Failure of Knight Capital; Collapse of EURCHF to 1.0000
2012, September	SNB imposes EURCHF floor (cap on value of Swiss franc)
2013, December	Closure of Deutsche Bank's Commodities department
2015, January	SNB abandons the EURCHF floor
2016, October	Cable Flash Crash

Notes

Chapter 1

1 'Deutsche Bank Guide to Currency Indices', George Saravelos et al., October 2007, p14, http://cbs.db.com/new/docs/DBGuideToFXIndices.pdf

2 'Interdealer Broking History', Tullett Prebon, http://www.tullettprebon.com/about/about_ourstory.aspx

Chapter 3

1 'Electronic Platforms in Foreign Exchange Trading', Celent E-Forex Report 2007, Figure 10, http://www.e-forex.net/Files/surveyreportsPDFs/Celent%20FX%20report.pdf

2 Since then, a cap has been set on this multiple (so-called 'leverage') by regulators. '50 times as from August 2010, lowered again to 25 times as from August 2011' in 'High-frequency trading in the foreign exchange market', Bank for International Settlements, September 2011, p17, http://www.bis.org/publ/mktc05.pdf

3 'Retail FX Margin Trading', Hjalmar Schröder and Reto Stadelmann, UBS, August 2007, http://www.ecb.europa.eu/paym/groups/pdf/FXCG_RetailFX_070904.pdf??f6482146958a17d0d2392073ee0cfa21

4 'ICAP Agrees to Buy Electronic Currency Broker EBS', Hamish Risk and Andrew Reierson, Bloomberg, 21 April 2006, http://www.bloomberg.com/apps/news?pid=newsarchive&sid=aB9rtJu7IEFs&refer=top_world_news

5 'AFME Liquidity Conference, FX Market Structure', Oliver Wyman, February 2015, http://www.afme.eu/uploadedFiles/Events/2015/Market_Liquidity/AFME%20Market%20Liquidity%20Conference%202015%20-%20OW%20FX%20Market%20Structural%20Review%20Presentation.pdf

6 'Triennial Central Bank Survey of Foreign Exchange and Derivatives Market Activity in 2007', Bank for International Settlements, 2007, http://www.bis.org/publ/rpfxf07t.htm

7 'Deutsche releases Next Gen FX Pricing API', Paul Blank, SingleDealerPlatforms.org, 20 September 2012, http://singledealerplatforms.org/2012/09/20/deutsche-releases-next-gen-fx-pricing-api/

8 'Triennial Central Bank Survey, Foreign exchange turnover in April 2013: preliminary global results', Bank for International Settlements, September 2013, http://www.bis.org/publ/rpfx13fx.pdf

9 'High-frequency trading in the foreign exchange market', Bank for International Settlements, September 2011, http://www.bis.org/publ/mktc05.htm

10 Ibid.

11 'In the Matter of Knight Capital Americas LLC', Securities and Exchange Commission, October 2013, https://www.sec.gov/litigation/admin/2013/34-70694.pdf

12 'High-frequency trading in the foreign exchange market', Bank for International Settlements, September 2011.

13 Swiss National Bank press release, SNB, 6 September 2011, http://www.snb.ch/en/mmr/reference/pre_20110906/source/pre_20110906.en.pdf

14 'FXCM Releases Detailed Data on the SNB Flash Crash', FXCM press release, 11 March 2015, http://ir.fxcm.com/releasedetail.cfm?ReleaseID=901193

15 'Alpari UK currency broker folds over Swiss franc turmoil', BBC News, 16 January 2015, http://www.bbc.co.uk/news/business-30846543

Chapter 4

1 'Causes of the Recent Financial and Economic Crisis', Testimony of Chairman Ben S. Bernanke before the Financial Crisis Inquiry Commission, Washington, D.C., 2 September 2010, http://www.federalreserve.gov/newsevents/testimony/bernanke20100902a.htm

2 'The Pricing of Options and Corporate Liabilities', Fischer Black and Myron Scholes, *Journal of Political Economy*, May–June 1973, https://www.cs.princeton.edu/courses/archive/fall02/cs323/links/blackscholes.pdf

3 US Treasury data, http://www.treasury.gov/resource-center/data-chart-center/interest-rates/Pages/Historic-LongTerm-Rate-Data-Visualization.aspx

4 'Procter & Gamble's Tale of Derivatives Woe', *NY Times*, 14 April 1994, http://www.nytimes.com/1994/04/14/business/worldbusiness/14iht-procter.html

5 'The Bankers Trust Tapes', *Business Week*, 16 October 1995, http://www.businessweek.com/1995/42/b34461.htm

6 'The Progress of Computing', Willam D. Nordhaus, Yale University and the NBER, August 2001 http://www.econ.yale.edu/~nordhaus/homepage/prog_083001a.pdf

Chapter 5

1 Quoted in 'Debt Investors Turn Page on Russia', *Wall Street Journal*, 19 December 2012, http://www.wsj.com/articles/SB10001424127887324677204578186063726167542

2 US Treasury data, http://www.treasury.gov/resource-center/data-chart-center/interest-rates/Pages/Historic-LongTerm-Rate-Data-Visualization.aspx

3 *When Genius Failed*, Roger Lowenstein, Fourth Estate, 1999, p4.

4 'Bankers Trust and the Birth of Modern Risk Management', Gene D. Guill, Wharton Financial Institutions Center, March 2009, Table 1, http://fic.wharton.upenn.edu/fic/case%20studies/Birth%20of%20Modern%20Risk%20Managementapril09.pdf

5 Ibid., Section IV.

6 'Amendment to the Capital Accord to Incorporate Market Risks', Basle Committee on Banking Supervision, January 1996, http://www.bis.org/publ/bcbs24.pdf

7 'The arb boys ride again', *Businessweek*, 12 September 1993, http://www.bloomberg.com/bw/stories/1993-09-12/the-arb-boys-ride-again

8 *When Genius Failed*, Roger Lowenstein, Fourth Estate, 1998, p39.

9 Ibid., p120.

10 'Long-Term Capital Management, L.P. (A)', Harvard Business School Case Study, 9-200-007, 5 November 1999.

11 Ibid., p13.

12 Ibid., p12. Study gives daily standard deviation as $45 million. Scaled up by factor of 2.33 by author to translate to p99 risk.

13 Ibid., p12.

14 'Key Indicators of Developing Asian and Pacific Countries', published by the Asian Development Bank online at adb.org.

15 'The Asian Crisis: Causes and Cures', IMF Staff in Finance and Development, June 1998, http://www.imf.org/external/pubs/ft/fandd/1998/06/imfstaff.htm

16 'Global Development Finance, Analysis and Summary Tables', World Bank, May 2000, Table 2.1, http://siteresources.worldbank.org/INTPROSPECTS/Resources/334934-1325713584429/8351805-1325714533083/GDF2000CH2.pdf

17 Author's calculations using data from Pacific Exchange Rate Service, University of British Columbia, Saunder School of Business, http://fx.sauder.ubc.ca/data.html

18 Ibid.

19 US Energy Information Administration, http://www.eia.gov/dnav/pet/hist/LeafHandler.ashx?n=PET&s=RWTC&f=D

20 Central Bank of Russia statistics website, http://www.cbr.ru/eng/statistics/print.aspx?file=b_sector/interest_rates_98_e.htm&pid=procstavnew&sid=svodProcStav

21 Letter to investors, John W. Meriwether, Bloomberg, 2 September 1998, http://www.businessweek.com/1998/38/b3596001.htm

22 'Long-Term Capital Management, Report to Congressional Requesters', United States General Accounting Office, October 1999, http://www.gao.gov/assets/230/228446.pdf

Chapter 6

1 'Weather risk market remains buoyant, claims Clemmons', Paul Lyon, Risk.net, 24 October 2002, http://m.risk.net/risk-magazine/news/1503229/weather-risk-market-remains-buoyant-claims-clemmons

2 Presentation to Merrill Lynch European Banking & Insurance Conference London, Anshu Jain, 8 October 2002, https://www.db.com/ir/en/download/1382.pdf

3 Stern Business School, NYU, datasets, http://pages.stern.nyu.edu/~adamodar/New_Home_Page/datafile/histretSP.html

4 US Treasury data, http://www.treasury.gov/resource-center/data-chart-center/interest-rates/Pages/Historic-LongTerm-Rate-Data-Visualization.aspx

5 *2015 Investor Company Handbook*, Investment Company Institute, May 2015, Chapter 2, http://www.icifactbook.org/fb_ch2.html#popularity

6 'Studies on Stock and Bond Picking Performance', Mark Hebner, Index Fund Advisors, May 2013, https://www.ifa.com/articles/studies_on_stock_picking_performance/

7 'Speculators Have Discovered Palladium and Sugar', William Baldwin, *Forbes*, March 2011, http://www.forbes.com/forbes/2011/0411/investing-william-baldwin-investment-strategies-palladium-sugar.html

8 Presentation to Merrill Lynch European Banking & Insurance Conference London, Anshu Jain, 8 October 2002, Slide 17, https://www.db.com/ir/en/download/1382.pdf

9 Ibid., Slide 14.

10 Market Surveys Data, 1987–2010, ISDA, 2010, http://www.isda.org/statistics/pdf/ISDA-Market-Survey-annual-data.pdf

11 'Introducing CCOs', *Credit* magazine, February 2005, http://db.riskwaters.com/public/showPage.html?page=credit_feb05_productlaunch

12 'CDO Evaluator Applies Correlation and Monte Carlo Simulation to the Art of Determining Portfolio Quality', Sten Bergman, Standard and Poor's, 12 November 2001, http://www.globalriskguard.com/resources/crderiv/sp_portf_qual.pdf

13 '"The Formula That Killed Wall Street"? The Gaussian Copula and the Material Cultures of Modelling', Donald MacKenzie and Taylor Spears, School of Social & Political Science, University of Edinburgh, June 2012, http://www.sps.ed.ac.uk/__data/assets/pdf_file/0003/84243/Gaussian14.pdf

14 Ibid., p31.

15 'On Default Correlation: A Copula Function Approach', David X. Li, *Journal of Fixed Income*, 9/4:43–54, http://www.defaultrisk.com/pp_corr_05.htm

16 Standard & Poor's Ratings Definitions, Standard & Poor's Ratings Services, 20 Nov 2014, http://www.standardandpoors.com/en_US/web/guest/article/-/view/sourceId/504352

17 Deutsche Bank to acquire MortgageIT Holdings, Inc., Deutsche Bank press release, 12 July 2006, https://www.db.com/newsroom_news/archive/medien/deutsche-bank-to-acquire-mortgageit-holdings-inc-en-11232.htm

18 *Traders: Risks, Decisions, and Management in Financial Markets*, Mark Fenton-O'Creevy, Nigel Nicholson, Emma Soane and Paul Willman, Oxford University Press, 2005, Chapter 6.

19 For evidence of this, see for example Table 1 in 'Pay, Politics and the Financial Crisis', Kevin J. Murphy, University of Southern California, Marshall School of Business, 16 February 2012, http://risk.econ.queensu.ca/wp-content/uploads/2013/10/Murphy-PayPoliticsCrisis-2-16-12-1.pdf

20 'S&P/Case-Schiller Home Price Indices', us.spindices.com

21 Securities Industry and Financial Markets Association (SIFMA), Statistics, http://www.sifma.org/research/statistics.aspx

22 'Russian Debt Restructuring', Alexander Nadmitov, Harvard Law School, 2004, p47, http://www.law.harvard.edu/programs/about/pifs/education/llm/2003---2004/sp26.pdf

23 *The Greatest Trade Ever*, Gregory Zuckerman, Broadway Books, 2009, p176.

24 All Deutsche Bank numbers in this chapter are taken from annual reports issued from 2000 to 2007, https://www.deutsche-bank.de/ir/en/content/reports_2011.htm. Asset figures mentioned in the text were calculated under US GAAP accounting. In 2007, a new accounting standard called IFRS was introduced which increased 2006 reported assets to €1,468 billion (vs. US GAAP €1,012 billion) and 2007 assets to €1,895 billion.

25 Deutsche Bank, Investor Relations, https://www.db.com/ir/en/content/share_price_information.htm

26 From $1.48 trillion in 2004 to $2.19 trillion in 2007, Citibank 2007 form 10-K, http://www.citigroup.com/citi/investor/data/k07c.pdf?ieNocache=32

27 Ibid.

28 'Changes in the Size Distribution of U.S. Banks: 1960–2005', Hubert P. Janicki and Edward Simpson Prescott, Federal Reserve Bank of Richmond, *Economic Quarterly*, 92/4, Fall 2006, Figure 2, https://www.richmondfed.org/~/media/richmondfedorg/publications/research/economic_quarterly/2006/fall/pdf/janicki_prescott.pdf

29 JPMorgan Chase 2006 annual report.

30 'Chase buying J. P. Morgan', Chris Isidore, CNN Money, 13 September 2000, http://money.cnn.com/2000/09/13/deals/chase_morgan/

31 'Chase and Chemical in $300bn merger', Michael Marray, *Independent*, 29 August 1995, http://www.independent.co.uk/news/business/chase-and-chemical-in-300bn-merger-1598520.html

32 'S&P/Case-Schiller Home Price Indices', us.spindices.com.

33 'Nightmare Mortgages', *Businessweek*, 10 September 2006, http://www.bloomberg.com/bw/stories/2006-09-10/nightmare-mortgages

34 *All the Devils Are Here*, Bethany McLean and Joe Nocera, Portfolio / Penguin, November 2010, Chapter 18.

35 Lehman Brothers Annual Report 2007, https://www.zonebourse.com/NB-PRIV-EQ-PARTN-56192/pdf/87896/NB%20PRIV%20EQ%20PARTN_Rapport-annuel.pdf

36 Bear Stearns Annual Report 2006, http://www.slideshare.net/QuarterlyEarningsReports3/bear-stearns-annual-report-2006

37 'Risk Off', paper by Andrew G. Haldane, Bank of England, August 2011, http://www.bankofengland.co.uk/archive/Documents/historicpubs/speeches/2011/speech513.pdf

38 Deutsche Bank Roadshow, Dr Clemens Börsig, CFO, 1 September 2004, Slide 6, https://www.db.com/ir/en/download/Roadshow_Boston_Dr_Boersig_1_Sep_2004.pdf

39 Deutsche Bank Annual Report, 2008, https://annualreport.deutsche-bank.com/2008/ar/servicepages/downloads/files/dbfy2008_entire.pdf

40 Ibid.

41 Ibid.

Chapter 7

1 'Bankers Are Almost as Unloved as Prostitutes, Playboy Reports', Jann Bettinga and Stefanie Haxel, 12 November 2008, http://www.bloomberg.com/apps/news?pid=newsarchive&sid=aGZhsQhm0gYc

2 'Libor: The Crime of the Century', *The Nation*, Robert Scheer, 6 July 2012, http://www.thenation.com/article/libor-crime-century/

3 'A Greek Banker Spills On The Early Days Of The Libor And His First Deal With The Shah Of Iran', Kirstin Ridley, Huw Jones, Reuters, 8 August 2012, http://www.businessinsider.com/history-of-the-libor-rate-2012-8?IR=T

4 Market Surveys Data, 1987–2010, ISDA, 2010, http://www.isda.org/statistics/pdf/ISDA-Market-Survey-annual-data.pdf

5 'The Wheatley Review of LIBOR: final report', Her Majesty's Treasury, September 2012, https://www.gov.uk/government/uploads/system/uploads/attachment_data/file/191762/wheatley_review_libor_final-report_280912.pdf

6 Ibid., Chart 4.A.

7 'Fixing LIBOR: some preliminary findings', www.parliament.uk, 18 August 2012, paragraph 27, http://www.publications.parliament.uk/pa/cm201213/cmselect/cmtreasy/481/48104.htm

8 Ibid., paragraph 30.

9 Ibid., paragraph 50.

10 'Traders Said to Rig Currency Rates to Profit Off Clients', Liam Vaughan, Gavin Finch and Ambereen Choudhury, Bloomberg, 12 June 2013, http://www.bloomberg.com/news/articles/2013-06-11/traders-said-to-rig-currency-rates-to-profit-off-clients

11 Ibid.

12 Ibid.

13 'FCA fines five banks £1.1 billion for FX failings and announces industry-wide remediation programme', Financial Conduct Authority, 12 November 2014, http://www.fca.org.uk/news/fca-fines-five-banks-for-fx-failings

14 'Six banks fined $5.6bn over rigging of foreign exchange markets', *Financial Times*, Gina Chon, Caroline Binham and Laura Noonan, 20 May 2015, http://www.ft.com/cms/s/0/23fa681c-fe73-11e4-be9f-00144feabdc0.html#slide0

15 Slightly clarified transcript from 'Examples of Misconduct in Private Chat Rooms', Commodity Futures Trading Commission, Office of Public Affairs, 2014, http://www.cftc.gov/ucm/groups/public/@newsroom/documents/file/hsbcmisconduct111114.pdf

16 '"Flash crash trader" Navinder Singh Sarao loses bail appeal', Simon Goodley, *Guardian*, 20 May 2015, http://www.theguardian.com/business/2015/may/20/flash-crash-trader-navinder-singh-sarao-loses-bail-appeal

17 'Disruptive Practices Prohibited / Rule 575', CME, CBOT, NYMEX & COMEX, 15 September 2014, http://www.cmegroup.com/rulebook/files/ra1405-5r.pdf

18 'Recommendations for Equitable Allocation of Trades in High Frequency Trading Environments', John W. McPartland, Federal Reserve Bank of Chicago, July 2013, revised July 2014, https://www.chicagofed.org/publications/policy-discussion-papers/2013/pdp-1

19 'Deutsche Bank steps up e-mail snooping', Dan Thomas, *Personnel Today*, 1 February 2006, http://www.personneltoday.com/hr/deutsche-bank-steps-up-e-mail-snooping/

20 'UBS to Avoid Fine In EU Libor Probe', David Enrich and Charles Forelle, *Wall Street Journal*, 21 November 2013, http://www.wsj.com/articles/SB10001424052702303653004579211592922244248

21 'JPMorgan Algorithm Knows You're a Rogue Employee Before You Do', Hugh Son, Bloomberg, 8 April 2015, http://www.bloomberg.com/news/articles/2015-04-08/jpmorgan-algorithm-knows-you-re-a-rogue-employee-before-you-do

22 Ibid.

Chapter 8

1 'Forms and paradoxes of principles-based regulation', Julia Black, Professor of Law and Research Associate, Centre for the Analysis of Risk and Regulation, London School of Economics and Political Science, *Capital Markets Law Journal*, 3/4, 10 September 2008, http://www.lse.ac.uk/collections/law/staff%20publications%20full%20text/black/forms%20and%20paradoxes%20of%20pbr%202008.pdf

2 *The Age of Turbulence*, Alan Greenspan, Penguin Books, 2008, p52.

3 'Testimony of Chairman Alan Greenspan, The regulation of OTC derivatives, Before the Committee on Banking and Financial Services, U.S. House of Representatives', 24 July 1998, http://www.federalreserve.gov/boarddocs/testimony/1998/19980724.htm

4 For more on this fascinating topic, see *The Myth of the Rational Market*, Justin Fox, Harper Business, 2011.

5 *The End of History and the Last Man*, Francis Fukuyama, Penguin Books, 1992.

6 'The Financial Crisis and the Role of Federal Regulators', Committee on Oversight and Government Reform, House of Representatives, 23 October 2008, http://www.gpo.gov/fdsys/pkg/CHRG-110hhrg55764/html/CHRG-110hhrg55764.htm

7 *Stabilizing an Unstable Economy*, Professor Hyman Minsky, McGraw-Hill Professional, 1986.

8 'Working Paper No. 74, The Financial Instability Hypothesis', Hyman Minsky, The Jerome Levy Economics Institute of Bard College, May 1992, http://www.levyinstitute.org/pubs/wp74.pdf

9 *Unsettled Account: The Evolution of Banking in the Industrialised World since 1800*, Richard S. Grossman, Princeton University Press, 2010, p65.

10 'Regulatory Capital Reform under Basel III', Latham & Watkins, March 2011, http://www.garp.org/media/583507/regulatorycapitalreformbaseliii_nicolaides032311.pdf

11 'Banks and capital requirements: channels of adjustment', BIS Working Papers No. 443, Benjamin H. Cohen and Michela Scatigna, March 2014, http://www.bis.org/publ/work443.pdf

12 'Implementing OTC Derivatives Market Reforms', Financial Stability Board, 25 October 2010, http://www.financialstabilityboard.org/wp-content/uploads/r_101025.pdf

13 'How much capital should banks have?', Lev Ratnovski, Economist, Research Department, IMF, 28 July 2013, http://www.voxeu.org/article/how-much-capital-should-banks-have

14 Ibid.

15 *The Bankers' New Clothes: What's Wrong with Banking and What to Do about It*, Anat Admati and Martin Hellwig, Princeton, 2013.

16 'Results of 2014 EU-wide stress test', European Banking Authority, 2014, http://www.eba.europa.eu/documents/10180/851779/2014%20EU-wide%20ST-aggregate%20results.pdf

17 'US companies unleash share buyback binge', Eric Platt, *Financial Times*, 14 April 2015, http://www.ft.com/cms/s/0/48da55fe-e1f7-11e4-bb7f-00144feab7de.html#axzz3jLIkbP91

18 'OTC Derivatives Market Reforms: Eighth Progress Report on Implementation', Financial Stability Board, 7 November 2014, http://www.financialstabilityboard.org/wp-content/uploads/r_141107.pdf?page_moved=1

19 Ibid., Figure 2.1.

20 'Central Counterparties: Addressing their Too Important to Fail Nature', Froukelien Wendt, IMF Working Paper, January 2015, https://www.imf.org/external/pubs/ft/wp/2015/wp1521.pdf

21 'The FSB publishes its 2014 Global Shadow Banking Monitoring Report', Financial Stability Board, 4 November 2014, http://www.financialstabilityboard.org/2014/11/fsb-publishes-its-fourth-global-shadow-banking-monitoring-report-2014/

22 'U.S. regulators struggle in effort to tackle shadow banking', Michael Flaherty and Howard Schneider, Reuters, 1 April 2015, http://www.reuters.com/article/2015/04/01/usa-fed-shadowbanks-idUSL3N0WY4O420150401

23 '2015 update of list of global systemically important banks (G-SIBs)', Financial Stability Board, 3 November 2015, http://www.financialstabilityboard.

org/wp-content/uploads/2015-update-of-list-of-global-systemically-important-banks-G-SIBs.pdf

24 'A Fair and Substantial Contribution by the Financial Sector: Final Report for the G-20', International Monetary Fund, June 2010, https://www.imf.org/external/np/g20/pdf/062710b.pdf

25 'The Volatility of Firm's Assets and the Leverage Effect', Jaewon Choi and Matthew Richardson, University of Illinois and Stern School of Business, September 2012, http://www.apjfs.org/conference/2012/cafm-File/10-4.pdf

26 '"The Formula That Killed Wall Street"? The Gaussian Copula and the Material Cultures of Modelling', Donald MacKenzie and Taylor Spears, School of Social & Political Science, University of Edinburgh, June 2012, http://www.sps.ed.ac.uk/__data/assets/pdf_file/0003/84243/Gaussian14.pdf

27 'What Will Happen to a Generation of Wall Street Traders Who Have Never Seen a Rate Hike?', Callie Bost and Jeanna Smialek, Bloomberg, 29 May 2015, http://www.bloomberg.com/news/articles/2015-05-28/wall-street-s-young-guns-brace-for-first-big-test-as-fed-looms

28 Deutsche Bank Annual Report 2007, https://www.deutsche-bank.de/ir/en/download/Annual_Report_2007_entire.pdf

29 'Subprime Crisis: SFBC Investigation Into the Causes of the Write-downs of UBS AG', Swiss Federal Banking Commission, 30 September 2008, https://www.finma.ch/FinmaArchiv/ebk/e/publik/medienmit/20081016/ubs-subprime-bericht-ebk-e.pdf

30 'Land and Property Values in the U.S.', Lincoln Institute of Land Policy, www.lincolninst.edu

31 'Bank Size and Systemic Risk', Luc Laeven, Lev Ratnovski and Hui Tong, IMF Staff Discussion Note, May 2014, http://www.imf.org/external/pubs/ft/sdn/2014/sdn1404.pdf

32 'Jamie Dimon memo outlines simplified JPMorgan structure', Tom Braithwaite and Kara Scannell, Financial Times, 17 September 2013, http://www.ft.com/cms/s/0/1b6961c2-1f9e-11e3-aa36-00144feab7de.html#axzz3kHdXjDG1

33 'HSBC: Shrink and simplify', Martin Arnold and Patrick Jenkins, *Financial Times*, 22 April 2015, http://www.ft.com/cms/s/0/55cc51ac-e82f-11e4-894a-00144feab7de.html#axzz3kHdXjDG1

34 'Deutsche Bank quits commodities, but keeps index funds', Barani Krishnan, Reuters, 5 December 2013, http://www.reuters.com/article/2013/12/05/us-deutsche-commodities-idUSBRE9B40P820131205

35 'Can America's Big Banks Get Less Complex?', Yalman Onaran, Bloomberg, 6 July 2015, http://www.bloomberg.com/news/articles/2015-07-06/u-s-banks-keep-thousands-of-units-after-push-to-simplify-them

36 'Deutsche's former FX head says the transformation is coming', Kevin Rodgers, *Euromoney*, May 2015, http://www.euromoney.com/Article/3456242/Deutsches-former-FX-head-says-the-transformation-is-coming.html

37 'Atom Bank approved as UK's first digital-only lender', Emma Dunkley, *Financial Times*, 24 June 2015, http://www.ft.com/cms/s/0/d44266e4-1a60-11e5-a130-2e7db721f996.html#axzz3kZKcH71i

38 'Banks Face Powerful Competitors In The Payments Business', Tom Groenfeldt, *Forbes*, 14 October 2014, http://www.forbes.com/sites/tomgroenfeldt/2014/10/14/banks-face-powerful-competitors-in-the-payments-business/

39 'Bank inquiry: Regulator says IT systems "antiquated"', John Campbell, BBC, 8 January 2014, http://www.bbc.co.uk/news/uk-northern-ireland-25661105

Glossary

agency business
Services provided by a bank that do not require it to take risk and are performed in return for a fee. A good example is that of merger advice. See also **principal business**.

API
Application Program Interface: a set of tools, routines and protocols to allow the development of software. Specifically, in the field of finance, the term API is used as shorthand for a predetermined, often standardised way of allowing different computer systems to 'talk' to each other.

arbitrage
Trading risklessly for profit – usually, in the context of finance, as a result of exploiting pricing inconsistencies between different markets or financial instruments.

ARM
Automated Risk Manager: Deutsche Bank's FX department's system to price and risk-manage **spot FX**.

asset
Anything tangible or intangible that is capable of being owned or controlled to produce value and that is held to have positive economic value. Within banks, assets include cash, purchased **bonds** or shares, loans that have been made, buildings that are owned by the bank, positive valuations of trading positions etc.

Autobahn
Deutsche Bank's system to allow its customers to trade various products (including FX) electronically.

back-to-back
A practice whereby a trade is booked with one counterparty and an identical and offsetting trade is booked with another; an important

part of **prime brokerage** or central clearing by a Central Counterparty (see **CCP**).

balance sheet
The account, at one particular moment in time, of all **assets** and **liabilities** that are owned or owed by a bank. Assets equal liabilities plus **capital**.

bank run
A panic in which depositors suddenly withdraw their money from a bank causing it to run out of ready **funding**.

Basel
Shorthand for a series of accords, issued by the *Basel Committee on Banking Supervision*, under the auspices of the Bank for International Settlements in Basel, Switzerland, that deal with the amount of **capital** and (latterly) **funding** that a bank should have. Basel I ran from 1988 to 2004; Basel II from 2004 to 2008; Basel III (the current version) will be implemented fully by 2019.

bid
The price at which a market participant is willing to buy – compare with **offer**. Slang for something worthy of approval: 'I'm well bid for that restaurant.'

bond
A pre-packaged and tradable way for a company, country, fund or bank to borrow money. Normally denominated in one specific currency, a bond will typically pay a series of **coupons** that are a fixed or floating percentage of the amount borrowed.

broker
A person employed at an *interdealer brokerage house* whose job is to match buyers and sellers in a market in return for a fee. Typically, broking is an **agency business**.

BTAnalytics
A suite of computer programs developed by Bankers Trust to allow the pricing and risk management of **derivatives**. See also **DBAnalytics**.

business
In banking terminology, a 'business' is simply another way of referencing a **department**. For example: 'the FX business'.

call
An **option** to buy a financial instrument or other asset. See also **put**.

capital
The difference between a bank's **assets** (what it owns) and **liabilities** (what it owes). Capital represents the value of the bank to its owners and is the buffer protecting a bank's creditors (owners of its liabilities) from loss if the bank's assets decline in value.

capital adequacy ratio
The ratio of a bank's **capital** to the risk-weighted value of its **assets** (**RWA**). Minima are defined under **Basel**.

cash settlement
A technique for settling trades that does not require the physical transfer of assets but rather calculates the amount won or lost on a position by reference to a published benchmark. For example: a **call option** to buy a share at a **strike** of £110 comes to maturity with the share price trading at £130. If the option buyer hands over £110 and gets the actual share in return, that is known as *physical settlement*. If, on the other hand, the contract specifies cash settlement then the price of the share will be observed (possibly at the closing price on the relevant exchange) and the difference between the **strike** and the settlement price (i.e. £20) will be paid by the option seller to the option buyer – no share changes hands. An accountant once asked one of our weather derivatives traders if weather derivatives were cash settled. 'Normally, yes,' came the reply, 'it's tricky to take delivery of rainfall.'

CCP
A *Central Counterparty* (e.g. the London Clearing House) that stands between all transactions between market participants for various financial products.

CDS
Credit default swap: a financial instrument whereby the seller, in return for a stream of cash flows, is obliged to recompense the buyer for any losses resulting from **default** (or other credit event) on a predetermined 'reference security' like a **bond** or a loan.

CDO
Collateralised debt obligation: a type of **structured bond** that pays out the cash flows arising from a pool of underlying assets, normally **bonds**. Typically, a CDO is split into **tranches** with various levels of **seniority**.

CDO-squared
A **CDO** that is based on a pool of assets that contains (or is entirely made up of) tranches of other, different CDOs.

collateral
Assets that are delivered or legally 'pledged' to a lender and which would be sacrificed to the lender in the event of a borrower's **default**. A common, everyday example is that of a house acting as collateral for a mortgage loan.

commercial bank
A bank (or a part of a **universal bank**) that provides loans to, accepts deposits from and offers other transactional services to commercial enterprises – but does not offer the services of an **investment bank**.

Compliance
A **department** within a bank responsible for making sure that the bank obeys all applicable regulations throughout the world.

coupons
The regular interest payments to the holder of a **bond** – so called because, in years gone by, some bonds (called bearer bonds) were made of paper and had physical coupons to be torn off and posted to the bond issuer in order to get the payment.

Credit
Credit Trading is the business line responsible for pricing and trading credit products, like **CDSs** or **CDOs**. *Credit Risk* is the department that monitors and controls the degree to which a bank is exposed to credit risk – especially that of **default**.

DBAnalytics
A suite of computer programs developed by Deutsche Bank to allow the pricing and risk management of **derivatives**. See also **BTAnalytics**.

decimalisation
The change, from 2005 onwards, in the number of decimal places quoted for any FX rate from four to five. A similar process occurred earlier in the **equity** markets.

default
The failure of a borrower to meet the legal obligations of a loan or **bond** – usually, but not exclusively, because of a failure to pay.

department
A business unit within a bank normally employing several hundred people and dedicated to a coherent set of products, activities, clients or geographies. Examples: *Emerging Markets* department; *Risk Management* department.

deposits
A type of loan, usually short-dated in nature, between one market participant and another. Retail deposits are deposits made by private individuals to their clearing bank and are **liabilities** of the bank.

deposit insurance
A scheme whereby governments guarantee retail **deposits** in return for fees from banks.

derivatives
Financial products that 'derive' their value from that of one or more underlying assets; examples include **options**, **swaps**, **CDOs**, **MBSs** etc. They are used as means of taking or reducing risk by transferring it from one counterparty to another.

desk
A business unit within a bank normally employing tens of people and forming part of a **department**. Examples: the London FX spot desk; the US dollar swaps desk.

EBS
Electronic Broking Services: a computerised platform for trading **spot** (and, to a lesser extent, **forward**) FX. Due to its role in replacing the role of voice brokers, occasionally referred to as 'Every Broker's Screwed'.

ECN
Electronic Communication Network: an automated system that matches buy and sell orders for financial products.

the Engine
Nickname for the computer system at Bankers Trust that calculated **RAROC** and **VaR**.

equity
The claim on the value of the bank by the bank's owners, accounted for on the liability side of a bank's **balance sheet**. For most banks equity exists in the form of shares.

Equity department
The business within a bank responsible for issuing and trading shares (as opposed to **bonds** or other **fixed income** products).

ERM
The *Exchange Rate Mechanism*: a system introduced in 1979 by the European Union to manage currency fluctuations. It attempted, by means of interest rate policy and FX market intervention by central banks, to maintain currencies in predefined bands around central parities with each other. Replaced by the euro after a series of crises in the 1990s.

e-trader
A trader whose job is to design, help build and run electronic trading systems like **ARM**. See also **voice trader**.

Euromoney
A publication concentrating on reporting on the activities of the financial service industry; also, shorthand within FX for the annual 'Euromoney FX Survey' – a volume-based survey of customer dealing patterns.

exchange
A centralised financial marketplace where standardised **securities** (e.g. shares or **futures**) can be traded.

exchange-traded
A description of deals that are transacted on an **exchange** rather than bilaterally in the **OTC** market.

exotic

A term used to describe variants of a **derivative** with more features than the simplest possible version (see **plain vanilla**).

fixed income

The set of financial products that are not **equities**. It includes loans, **bonds**, FX, credit products, commodities etc.

forward

A transaction to buy or sell a financial instrument for a fixed price at a date in the future; for example: an *FX forward* is the exchange of one currency for another; a *share forward* is the purchase or sale of a share.

funding

The way in which a bank finances its cash requirements by borrowing: retail **deposits** are considered the most stable funding source and 'wholesale deposits' (short-term loans in the **money markets**) the least. Also, colloquially, funding refers to cash on hand ready to meet short-term needs.

future

A contract to buy or sell a financial instrument for a fixed price at a date in the future. It closely resembles a **forward** but is a standardised **security** that trades on an **exchange** and is **margined**.

give up

The process whereby a trade is reported by a client to its **prime broker** in order for it to be **back-to-backed** with the original counterparty.

GKO

A class of Russian, short-dated, rouble-denominated, zero-coupon bonds heavily traded between 1996 and 1998.

Greeks

The generic name for the risks of any portfolio of assets and liabilities, but most particularly those arising from **derivative** positions. The term arises because Greek letters are often used to denote the risk sensitivities of derivatives. For example:

> **delta** – the change in the value of a derivative with moves in the price of the underlying asset.

gamma – changes in delta with moves in the underlying asset. A so-called 'second-order' Greek: that is, a change on a change.

rho – the change of the value of a derivative with respect to interest rates.

theta – the change of the value of a derivative with respect to time. Also known as 'time decay'.

vega – the change of the value of a derivative with respect to changes in the market estimation of future (or 'implied') **volatility**.

hedge fund

A fund set up to trade and invest on behalf of wealthy and – supposedly – sophisticated investors. Lightly regulated as a consequence of their investor profile.

HFT

High-frequency trading: a type of computerised trading characterised by large numbers of deals in small size done at high speed in order to exploit market inefficiencies. Usually done by HFT funds – a type of **hedge fund**.

investment bank

A bank (or a part of a **universal bank**) that offers investment banking services. These include issuing **securities**, selling and trading those securities (and other products), and offering advice for a fee. Examples: Goldman Sachs, Morgan Stanley, Lehman Brothers, Bear Stearns.

latency

Delay in the processing of buying or selling signals caused by physical effects or the design of software. 'Latency **arbitrage**' is the activity of exploiting other market participants' latency for profit.

leverage

Using borrowing to enhance the returns on an investment strategy. An everyday example is using a mortgage to purchase a house: the buyer only provides a part of the purchase price; the rest is borrowed. Any increases (or decreases) in the value of the property accrue to the buyer alone. In trading, leverage is commonly applied when positions are **margined**.

leverage ratio

The raw ratio of a bank's **assets** to its **capital**, unadjusted by any consideration of risk.

liabilities

Debts or other obligations that arise during the course of business operations. In banks, liabilities include **deposits** from customers or other banks, issued **bonds**, loans taken out and shareholders' **equity**.

LIBOR

The *London Interbank Offered Rate*: an interest rate reference which measures the borrowing costs of banks in the London market for a set of currencies over different tenors and which is used in the **cash settlement** of various interest rate products, most commonly interest rate **swaps**.

liquidity

A measure of the ability of market participants to transact within a reasonable time frame and at a price close to the price pertaining in the market when the decision to trade was made. A liquid market allows risk to be transferred quickly with little 'slippage' in price.

long

A description of the situation whereby a rise in the price of a financial instrument (e.g. a share, **bond** or **future**) or of a market parameter (e.g. implied **volatility**) will result in a gain. Being 'long' a financial instrument arises from a purchase. See also **short**.

LTCM

Long-Term Capital Management: a highly **leveraged hedge fund** engaged in **arbitrage** and **relative value trading** that came to grief in 1998 with disastrous consequences.

margin

The provision of **collateral** to a trading partner to offset the credit risk of potential losses. *Upfront* or *initial* margin (aka 'haircut') is provided at the outset of the deal. *Variation* margin is provided as the value of the deal (or portfolio of deals) changes in value over time.

market making

Providing prices to allow clients to execute transactions when they want to.

MBS

Mortgage-backed security: a type of **structured bond** that pools a number of mortgages and pays out the cash flows of this pool in various **tranches** of different **seniority**.

money markets
Financial markets which participants (banks, corporations and funds) use as a means for **funding** (borrowing and lending) in the short term – from several days to just under a year.

Monte Carlo pricing
A mathematical technique that generates the price and the **Greeks** of a **derivative** by modelling thousands of hypothetical 'experimental' scenarios and averaging the value of the derivative observed in all of them.

Mrs Watanabe
A slang term for the aggregate of all Japanese retail FX speculators trading via **retail aggregators**.

offer
The price at which a market participant is willing to sell – compare with **bid**. Slang for something worthy of disapproval: 'I'm well offered on this book.' Source of endless confusion when traders are asked to put in 'an offer' for a house they actually want to buy.

one-day p99
A descriptor related to the calculation of risk in a bank using the **VaR** methodology. 'P99' refers to the way that the calculation attempts to quantify the 99 per cent worst-case outcome; 'one-day' refers to the time period over which the quantification is attempted. A 'one-day p99 bump' is a move in an asset price or risk factor (e.g. implied **volatility**) that forms an input to the calculation. 'One-day p99 VaR' or 'one-day p99 risk' is the output of the calculation and is meant to represent the monetary loss that will not be exceeded for one day's trading on more than 1 per cent of days.

one-stop shop
The strategic doctrine in many large banks in the 1990s and early 2000s which held that the financial services market would become dominated by a few banks that could offer their clients a full suite of all products and services in every geographical location.

OPTICS
An FX **derivatives** risk management system developed at Merrill Lynch.

option

A **derivative** financial instrument that gives the buyer the right, but not the obligation, to buy (or sell) an asset at a future date for a predetermined price (the **strike** price).

OTC

Over-the-counter: a description for deals (normally **derivatives**) that are transacted bilaterally between two counterparties. Compare with **exchange-traded**.

out trade

An incorrectly booked transaction that misleads traders (and others) as to the true risk their bank has assumed. Slang for a mistake: 'Did you go to Steve and Julia's wedding?' 'Yep. I think it's an out trade, to be honest.'

Panopticon

An architectural design created by the English philosopher Jeremy Bentham (1748–1832) that allows a single watchman to observe all the inhabitants of a building without their being able to tell whether or not they are being watched; ideal for prisons or trading floors.

physical settlement

See **cash settlement**.

pips

The last decimal places of an FX price – commonly quoted as shorthand for the price for reasons of sloth. If the exchange rate of US dollars to euros is 1.1182, the pips are 82.

plain vanilla

A term used to denote the simplest variant of a **derivative**; for example, a regular **call** or **put option**. Compare with **exotic**.

position

The sum of risks of a number of deals – if a trader starts with nothing then buys a lot of shares he will have a **long** position in the shares.

premium

The price paid up front for an **option**.

prime brokerage
A service whereby a bank, for the convenience of its client, interposes itself between the client and the client's trading counterparties in return for a fee.

principal business
Services provided by a bank that require it to take risk. Most trading **departments** are principal businesses. See also **agency business**.

Prisoners' Dilemma
A classic example in game theory of a situation where two rational entities might behave in a way that harms their own interest. Two prisoners, accused of a crime, are held in separate cells by the police. Each is offered the same bargain: betray the other prisoner or stay silent. If they both stay silent they will only serve a year in jail. But if either prisoner remains silent and is betrayed by the other, the silent one will serve three years and his treacherous partner will walk free. If they both squeal they each serve two years. The rational course of action is for both to betray the other, despite the fact that they would serve a shorter term if they both remained silent. The term 'Prisoners' Dilemma' is used in this book as shorthand for a variety of game-theoretical processes whereby banks, regulators and individuals reach decisions that seem rational but might not be in their collective self-interest.

production credits
An accounting method that credits a salesperson for business that is brought in without necessarily linking the sum to the money made on the deal (which may be unknown or unknowable at time of trade).

proprietary trading
Trading (also called 'prop' trading) in which traders in a bank trade purely on the bank's account for profit rather than as part of a **market making** effort.

put
An **option** to sell a financial instrument or other asset. See also **call**.

range trade
A type of **derivative** that pays a fixed amount to the buyer if the price of a specified financial product remains with a certain range for the lifetime of the deal; a form of **exotic option**.

RAPID

Revolutionary **API** *Developm*ent: Deutsche Bank's FX department's modern-day system to price and risk-manage certain flows in **spot FX.**

RAROC

Risk-adjusted return on capital: a measurement framework for risk and return in Bankers Trust that compared potential gain to maximum potential loss (a forerunner of **VaR**).

relative value trading

Closely related to **arbitrage** but, instead of being certain of a profit, transacting in situations where a profit is merely statistically very likely.

retail aggregators

Firms that allow private individuals to trade FX on the basis of **cash settlement** and **margin.**

retail bank

A bank (or a part of a **universal bank**) that provides loans to, accepts deposits from and offers other transactional services to private individuals and – occasionally – small enterprises.

Rizla

A brand name for small pieces of paper, each with a strip of adhesive gum, used to roll cigarettes by hand.

RWA

Risk-weighted assets: a measurement of the size of the **asset** side of a bank's **balance sheet** weighted according to the risk of those assets as defined by the **Basel** rules. The higher the risk, the higher the weighting; RWA is used in the calculation of **capital adequacy ratios.**

securities

Tradable financial assets of any kind. Bonds and shares are securities.

seniority

Where a financial claim ranks, in legal terms, in the priority of claiming cash flows from a company or from a **structured bond**, most particularly in the event of bankruptcy or failure. In **CDOs** and **MBSs** seniority refers to the various **tranches** (or slices) of the bond. When it comes to claims on a company (e.g. a bank) it refers to the precedence of various types of

liability: typically senior bonds outrank junior bonds, which, in turn, outrank **equity**.

short

A description of the situation whereby a decline in the price of a financial instrument (e.g. a share, **bond** or **future**) or of a market parameter (e.g. implied **volatility**) will result in a gain. See also **long**.

skew

To quote a **two-way price** higher or lower than the current market price in order to gain information or dissuade a client or bank from dealing on one side of the price.

spot FX

The exchange of one currency for another for 'spot delivery' (typically two business days after the deal is done); the cornerstone of the FX markets.

spread

The difference in price between the **bid** and the **offer**; thus *bid-offer spread*.

SSF

Spreadsheet Solutions Framework: a system developed by Bankers Trust to allow deals priced and booked on Microsoft Excel spreadsheets to be managed centrally.

strike

The predetermined price at which an **option** can be exercised.

structured bond

A bond which, in some way, is structured to be more complex than a regular bond, often by using asset pooling or other techniques. Examples include **CDOs and MBSs**.

swap

A very common form of **derivative**, in which a set of cash flows is exchanged or 'swapped' for another. For example: the most common type of interest rate swap exchanges fixed interest payments for floating payments; credit default swaps (**CDSs**) exchange premiums for the promise of financial recompense in the event of a **default**.

synthetic CDO
A **CDO** that is not based on the cash flows of a pool of real bonds but rather on a series of **CDSs** that reference the bonds.

tranche
A 'slice' of a **structured bond** such as a **CDO** or an **MBS** that offers a particular priority (or **seniority**) of claim on the cash flows of the underlying pool of assets.

TRS
Total return swap: a type of **swap** whereby the returns of holding a bond purchased using borrowed money are packaged into one instrument. TRSs allow an investor to get the **leveraged** financial return of holding a bond without owning it.

two-way pricing
To provide a **bid** and an **offer** simultaneously for the same financial product at the request of a client.

universal bank
A bank that comprises divisions that offer the services of **retail**, **commercial** and **investment banks** under one corporate umbrella. Examples: Deutsche Bank, Citigroup, JPMorgan, HSBC, RBS.

VaR
Value at risk: a modelled measure of the risk of a portfolio of assets and liabilities that states the estimated maximum loss given a certain probability of the occurrence of that loss (say, 1 per cent) over a defined time period (say, one day).

voice trader
A trader who prices deals and manages positions himself and who isn't the meat-based servant to the demands of an electronic trading system. See also **e-trader**.

volatility
The degree of choppiness in the price movements of a financial instrument and thus the potential for its price to change from its current level over time. In derivative pricing it is commonly defined as the standard deviation of the natural logarithms of the returns on the asset over a defined period. Two ways of thinking about volatility exist. The measure of volatility that

has occurred in the past is termed 'actual', 'past' or 'observed' volatility. The market's view on how volatile a financial instrument will be in the future is called 'implied' volatility because it can only be gauged by observing the prices of derivatives and working out what those prices imply for volatility. However, so central to pricing is this term, that it is now actually used as a proxy for derivative price in various markets, including FX.

weather derivatives
Financial contacts that pay out depending on observations of various weather phenomena – for example, temperature, rainfall, etc. Used in order to hedge businesses against the negative impact of weather events.

Index